How to Read the Qur'an

How to Read the Qur'an

A New Guide,
with Select Translations

Carl W. Ernst

The University of North Carolina Press
Chapel Hill

This book was published with the assistance of the
William R. Kenan Jr. Fund of the University of North Carolina Press.

Manufactured in the United States of America
Set in Iowan Old Style
by Tseng Information Systems, Inc.
The paper in this book meets the guidelines for
permanence and durability of the Committee on
Production Guidelines for Book Longevity of the
Council on Library Resources.

The University of North Carolina Press has been a member
of the Green Press Initiative since 2003.

Library of Congress Cataloging-in-Publication Data

Ernst, Carl W., 1950–
How to read the Qur'an : a new guide, with select translations / Carl W. Ernst.
p. cm.
"This book was published with the assistance of the
William R. Kenan Jr. Fund of the University of North Carolina Press."
Includes bibliographical references and index.
ISBN 978-0-8078-3516-6 (cloth : alk. paper)
1. Koran—Introductions. 2. Koran—Reading. 3. Koran—Criticism,
interpretation, etc. 4. Koran as literature. I. Title.
BP130.E76 2011
297.1'2261—dc23   2011020424
15 14 13 12 11   5 4 3 2 1

Contents

Figures and Charts

Figures

Charts

Acknowledgments

A book like this cannot come about without the support of many talented people and generous institutions, and it is a pleasure to take the opportunity here to express my thanks for that support.

The idea of a literary introduction to the Qur'an started some years ago with a suggestion by Rick Todhunter. I sharpened the concept of a chronological reading of the Qur'an in a course taught over several years, with stimulating feedback from my students at the University of North Carolina at Chapel Hill. Among my research assistants, Aya Okawa contributed brilliant charts of Qur'anic chronology, and Brannon Ingram worked ably to obtain permission for illustrations. Several colleagues and graduate students provided astute criticisms of earlier drafts; many thanks to Bruce B. Lawrence of Duke University, Peter Wright of Colorado College (whose UNC dissertation opened a stimulating window on the rhetoric of the Qur'an), Timur Yuskaev of Hartford Seminary, and Tehsin Thaver of UNC for their helpful comments. Zafar Ishaq Ansari of the International Islamic University (Islamabad) made important critical observations at an early stage. Azizan Baharuddin of the University of Malaya and her colleagues gave a generous reception to materials from chapter 4. Two anonymous readers for UNC Press made helpful suggestions for improving the argument. I appreciate all these readers' comments, and if I have not always followed them, any defects in this presentation are entirely my own responsibility.

My editor at UNC Press, Elaine Maisner, has been incredibly patient and supportive of this project. Thanks to her and all the hard-working staff at the press, who set the standard for quality academic publishing. I would also like to thank Raymond Farrin of the American University of Kuwait for kindly sharing with me the proofs of his forthcoming study of early Arabic literature, *Abundance from the Desert*. Christiane Gruber of Indiana University generously shared her expert knowledge of suitable illustrations.

A special debt of gratitude goes to artist Ahmed Moustafa, who graciously gave permission for an expanded image of his superb painting, *God Is the Light of the Heavens and the Earth*, to appear on the cover of the book. The title translates the opening words of the famous "Light Verse" of the Qur'an (24:35), the complete text of which is presented eight times in the rectangular bands of the original image (four times in a clockwise, and four times in a counterclockwise direction). This is overlaid on a repeating geometric grid containing the first words of the "Throne Verse" (Qur'an 2:255), "God! There is no god but He, the Living, the Everlasting." The color palette of this remarkable composition shifts from earth hues below to sky blue above, and the illuminated clouds in the center convey an unmistakable sense of going through the text to what lies beyond—a marvelous image to suggest engagement with the text of the Qur'an.

On a personal note, I would like to salute my first cousin once removed, Emeritus Professor L. Carl Brown of Princeton University, the senior Arabist in the family, who for many years has set an admirable example of scholarship and teaching. As always, I owe more than I can say to my wife, Judith Ernst.

Portions of the research for this book were supported by a residency at the Doris Duke Foundation for Islamic Art, a fellowship from the John Simon Guggenheim Memorial Foundation, and a fellowship from the Mellon-supported Program in Medieval and Early Modern Studies at UNC. I also gratefully acknowledge the support of the William R. Kenan Jr. Charitable Trust and the UNC College of Arts and Sciences.

Finally, this book is dedicated to the memory of Dr. Nasr Hamid Abu Zayd (1943–2010), a gifted scholar and pioneer in the literary study of the Qur'an.

How to Read the Qur'an

The Problem of Reading the Qur'an

Obstacles to Reading the Qur'an

The genesis of this book comes from a simple question: how should non-Muslims read the Qur'an? On one level, this would seem to be a relatively straightforward issue. The Qur'an is a sacred text, comparable to the Bible and the scriptures of other religious traditions, which are often read and studied in academic and literary contexts. From that point of view, the questions might seem to be primarily technical—how is the text organized, what are its primary features, and what is its audience and principal interpretive traditions? Surely the Qur'an should be approached like any other text.

But with the Qur'an the situation is different. The Qur'an is the source of enormous anxiety in Europe and America, for both religious conservatives, who are alarmed about a competitive postbiblical revelation, and secularists, who view Islam with deep suspicion as an irrational force in the post-Enlightenment world. Neither of those worldviews takes the Qur'an very seriously as a text; according to these views, it is instead a very dangerous problem. It is even the case that a number of attempts have been made to outlaw the sale and distribution of the Qur'an completely, as a text that promotes violence, an argument made by fundamentalist Hindus in India during the 1980s and more recently by a right-wing anti-immigration party in the Netherlands. In 2002, outside religious groups sued the University of North Carolina at Chapel Hill for violating the freedom of religion, when (at my suggestion) it assigned a translation of selections from the Qur'an as its summer reading program for all incoming students that year.[1] In 2010, an obscure Christian pastor in Florida drew worldwide attention when he threatened to burn copies of the Qur'an, claiming that it was the cause of the terrorist attacks against American targets in September 2001. These are only a few manifestations of contemporary nervousness about reading the Qur'an. I would argue that such an attitude of suspicion is hardly conducive to a fair-minded understanding of the text.

Hostile readers of the Qur'an use a literary approach that is the equivalent of a blunt instrument. They make no attempt to understand the text as a whole; instead, they take individual verses out of context, give them the most extreme interpretation possible, and implicitly claim that over 1 billion Muslims around the world robotically adhere to these extremist views without exception. This is, in effect, a conspiracy theory that has virally multiplied in significant sectors of modern Euro-American society. It is irrational, it is paranoid, and it is out of touch with the realities of the lives of most Muslims around the world today. It ignores the existence of multiple traditions of interpreting the Qur'an in very different fashions (see chapter 1). Unfortunately, a small minority of extremists, who quote the Qur'an in support of terrorist violence, have been magnified by the media into a specter that is now haunting Europe (and the United States) more intensely than Marxism ever did.[2] In part because of these contemporary anxieties, it is difficult for most Europeans and Americans to read the Qur'an.

What is the Qur'an, actually? The historical evidence regarding the origin of the Qur'an is discussed in greater detail in chapter 1, but a brief summary is offered here for those who are unfamiliar with the text. The Qur'an (the title literally means "recitation"—the older spelling "Koran" is no longer used by scholars) can be described as a book in the Arabic language that is divided into 114 chapters known as suras; these suras in turn are divided into numbered verses (*ayas*), of which there are nearly 6,000 in all. While there is debate over exactly how the Qur'an was transmitted and collected, there is widespread agreement among both Muslim authorities and modern Euro-American scholars that the basic text emerged in sections during the lifetime of the Prophet Muhammad over a period of some twenty-three years (roughly 610–32 CE). Then, by a process that is still quite unclear, these portions were assembled into the present form over the next few decades.[3] The text features numerous indications of oral composition techniques, such as repetition, argumentative ("agonistic") style, building blocks, symmetry, and formulaic utterances, which are often difficult for modern readers to appreciate.⁴ In terms of chronological sequence, the most significant division of the suras of the Qur'an is marked by the emigration (*hijra*) of the Prophet Muhammad in 622 CE, when he left the unfriendly environment of pagan Mecca and took leadership over the town of Medina; this was roughly halfway through his prophetic career. The Meccan and Medinan suras show quite different qualities. The short and rhythmically powerful Meccan suras sustained the worship services of a small community of believers under pressure from a hostile pagan establishment. In contrast, the lengthy and prosaic Medinan suras debated scriptural and legal issues with Jews and Christians, at a time when Muhammad's followers were striving to survive as a community during a difficult struggle with opposing military forces and political treachery. The differing characteristics of the Meccan and Medinan suras will be crucial for understanding the changes in the way the Qur'an unfolded over time.

The other basic point to be made about the Qur'an is that it has a central importance in Islamic religious practice. Muslims (who number well over 1 billion souls today) consider the Qur'an to be the word of God, transmitted through the Prophet Muhammad. Although over 80 percent of Muslims worldwide are not native speakers of Arabic, all observant Muslims need to know at least portions of the Qur'an by heart in the original language, to recite in their daily prayers. Recitation of the Arabic text of the Qur'an is a demanding art; at the highest level, virtuoso Qur'an reciters demonstrate vocal skills comparable to those of an opera singer. Handwritten copies of the Qur'an, often in lavish and lovingly created calligraphic styles, represent one of the most revered forms of Islamic art. The Qur'an is a major source of Islamic religious ethics and law, and it has had a pervasive impact on the literatures of Arabic, Persian, Turkish, Urdu, and many other languages spoken by Muslims.

In comparison with the Bible, the Qur'an exhibits much greater textual stability, and the variant readings found in different manuscripts are largely trivial differences in pronunciation or vocabulary. A number of theories have been advanced in recent years by European writers, questioning the traditional account of its composition. Some have proposed that the Qur'an was actually assembled as long as two centuries after the time of the Prophet Muhammad. This hypothetical argument has not gained much traction, because of a lack of supporting evidence. Other more bizarre theories have been advanced, claiming that the Qur'an is really based on a Christian text, or that it is not written in Arabic at all, but in a form of

Syriac that is badly understood (see chapter 1). Scholars of biblical studies (and readers of *The Da Vinci Code*) are certainly familiar with breathless exposés that claim to overturn all of the history of Christianity. This kind of radical revisionism probably gets more of a hearing when it concerns Islam, in part because most people are less familiar with the subject, but also because of fantasy expectations about debunking the Qur'an; otherwise it is hard to understand why such eccentric publications would be featured on the front page of the *New York Times*.[5]

While the Qur'an overlaps with the Bible on certain subjects, it is unfamiliar enough in its distinctive narratives and in its stylistic peculiarities that many first-time readers have pronounced it to be impenetrable. The strangeness of the Qur'an for the Jewish or Christian reader lies in the fact that it does not repeat earlier biblical texts but instead makes brief allusions to them while providing a new and original synthesis that departs from familiar ways of reading the Old and New Testaments. Though the Bible, especially in the King James Version, has had centuries of powerful impact on the development of English prose, the Qur'an remains an unknown cipher for most English speakers, despite its tremendous influence on the literatures and languages of the Middle East, Africa, and Asia.

Given the blank slate of sheer unfamiliarity with the Qur'an among Americans and Europeans, it is perhaps inevitable that certain cultural habits have become obstacles to an understanding of it. In the mood of anxiety and fear of the post-9/11 era, it is perhaps understandable that one of these habits would be the temptation to find quick answers in this ancient text, to provide simple solutions to an urgent modern political problem. Unfortunately, nervous haste all too readily leads to serious problems of misrepresentation, as isolated phrases are made to stand in for a whole text, a single text is made to stand for an entire religion, and extremist individuals magnified by the media are taken to be representative of hundreds of millions of people in dozens of different countries. These are not trivial mistakes; weighty and unfortunate consequences flow from any distorted prejudice that substitutes for real knowledge.

At this point, I would like to draw attention to several ways in which it has been common to approach a text like the Qur'an superficially. One is what Professor Peter Wright of Colorado College calls "religious tourism," which he defines as "the presumption shared by many people that learning about religion consists in hearing various dogmas and then arguing about whether or not one finds those dogmas compelling."[6] Put another way, reli-

gion is thought of as a marketplace in which the commodities are "beliefs," which supposedly can be determined and evaluated by a quick look at a few lines, regardless of their meaning in context. Obviously, one does not need to actually read much, or take any classes, in order to decide what one likes or does not like; advertising and the media typically fill in the blanks for consumers of religion, just as they do for buyers of other commodities.

But it turns out that texts like the Qur'an, which come from far away and which have been held in reverence by many people over centuries, have multiple meanings. There are major groups of believers who accept the Qur'an (or the Bible) as an authority but who have radically different understandings of what it is all about. To imagine that one can pick up a complicated text like this, read a few lines, and know what it "says" on any given topic is unrealistic, to say the least. As one early Muslim leader observed, the Qur'an does not speak, but it does require an interpreter (see chapter 1). One of the key points of this book is that the focus of the Qur'an underwent significant changes during the twenty-three years when it was being delivered. If in fact the Qur'an altered its expression and emphasis for changing audiences and circumstances on its first appearance, how could one decide what the Qur'an says on any given subject for all times? Another major conclusion of this book is that the central messages of the Qur'an are embedded in its structure, in the way that its component parts are put together, so pulling a random verse out of context is as likely as not to produce misinformation. The good news is that, with a little more effort, one can come to understand both the structures by which the Qur'an is composed and the changing literary and historical situations within which it had meaning for its audiences.

Another questionable assumption is the idea that if one understands the Qur'an, one understands the entire Islamic faith, and therefore one understands all Muslims. This breathtakingly simple concept, a by-product of Protestant views of scripture, is no doubt convenient; it means that in order to understand Muslims one does not really have to take seriously things like hundreds of years of history and politics, social and economic conditions, the cultures of different regions, and so on. It would be easy if, from a few lines in a sacred text, one could predict everything about the behavior of hundreds of millions of people in widely separated countries, as if they were programmed from a central computer. A simple thought experiment should indicate otherwise. What does the New Testament tell us about modern American Christian attitudes on issues like abortion, homo-

sexuality, and environmentalism? Since Christians fall on all sides of these issues (let alone the debate about which groups count as Christian), many additional factors would have to be introduced to provide convincing explanations of these questions. Likewise, the Qur'an by itself is far from explaining the history of Muslim majority societies. Even in a relatively specialized subject like classical Islamic law and ethics, the Qur'an is only one of several sources of authority. Those who wish to understand Muslims today will need to look at a great many other subjects besides the Qur'an.

Another obstacle that needs to be addressed is the assumption that the Qur'an, unlike the Bible or the Greek and Latin classics, is an exotic oriental text that is foreign to the traditions of "the West." Elsewhere I have attempted to point out that Islam plays a significant role in both European and American history, and that it would be a mistake to pretend otherwise.[7] More important, recent research is making it possible to understand how closely the Qur'an is related to other ancient texts, both biblical and later in origin. The intertextual relationship between the Qur'an and other writings of "Western civilization" is a controversial subject only in theology. That is, for Christian theologians, and later for post-Enlightenment European scholars, the Qur'an was viewed as an inferior derivative work, a travesty of the Bible. Conversely, for Muslim scholars, divergences between the Qur'an and biblical texts were proof of the distortions of the Bible. For neither of these groups has it been considered worthwhile to investigate the way that the Qur'an engages with earlier texts, as part of a shared civilization. If one sets aside such theological competition, however, once this barrier is removed it becomes wonderfully apparent that the Qur'an was aimed at an audience that was quite aware of a wide range of ancient religious literature that is also claimed by the West. Moreover, like other prophetic writings, the Qur'an engages in critical rewriting of those previous texts as a way of establishing its own voice. While we are far from having a comprehensive view of this intertextual relationship, one of the aims of this book is to acquaint readers with examples of the ways in which the Qur'an references and grapples with earlier sacred writings. Seeing the text in this way makes it clear that the Qur'an is in fact a part of the same tradition as the Bible.

The problem of reading the Qur'an is compounded by the fact that the scholarship surrounding this text is one of the most forbidding and technical fields of what used to be called Oriental studies. Much of the modern scholarship on the subject is published in German and French, and even

the English-language materials are located mostly in specialized journals or in hard-to-find collections of articles. Moreover, Qur'anic studies as an academic field has been pursued by a relatively small number of researchers, so that it can scarcely compare with the vast number of publications that have been produced in biblical studies over the past century or so. Still, there have been significant advances made in Qur'anic scholarship in recent years, which include the first specialized academic journal devoted to the subject, plus a number of excellent academic syntheses and reference works, including the extremely valuable *Encyclopaedia of the Qur'an*.[8] But it is still difficult for the average interested reader to get access to the most important available scholarship on the Qur'an. The media and popular writings about Islam are much more interested in oddball attempts at discrediting the Qur'an than in the more challenging task of reading the text seriously. Internet sites operated by religious organizations (whether attacking Islam or defending it) shed more heat than light upon the subject. What is needed at this point is a clear and straightforward presentation of the main issues and debates in modern scholarship concerning the structure and characteristics of the Qur'an, which will enable readers to come to a significant understanding of this complicated text, its relationship to other scriptures, and its historical context. That rather urgent need is the pretext for this guide to reading the Qur'an.

Aims of This Book

This book is aimed at several overlapping groups of readers. The first audience I have in mind is college and university students taking a course on Islam, the Qur'an, Abrahamic religions, world religions, or comparative literature; this includes secondary school students who have the opportunity to take courses on some of these topics. Along with my students, several times I have worked through many of the problems explored in this book in my own course on the Qur'an as literature. An audience of students can be presumed to be intelligent and curious, though not necessarily as having any particular background on the subject. For them, my goal is to provide historical and literary access to the text, so that students can not only come to an understanding of significant parts of the Qur'an but can also develop the skills to read it (and other challenging texts) on their own. In accordance with the principles of the academic study of religion, this is presented in a nontheological fashion. It is not assumed that students or readers share any particular religious orthodoxy, and no judgment is made about whether or not the Qur'an is a divine revelation or the word of God. What is undeniable is the fact that the Qur'an is a very important text that has been taken seriously by hundreds of millions of people for well over a thousand years, and that it is related to a number of earlier scriptural texts. On that historical and literary basis, it is not only feasible but also important to pursue an understanding of how the Qur'an works. There are also quite a few general readers outside of the university who are genuinely curious about what kind of book the Qur'an is and how to understand it, and this literary and historical introduction is designed for them as well.

I am aware that there are other audiences, both religious and nonreligious, for this guide to reading the Qur'an who have interests that go beyond academic inquiry. For them too, I believe that a historical and literary approach will be of great importance. Although my approach is nontheological, I will return to the question of the theological implications of the literary study of the Qur'an in the conclusion of this book. Increasingly, members of other religious faiths are realizing that the study of the Qur'an can be relevant to their own traditions. Thus, students in Christian or Jewish theological seminaries and divinity schools (and religiously minded readers in general) will find that many of the intellectual tools developed in this book have an interesting relevance to their own religious investigations. For them, the question of the relationship of the Qur'an to biblical texts can have considerable significance when it is carried out in a nonpartisan fashion without predetermined agendas.

Finally, there will undoubtedly be Muslim readers who are curious about what non-Muslim scholars make of the Qur'an, whether these readers are concerned to defend their own faith or to ask questions about it. Having always had Muslim students in my classes and among my graduate students, I want to underline the fact that this historical and literary approach is impartial and respectful, and that it seeks the understanding that is the basis for real communication. From that perspective, I hope this book will be useful to Muslim readers as well, even though it does not reproduce the authoritative views of the Qur'an that would be found in Muslim religious institutions.

This guide to reading the Qur'an by its very nature assumes a literary approach to the text, which is a method that has already been well developed for the study of the Bible as literature. By referring to the Qur'an as literature, I have something very specific in mind: the Qur'an as a text is formulated with a language and style that may be understood in terms of its literary forms and contents. Like other sacred texts, the Qur'an may be studied through its use of literary features, such as hyperbole, metaphor, allegory, symbolism, personification, irony, wordplay, and poetry.[9] Regardless of whether or not one considers the Qur'an to be a divine communication, the fact remains that it is a text expressed in human language and aimed at human audiences and that it appeared in a particular historical context. It is therefore possible for any reader to ask questions about its form and content and to come to a better understanding about how it would have been received at the time of its delivery. The related issues of how the Qur'an connects to literary traditions in the languages of the Mediterranean and western Asia and how the Qur'an has been interpreted by Muslim scholars over the centuries are separate questions (and immense subjects) that are outside the scope of this book. The great advantage of this literary approach is that it can appeal to nonspecialists, and it does not require readers to declare any particular religious allegiance in advance. No doubt, a literary and historical approach carries with it a series of assumptions about the nature of texts, and those assumptions may be debated. Nevertheless, this method has the advantage of offering a relatively open space for discussion that is not dominated by confessional or ideological concerns.

How does this book differ from other introductions to the Qur'an? Simply claiming to use a literary and historical approach is not enough, since literary and historical frameworks also characterize the hostile and condescending studies of European Orientalists, who have seen the Qur'an as both foreign ("Oriental," that is, not Western) and the product of an inferior colonized civilization. Instead, I am working from the perspective of a post-Orientalist and cosmopolitan approach to the study of Islam (chapter 1). What this boils down to is that the Qur'an, like many other influential and important works of the past, is part of a global heritage that is relevant to any educated person, regardless of his or her religious persuasion—or lack of it. By starting out with that assumption, I am stating that the Qur'an is a work that is worth studying, on its own terms and in its own context, without the negative preconceptions that are all too commonly applied to it. In this way, the Qur'an can be seen in terms of broad humanistic and social-scientific issues, so it can be integrated into the curriculum of knowledge rather than isolated as an exotic item.

By looking at the Qur'an as a literary work that exists in history, I am also taking it out of the context of scriptural authority. What is striking about most recent general publications on the Qur'an is the way they treat it mainly as an authoritative text that has a certain number of particular themes and messages that can be discovered and defined. That is, they consider the Qur'an from a postcanonical perspective, which means that it is a finished work to be seen primarily as an unchallenged source of teachings and commandments for the community that accepts it as a sacred text. Thus the majority of presentations of the Qur'an, by proposing to explain how Muslims understand the Qur'an, end up deferring to the historic interpretations of it that are found in the dominant traditions of Islamic thought. Although that is certainly a legitimate project, such a subject-oriented approach is open to the objection that it assumes that all of the Qur'an is to be treated as equally authoritative and consistent, and it tends to accept uncritically the interpretive conclusions of current forms of Sunni (and, to a much lesser extent, Shi'i) orthodoxy. Aside from the conspiracy theorists who wish to debunk and deconstruct the Qur'an, nearly all general treatments of the Qur'an (whether written by Muslims or by non-Muslims) adopt some notion of traditional Islamic scholarship as the baseline for interpretation. This observation is true of the anti-Islamic activists who wish to ban the Qur'an as a dangerous incitement to violence, and it is also applicable to fundamentalist Muslim engineers who think of the Qur'an as an instruction manual, which they distribute on numerous look-alike websites. All of these sources purport to tell the reader what the Qur'an "says."

What is missing from nearly all these approaches is any sense of the exciting scholarship that has been done on the Qur'an as a text that has developed over time and which unfolded in interaction and dialogue with a contemporary audience.[10] Instead of offering the reader selections from the Qur'an organized around topical themes, I present a chronological reading of the Qur'anic text, following and building on the best research of modern scholarship. The historical approach to the unfolding of the Qur'an was initially proposed by Theodor Nöldeke a century and a half ago, and it has proven to be a sturdy method that continues to be fruitful, especially as developed more recently by scholars such as Angelika Neuwirth. This approach to the Qur'an offers an attractive alternative to the usual method of reading the text. This is because the official edition of the Qur'an arranges the 114 suras more or less in decreasing order of size, and it turns out that the parts of the Qur'an that were the last to be delivered are found at the beginning, since they are the longest. The result is that if one reads the Qur'an in its official order, it is extremely difficult for the new reader to understand what is going on; it is the equivalent of starting a novel by reading the last chapter first. But if one approaches the text chronologically, beginning with the short suras toward the end, which were the first to be delivered, a very different reading experience results that arguably makes a great deal more sense to new readers. This chronological approach also recapitulates the sequence of the Qur'an that was experienced by its first audience. That, in short, is the method adopted in this guide to reading the Qur'an. It is, of course, quite different from the ritual study of the Qur'an as a divine liturgy, as practiced in Muslim communities. There, accurate pronunciation and recitation of the richly poetic Arabic text according to complex rules provides an experience quite different from silently reading a prosaic English translation. But such a gap is to be expected in a literary and historical study that does not claim to duplicate the reading of an insider.[11]

There are four basic elements of the chronological and literary approach to the Qur'an used in this book: development, structure, intertextuality, and historical context. These four elements can be briefly explained as follows.

First, establishing the chronological sequence of the suras of the Qur'an, even in a rough fashion, permits an appreciation of the development of the text over time. This means that one can pursue the question of how the first sections of the Qur'an were received by its audience, prior to the formulation of the Qur'an as a completed book; this may be considered the precanonical understanding the Qur'an. To give one simple example, the very word *qur'an* ("recitation"), when it first occurred in the earliest Meccan suras, would not have signified to listeners the completed text "between two covers" that we know today, since only a portion of the text had come into existence at that time. By comparing the different meanings that such a term undergoes chronologically, or by looking at the distinctive styles, structures, and vocabularies of different periods, one can build up a sense of the way that Qur'anic discourse developed in relation to its audience. In addition, there is the very important phenomenon of later insertions in early suras, which in many cases can be explained as the result of questions that listeners asked about passages that needed clarification or comment.

Detecting these phases in the composition and construction of Qur'anic passages allows the reader to understand why the text took on its current form.

Second, appreciation of the internal structure and organization of the Qur'an is extremely helpful for grasping its overall message, and it offers ways to comprehend the relation of one passage to another. Within the chronological framework, the primary unit of analysis is the sura, which needs to be understood as a literary whole rather than a random assortment of unrelated verses. And the sura, which to the new reader may indeed look like a random composition, must be broken down into sections that illustrate the way meaning is expressed. Stylistic analysis, for example, has demonstrated that many suras of the Qur'an exhibit a tripartite structure, in which the opening and closing sections affirm revelation, while the central section often relates a scriptural narrative concerning prophecy and its reception. Having a sense of this kind of structure helps readers to understand the dynamics within a given sura. This threefold organization, especially in the Meccan suras, follows established models, evoking not only the performance of a monotheistic worship service but also the odes of the pre-Islamic Arabic poets (chapter 3). There are also many instances of distinctive literary forms and genres, such as oaths, end-times or apocalyptic, signs of God in nature, and debate (explored in chapter 1), that are helpful to understanding different expressions in the Qur'an. Especially noteworthy is the strong presence of symmetrical organization or ring composition in many sections of the Qur'an (discussed at length in reference to Medinan suras in chapter 4). This structural feature, in which central messages are surrounded by contrasting frame sections, is very helpful for determining the most important points of emphasis in the Qur'an; ring composition indicates that the central points have priority and furnish principles of interpretation that govern the apparently conflicting statements that are typically found in adjacent verses.

Third, intertextuality is the relationship of one literary text to another, which can range from outright quotation to the subtlest of echoes. The Qur'an contains extensive reflections on earlier religious texts, mainly the Bible and to a lesser extent other writings. Theological concerns over the possible corruption of earlier scriptures have led later Muslim commentators to discount these connections, in order to preserve the purity of the Qur'anic revelation. Hostile readers of the Qur'an have often overemphasized what they saw as the dependence of the Qur'an on biblical sources, which allowed them to depict the Qur'an as an inferior and derivative work. Leaving these agendas aside, it turns out to be surprisingly useful to examine the way that the Qur'an alludes to and revises earlier scriptures, presenting itself as their fulfillment. This is not a new technique. The New Testament takes much the same approach with the Old Testament; and within the Hebrew Bible, later prophets revise earlier ones.[12] This literary relationship by way of allusion also clarifies the way in which the Qur'an forms part of a long tradition of scriptural reflection.

Fourth, historical context is extremely important in providing clues for the interpretation of particular passages. A great deal can be done with rhetorical analysis of internal elements of the text, such as formulas of address, and implied audiences, to provide convincing explanations of the significance of Qur'anic language. External sources need to be used with some caution, however, since some parts of the interpretive and historical traditions of early Islam seem to have been constructed precisely in order to fill in gaps and clarify unclear aspects of the Qur'an. Biographies of the Prophet Muhammad, for example, tend to be much more historically useful for the Medinan suras than for the Meccan suras.[13] Nevertheless, it is useful to consider information about historical context to provide interpretive frameworks for understanding the Qur'an.

When these elements of literary and historical analysis are applied in a careful reading of the Qur'an, new perspectives emerge on fundamental issues. Regarding the initial audience of the Qur'an in Mecca, archeological evidence of the widespread extent of tombs in the Arabian Peninsula (chapter 2), combined with analysis of debate passages from the middle and late Meccan suras (chapter 3), suggests that the "pagans" of Mecca were far more knowledgeable about prophetic religious themes than is commonly acknowledged. The existence of later insertions in early Meccan suras (chapter 2) indicates that the Qur'an was revised in dialogue with its first audience, who recited these suras frequently in worship services and asked questions about difficult passages. Application of this principle to sura 53 ("The Star") leads to the conclusion that the so-called Satanic verses in all likelihood never existed as part of the Qur'an (chapter 2). The intensive liturgical use of early Qur'anic texts is demonstrated by the many references that sura 15 (al-Hijr) makes to early Meccan texts, particularly the ritually important sura 1 (chapter 3). Sura 18 ("The Cave") draws upon mythical, folkloric, and epic narratives (the Seven Sleepers, al-Khidr, the romance of Alexander) from Christian and other Near Eastern sources and reframes them to provide a distinctive new interpretation. A close study of debates in selected Medinan suras (chapter 4) indicates that the sharp demarcations of religious identity that we assume today were not nearly as clear for listeners presupposed by the Qur'an. In fact, the evidence supports the notion that the "believers" in Medina who accepted the authority of Muhammad included Jews and Christians along with converted pagans. Rhetorical analysis in terms of symmetrical "ring composition" makes it possible to locate the central points of emphasis in the lengthy and complicated Medinan suras, revealing the Qur'an's firm articulation of the principle of religious pluralism, despite circumstances of historical conflict. The presence in the Medinan suras of revised versions of key liturgical texts from the Bible (including Psalms and New Testament canticles) illustrates a typical prophetic rewriting of previous revelations. These are examples of the conclusions resulting from the literary and historical analysis offered here.

In summary, the overall approach of this book is to provide the interested reader access to a scholarly approach to the Qur'an based upon recent research, but without the jargon and overly technical language typical of specialized research in this field. This is what the French call *un livre de diffusion*, an accessible book that presents and clarifies some of the best academic work on the Qur'an, laying out the debates and what is at stake, in a way that empowers the reader to do more reading independently.[14] In pursuing this task, I have drawn selectively upon what seem to me the most compelling examples of modern scholarship, pushing their conclusions further with new applications and synthesizing their insights in a way that has not been done before. I use notes to indicate the sources that I bring to the table for this discussion, and also for a few detailed comments that will be of interest primarily to specialists. But the main argument of the book has been designed for the motivated general reader with no particular background. This task is approached not by a complete translation of the Qur'an but by a "reading" of selected suras of the Qur'an in chronological order, including a liberal amount of translation, examining internal textual structure and relationships with textual predecessors as well as with other portions of the Qur'an. I hope that this book can be used as a model, both in classes and by motivated individual readers, to set up reading strategies for exploring portions of the Qur'an that I do not directly discuss (some suggestions for course instructors and for individual readers are provided in appendix C). Since this is an introductory work, it aims to illustrate a particular literary approach to the Qur'an without attempting to be exhaustive, with the added intention of encouraging other scholars to carry out further investigations of those parts of the Qur'an that are not covered here.

The purpose of this literary reading is understanding rather than the taking of theological sides. The title of this book, *How to Read the Qur'an*, indicates both the problem outlined in this chapter and the method demonstrated in the remainder of the book. I use the term "reading" deliberately, to indicate that a literary engagement with the Qur'an is necessarily an act of interpretation. This is, after all, only one reading of the Qur'an as literature, and others will surely produce different readings that either complement or challenge the conclusions offered here.

Style and Organization of This Book

My translations of passages from the Qur'an have several different formats, depending upon the focus of the argument at hand. Sometimes each verse is placed on a separate numbered line, especially in the case of the early suras with very short lines. Translations are also presented with short verses clustered in paragraphs, occasionally separated by slashes. For certain more complex and longer suras, each verse begins a new line, but successive phrases (the amount that can be easily recited in a single breath) start a new line that is indented beyond the first line. These different presentations are meant to clarify the structure of the sura. Because the voice of the implied speaker shifts frequently throughout the Qur'an, pronouns clearly referring to God and titles for revelation ("the Book," "the Reminder") are capitalized in translations from the Qur'an, in order to avoid confusion for readers.

Reference to the Qur'an follows the verse divisions of the standard Egyptian edition: thus, 5:3 indicates sura 5, verse 3. Occasionally, for longer verses, decimal points are used to indicate sections within a verse; 5:3.1 would be the beginning of that verse, 5:3.5 is the middle, and 5:3.9 designates the end. All translations of the Qur'an are mine unless otherwise indicated (the sura titles in chart 1.1 are A. J. Arberry's translations, by way of comparison). Translations of the Bible are from the New International Version. Dates are given according to the Gregorian calendar or Common Era (CE).

The style of translation is generally plain and strives to be idiomatic in modern American English. This often means departing from the ponderous and archaic style, reminiscent of the King James Bible, which many translators often implicitly accept as the norm for English translations of sacred texts. For problematic terms and passages, I find it very useful to reflect on the etymologies and classical usages found in specialized dictionaries.[15] Translations of the Qur'an into other languages are also helpful. At times, I may resort to unusual translation strategies for the sake of making a particular point or illustrating an issue under discussion. Occasionally, I employ informal, blunt, and contemporary usage, which works well to convey the direct emotional power of the Qur'an's language. The stilted tone and formal affect of many English Qur'an translations fail to deliver the urgency and commanding presence that, to my ear at least, are such strong characteristics of its style in Arabic. At times, I deliberately depart from "word for word" equivalence and translate the same Arabic word differently, depending on context and effect. Sometimes, translation will highlight one particular semantic field associated with an Arabic word, which may not show up in other translations. All this is part of the normal challenge that faces the translator of a text that can be read in multiple fashions. None of these translations is proposed here as a "final" or definitive version, since questions will continue to be asked that require new approaches to translating this text. Serious readers are generally advised, in any case, to have more than one English translation of the Qur'an at hand while reading this book to get a sense of the possibilities and the gaps between the different versions.[16] In that sense, all translation is provisional and subject to revision; my aim is to produce versions of the Qur'anic text that are alive and directly accessible to a modern literary sensibility.

The organization of this book is largely focused on questions of the structure and style of the Qur'anic text. In this respect, my approach differs from subject-oriented doctrinal presentations of the Qur'an, which in effect assume a single homogeneous viewpoint that can be decoded by comparing selected passages. The subject-oriented approach is also characteristic of legal interpretation of the Qur'an, which looks to this text as the primary source of authoritative Islamic teachings on religious norms and ethics. These legal interpreters have evolved elaborate interpretive strategies to flatten out the apparent inconsistencies between different Qur'anic passages, relying in particular on the notion of abrogation, discussed in chapter 1. That kind of harmonizing approach acknowledges a chronological dimension to the unfolding of the Qur'an, as is evident from the traditional labeling of suras as belonging to the earlier Meccan period or the later Medinan period. Abrogation also conveniently erases apparent inconsistencies by proclaiming the later text authoritative, leaving the significance of "abrogated" earlier verses unclear. Nevertheless, the commitment to finding authoritative rulings in the Qur'an is resistant to the notion of any development of Qur'anic style and message in dialogue with its audience. The rhetorical affirmation of scriptural authority, which is such a frequent message in practically every sura of the Qur'an, reinforces the expectation that the Qur'an, as the manifestation of the primordial heavenly book, should take on through time a form that had been decreed from all eternity.

The perspective offered in this book does not assume that canonical authority is the implicit and dominant characteristic of the Qur'anic text. Rather, it seeks to explore the initial reception of the text and the creative ongoing revision of prophetic messages as part of a dialogical process, which can be extrapolated from the internal evidence of the text itself. In other words, this book approaches the Qur'an not as it is constituted by its authoritative reception in later commentary and legal interpretation but in a pre-exegetical and precanonical sense, prior to the development of firm traditions of interpretation, and as a text that emerged in a particular historical context. Such a nontheological reading is not meant to be an antireligious rejection of the divine status of the Qur'an as accepted by Muslims. Rather, it brackets out the question of religious authority as something outside of the scope of the present inquiry. The literary understanding of the style and structure of the Qur'an is a question that any educated reader may explore, without having to make a theological commitment either for or against its sacred authority. In this sense, the study of the Qur'an should be no different than the study of the Hebrew Bible or the New Testament—in universities, these texts are not studied today primarily through the authoritative interpretations found in Midrashic commentaries or the writings of the Church Fathers, but as literary texts that emerged in particular historical contexts. In the same way, there is no reason why contemporary study of the Qur'anic text should privilege any particular later commentary tradition, if the aim is to understand how the text came together and was first received.[17]

The outline of the book follows the implications of the presuppositions just discussed. To begin, chapter 1 frames the Qur'an in its historical context and offers literary perspectives on its structure and chronological unfolding. This includes an overview of the literary forms present in the suras as the basic units into which the Qur'an is divided, and the chapter also surveys the different ways in which the Qur'an may be read, from both religious and literary perspectives. This survey is followed by three separate chapters that offer a chronological reading of the Qur'an according to the conclusions of modern scholarship. Chapter 2 addresses the early Meccan suras, chapter 3 covers the middle and later Meccan suras (which are treated together, because of their relative similarity), and chapter 4 is concerned with the Medinan suras. In each case, representative suras are presented in translation with accompanying analysis, to bring out significant literary and structural aspects of their composition. These examples include both relatively typical suras and some that are quite distinctive, in form or in content. In addition, while this literary approach steers away from the subject-oriented analysis that is characteristic of legal and authoritative interpretation of the Qur'an, in each chapter, one or more topical questions is explored, affording the opportunity for interrogating the way that the Qur'an relates to its environment and its audience. These questions include the implications of the apocalyptic "punishment stories," the rhetoric of debate in relation to the implied audience of the Qur'an, and the development of religious identity and conflict in the Medinan suras. The book ends with a concluding chapter briefly addressing the implications of a literary reading of the Qur'an that situates it in its historical environment.

Although it is not possible to provide a detailed commentary on every sura of the Qur'an within the scope of this book, the method of reading that is demonstrated here can be replicated by readers who are interested in exploring more broadly the texts of the Qur'an. Appendix A, "Reading the Structure of the Meccan Suras," presents outlines of all the Meccan suras of the Qur'an in such a way that the reader can break them down into manageable units for interpretation and in this way pursue a more complete chronological reading of the text. The Medinan suras have not yet been analyzed to the same degree, but it is to be hoped that the methods proposed here will still prove applicable, particularly when it comes to strong compositional features of the Qur'an, such as symmetry or ring composition within the sura. Detailed outlines of some proposed solutions to the structures of two Medinan suras are provided in appendix B. Additional interpretive exercises, suitable for an individual or for reading groups or classes, are suggested in appendix C. These tools are designed for those who wish to read actively and ask questions about how this important text has been organized. It is all too evident that a mere passive reading of the Qur'an in its normal and canonical order is both frustrating and unsatisfactory to the reader who approaches it for the first time.

The outlines and structural analyses of the suras as described here may strike some readers as arbitrary modern impositions, which lack the credibility of traditional interpretations. For those who are only willing to understand the Qur'an according to certain recognized authorities (never mind the fact that there are numerous conflicting traditions of interpretation), this purely literary study may be irrelevant and even useless. But the fact remains that the Qur'an is a text that appeared in a particular time and place, which a particular audience heard and responded to. This book seeks to understand to some extent how that happened, and it proposes a method to interpret the way that the Qur'an functioned as a literary document. This is not the only possible interpretation, but I hope it provides fresh ideas that readers can bring to the text. Those who may find unconvincing the particular analyses of the Qur'anic text offered here should take up the challenge of offering alternative explanations.

Finally, some readers may be surprised at the presence of a number of illustrations in this book, given that the Qur'an is itself not illustrated. These visual images are intended to indicate the connections that the Qur'an has with other cultural traditions, ranging from the monuments of Nabatean cities to portraits of Alexander the Great and memorials to the Seven Sleepers of Ephesus. The justification for the inclusion of these pictures is the presence of their subjects within the Qur'an. This in itself is another indication of the important links that tie the Qur'an to the legacy of a shared civilization.

1

The History and Form of the Qur'an
and the Practices of Reading

Situating the Qur'an in History

The Problem of the Historical Understanding of the Qur'an

The Qur'an is most frequently approached as a religious text that makes authoritative claims, which are to be either rejected or accepted. Certainly there are religious contexts where such an approach makes sense, whether it be in Muslim circles where reinforcement of Islamic religious teachings is the aim or in non-Muslim religious groups where the message of the Qur'an is fiercely opposed. Yet there are other ways of approaching the Qur'an as a literary text embodied in concrete historical situations; it is the argument of this book that situating the Qur'an in history with literary analysis is the most appropriate method both for the modern university and for the emerging global sphere of public culture.

The historical approach to religion as developed in modern universities, particularly in North America, is a way of addressing religious pluralism without either establishing or rejecting any particular form of religion. The university constitutes a public space in which everyone may take part, and the discussion of religion can be carried out by anyone without having to pay the price of a precommitment to any particular religious persuasion. In the academy, it is no longer acceptable (outside of explicitly religious schools) to quote one particular scriptural position as authoritative and beyond question. The proliferation of multiple religious views in modern society makes such an imposition impractical at best—at worst it is a tyrannical dream. Similarly, in the wider public arena, despite the existence of groups intent on imposing their own sectarian dogmas on society, it is increasingly possible for people to come to a positive appreciation of the religious views of others. Such a positive appreciation differs from the grudging acceptance known as tolerance, which only puts up with hated and distrusted others out of necessity. This is not to prejudge the outcome of a historical and literary reading of the Qur'an, but it is my observation that many people today have a genuine curiosity to understand the wellsprings of the religious beliefs of others. A historical and literary approach at least offers the prospect of a fair-minded and reasonable approach to other people's religions, which is why such a method seems both attractive and necessary today.

It might be argued that the Qur'an does not envision the possibility of a nonbeliever understanding the scripture of Islam. Indeed, being a rejecter of God's message is in effect the definition of disbelief. Qur'anic rhetoric treats the divine revelation as so transparently true that only willful disobedience could inspire its rejection. In a frequently repeated image, recalling the biblical language of God "hardening the heart" of Pharaoh, the Qur'an refers to God "putting a seal" on the hearts of unbelievers. "As for the unbelievers, it is the same for them if you warned them or you did not warn them; they do not believe. God has sealed their hearts and their hearing, and upon their sight there is a darkening; theirs is a great punishment" (2:7). At the same time, however, the Qur'an alludes to the possibility of non-Muslims—in this case, Christian monks—being deeply moved by the recitation of the text: "When they hear what was sent down to the messenger, you will see their eyes overflow with tears from that part of the truth that they recognize" (5:83). Admittedly, the Qur'an also envisions these monks proclaiming their faith and their status as witnesses of the revelation, so this ends up being a more or less triumphalist statement about the truth of the Qur'an. But the academic study of religion is necessarily something that stands apart from the endorsement of any particular religious message. What characterizes the academic approach is the application of humanistic and social scientific methodologies to the subject at hand; the scholarly analysis and reframing of a topic is different from the mere replication of its claims to authority.

Yet in another sense the Qur'an does offer a warrant for non-Muslims needing to understand the revelation. In a very profound sense, the Qur'an carries with it a recognition of the inevitable pluralism and multiplicity of humankind. "For everyone we have established a law, and a way. If God had wished, He would have made you a single community, but this was so He might test you regarding what He sent you. So try to be first in doing what is best" (5:48). If the existence of multiple religious groups is, as it were, part of the divine plan from a Muslim perspective, what conclusions may be drawn? Either non-Muslims must commit to endless (and ultimately insoluble) conflict with Muslims, or some kind of overlapping consensus or mutual recognition has to be worked out. Like it or not, non-Muslims will have their own perspectives on the Qur'an and the Islamic tradition, and the Qur'an does not appear to admit the possibility of the Islamic equivalent of evangelizing all humanity. It seems to me that an academic approach based on history and literature offers an important nontheological alternative to the implacable hostility and prejudice against Islam, which is such a prominent characteristic of the current climate of opinion in America and Europe.

There is, of course, a long history of more or less hostile academic study of Islam by non-Muslims, beginning with medieval theological polemics and transitioning to the modern academic enterprise known as Orientalism. Beginning with the first Latin translation of the Qur'an, completed in 1143 by Robert of Ketton, European Christian scholars embarked on a project of studying the Qur'an in order to refute it. The first successful translation of the Qur'an into English, done by George Sale in 1734, was in turn based on a more extensive Latin translation by an Italian Catholic priest named Louis Maracci (1698), which systematically attempted to disprove the Islamic scripture. While Maracci, ironically, viewed Islam as nearly as bad as Lutheran Protestantism, Sale (a Protestant) was content to dismiss Muhammad with faint praise as a minor lawgiver.

Most European intellectuals, even in the age of the Enlightenment, took it for granted that Muhammad was an impostor and that the Qur'an was a fabrication. Thomas Carlyle, who strikingly presented a rare positive portrayal of Muhammad in his book *On Heroes, Hero Worship, and the Heroic in History* (1841), gave the following frequently quoted negative review of Sale's translation of the Qur'an: "I must say, it is as toilsome reading as I ever undertook. A wearisome confused jumble, crude, incondite; endless iterations, long-windedness, entanglement.... Nothing but a sense of duty could carry any European through the Koran."[1] It may be asked in passing whether any of Carlyle's distaste for the Qur'an was due to the English style of George Sale's translation, though that would perhaps be unfair. In any case, Carlyle's jarringly negative verdict on Qur'an is fairly typical of what even the most open-minded European readers had to say on the subject. What Carlyle objected to was the organization and style of the Qur'an, which was believed to have been compiled in a haphazard fashion after the death of Muhammad. To his mind, it was not really a book at all. Still, it is noteworthy that Carlyle was aware that the chapters of the Qur'an were organized roughly by size (with the longest going first), in such a way that the first sections of the text were actually the last to be revealed. "The real beginning of it, in that way, lies almost at the end: for the earliest portions were the shortest. Read in its historical sequence it perhaps would not be so bad."[2] We shall return later to the topic of a chronological reading of the Qur'an.

In any case, there was a long tradition of religious animosity against the Qur'an in Christian Europe. This was followed by the disdain of enlightened intellectuals who viewed the Qur'an as at best a derivative work, definitely inferior to the Bible and to the classics of Greek and Roman antiquity. While there were undoubtedly impressive scholarly contributions in the early European study of Qur'an, it should nevertheless be taken into account that much of that scholarship on the Qur'an was negative in its approach.[3] In a rather different style defined by the Enlightenment, later Orientalist scholarship on the Qur'an would be marked to a considerable extent by the ambivalent projection of the Islamic "other," who was defined in every way as being the opposite of the European.[4]

Nevertheless, new investigations of the historical and literary character of the Qur'an began to appear in Europe by the middle of the nineteenth century. The single most important contribution came from the German scholar Theodor Nöldeke, in his *Geschichte des Qorans* (History of the Qur'an), first published in 1860. Nöldeke, a distinguished scholar of Arabic and Persian, built upon suggestions proposed two decades earlier by Gustav Weil to produce a reassessment of the Qur'an's traditional chronology, in order to refine with more detail the notion of the Meccan and Medinan phases of the Prophet Muhammad's career. Nöldeke employed considerations of not only content but also linguistic style and form to divide the Meccan period into three separate phases. Nöldeke's work was reissued in an expanded form in 1909, supplemented by an additional volume by Friedrich Schwally (1919) on the collection of the Qur'anic text and a concluding third volume (1938) by G. Bergsträsser and O. Pretzl on the variant readings of the Qur'an. This fundamental work of European scholarship, which will be discussed further below, is the basis for all modern academic study of the Qur'an.[5]

In many respects, this historical and literary investigation of the Qur'an was carried out alongside similar critical researches that European scholars were undertaking in the study of biblical texts. Julius Wellhausen's historical-critical analysis of the Old Testament (1883) brought to fruition a movement that questioned the traditional notion that Moses was the author of the first five books of the Bible; he proposed instead the "documentary hypothesis," according to which these books were actually compiled by different authors many centuries later and retroactively attributed to Moses. Similar revisionist approaches had been proposed for the study of the New Testament and the life of Jesus, culminating notably in Albert Schweitzer's *Quest of the Historical Jesus* (1906), which argued that modern authors inevitably projected their own understanding of Jesus in a way that had little to do with the actual historical context of Jesus. It must be acknowledged that such critical studies of the Bible caused dismay and controversy in some religious circles, leading for example to the Catholic Church's 1907 condemnation of modernism as a heresy. Likewise the birth of Protestant fundamentalism, articulated in the 1910 publication of *The Fundamentals*, was in good part a reaction against the German school of biblical criticism (along with Darwinian evolution). It is therefore not surprising that Orientalist scholarship on the Qur'an has been received with similar suspicion and resistance in some Muslim circles, where it has been seen as an attack on the basis of religion. In view of the long history of antagonistic Christian writings on the Qur'an, this negative reaction by Muslims to European scholarship is understandable. Moreover, despite the claims of European scholars regarding their own scientific objectivity, it was quite common until recently for them to make derogatory remarks about the inferior style of the Qur'an compared with European literatures.[6] A similar condescending attitude was typical of European attitudes toward classical Arabic poetry as well.[7] And, as we shall see, there are a number of new "revisionist" theories proposed in recent years, which attempt to cast major doubts on the authenticity of the Qur'anic text.

Despite the presence of theological prejudice and negativity in earlier European studies of the Qur'an, nevertheless, the approach of historical and literary scholarship still has much to offer, nor is it intrinsically anti-religious. After all, if we are not able to make judgments based on rationality and historical evidence, we will be left with appeals to authority, and this is hardly a solution, given the multiple authorities available today. If we are to have a serious academic discussion of this topic, the standard of debate must be characterized by analysis of evidence and argument and by the clarification of the consequences that are at stake. Special pleading on behalf of particular theological positions may be satisfying on one level, but what does genuine faith have to fear from history? Scholarly study should not be held hostage to the charge of deviation from anyone's religious orthodoxy.[8]

Although there certainly are serious problems with the legacy of Orientalist scholarship, of which readers should be aware, the shortcomings of earlier scholars do not in themselves invalidate the principles of historical research. Recent years have seen development of a post-Orientalist form of Islamic studies, in which both Muslim and non-Muslim scholars have joined in applying the methods of the humanities and social sciences to the study of Muslim societies and cultures, without accepting the old colonial antitheses that oppose Europe and America to an imagined "Islamic world."[9] Rather than perpetuate "false dichotomies and unnecessary dilemmas," the new approaches to Islamic studies acknowledge the cosmopolitanism that goes beyond the fixed identities of multiculturalism.[10] It is in this spirit that the present approach to the historical and literary study of the Qur'an is conceived.

A useful analogy for this project is the study of the Bible as literature or from a historical perspective, which is a subject firmly ensconced in the curricula of North American colleges and universities. Literary critics like Northrop Frye, Eric Auerbach, and Harold Bloom have brought critical questions to bear on the structure and function of biblical texts, as well as on their immense impact on later European literatures.[11] Bart Ehrman has produced a rigorously historical introduction to the New Testament that is the undisputed standard in its field, despite its complete avoidance of theological issues.[12] He and many other scholars of biblical studies for years have faced the gap between academic biblical studies and the Sunday school interpretations of the Bible that many students bring with them to college. The political and legal stance that governs American education distinguishes the academic "teaching about religion" from the authoritative "teaching of religion" that takes place in faith communities. Thus, while the teachings that students have received are interesting and worthy of study in their own right, the academic study of religion does not permit authoritarian claims to privilege one perspective over another. While perhaps difficult to implement in practice, the principle that governs this approach to religious studies in no way differs, whether one is speaking of the Bible or of the Qur'an.

History of the Qur'anic Text

The traditional history of the compilation of the Qur'an is fairly well known from early Arabic sources, and it may be summarized as follows. The prophetic career of the Prophet Muhammad took place roughly over the course of twenty-three years, from around 610 up to the time of his death in the year 632 CE. During that time, revelations that he received were delivered orally and were then written down as they appeared on materials of different types, including bone, wood, and leather. Members of the early Muslim community also memorized this material. Muhammad's oral recitation (which is the meaning of the Arabic word *qur'an*) seems not to have been collected into a single book during his lifetime. After his death, his companion and successor Abu Bakr (d. 634) is said to have ordered a collection of the written revelations, fearing for the preservation of the text because of the deaths of a number of those who had memorized it. He entrusted the compilation of the text to Zayd ibn Thabit (d. 655), who had formerly served the Prophet as a scribe. But variations began to emerge in the copies of the Qur'an preserved in different centers of the empire of the caliphate, and dissension resulted. Therefore, the third caliph, 'Uthman (d. 656), called for a standardization of the text, which was again supervised by Zayd ibn Thabit. Copies were distributed to the main centers of the empire, and alternate versions were suppressed. This 'Uthmanic version is regarded as the authoritative text of the Qur'an.[13] While the outlines of this account of the collection of the Qur'an are widely accepted in traditional sources, there are enough different versions of this story and enough references to variations in the text of the Qur'an to prompt questions and alternative theories, as we shall see.

When one turns to the nature of the assembled Qur'anic text, the first point to be addressed is the character of the Arabic language and script in which it is couched. Arabic is considered a West Semitic language, and it belongs to the family of languages with alphabetic scripts (such as Hebrew, Aramaic, and Ethiopic), which all ultimately descend from ancient Phoenician. Old written forms of the Arabic language are found in rock

Figure 1.1. Page from early Qur'an (9:31–32), ca. 900. Doris Duke Foundation for Islamic Art, Shangri La #11.25; photograph © 2002 Shuzo Uemoto.

inscriptions throughout the Arabian Peninsula, which employ several different scripts ultimately derived from South Arabia. Arabic speakers also used the Nabatean script from the second century BCE, notably in the city of Petra (in modern Jordan), and that became the basis for the distinctive Arabic script that emerged in Syria and northwest Arabia in the sixth century CE, sometimes in multilingual inscriptions that included Greek or Syriac.[14] One of the distinctive characteristics of Arabic and other Semitic languages is the formation of words on the basis of consonantal roots. In written form, until the invention of diacritical signs (which came considerably later), the Arabic alphabet depicted only consonants and long vowels; indeed, older manuscripts sometimes fail to distinguish between several different consonants that can be denoted by the same letter, and they can be quite difficult for modern readers to decipher (see figure 1.1). The result is that there are many written words that can be read in more than one way, depending on which short vowels are supplied (and early Arabic script is also inconsistent in the representation of long vowels). In practice, this does not create as much confusion as one might imagine, since experienced readers can generally determine the desired meaning from the context. But there is a sense in which early Arabic script was primarily a memory aid for readers who already knew the contents of the text. In many

ways, the written text of the Qur'an was inseparable from, and indeed relied upon, the authority of oral transmission. Over a period of several centuries, a system of diacritical signs gradually developed, to permit a clear
distinction not only between consonants represented by the same letter
shape but also between short vowels. In this way, non-Arabs who began to
study the text of the Qur'an (as well as secular literature and official docu-
ments in Arabic) would be able to decipher and pronounce the words of
the text more or less correctly.

As has been mentioned, there were a number of varying copies of the
Qur'an that were preserved by companions of the Prophet Muhammad,
which differed from the version established by 'Uthman. Chief among
these was the copy belonging to Ibn Mas'ud (d. 652–53), an eminent and
widely respected early Muslim scholar who was very close to the Prophet
and who had heard much of the Qur'an directly from his lips. As an illustration of some of the differences that existed in the pre-'Uthmanic copies
of the Qur'an, the case of Ibn Mas'ud is important, because later Qur'anic
commentary literature records dozens of variations preserved in his text,
differing from what later became the standard version. Commentators evidently found these alternative versions useful in explaining difficult passages, particularly where they offered synonyms for unusual words. Many
of these variants were simply based on different vowels read into the same
consonantal script, without much consequence in terms of widely differing
meaning, although there are a number of entirely different words in Ibn
Mas'ud's version.

In addition, there are reports that Ibn Mas'ud's copy had a slightly different order of suras and that it even omitted the first and the last two suras
altogether, evidently on the grounds that he considered them to be prayers
rather than part of the Qur'an itself. The notion that some early copies of
the Qur'an had a slightly different order of suras seems to be borne out by
the evidence of a cache of manuscripts discovered in a mosque in San'a,
Yemen, in the early 1970s, although these manuscripts do not otherwise
offer any major variations from the accepted text.[15] While some early Shi'i
scholars maintained that Qur'anic revelations concerning the Prophet's
cousin and son-in-law 'Ali ibn Abi Talib and the family of the Prophet were
eliminated and suppressed, this remained an argument from silence, since
there is no evidence of any surviving material that could prove this assertion. Shi'i authorities now uniformly accept the standard text as canonical.[16] Over the years, however, the 'Uthmanic version assumed primacy as

the standard text of the Qur'an, and by the tenth century the minor variant readings were preserved as acceptable alternatives, initially in a system of seven "readings" (*qira'at*), eventually expanded to fourteen. In practice today, a single reading (that of Hafs via 'Asim) is predominant, because of the widespread acceptance of the 1924 printing of the Qur'an by the Egyptian government using that standard, though the other readings are occasionally available in print or audio recordings.[17] In general, it is widely assumed that the text of the Qur'an has remained remarkably stable and that it has been more or less free from scribal insertions of the kind that crept into the manuscripts of the New Testament.[18]

The existence of variations in a sacred scripture such as the Qur'an will, nevertheless, raise questions in the minds of some readers about what the text of the Qur'an actually is. It is well known among scholars that, despite the efforts of scholars in the early twentieth century, no one has yet produced a critical edition of the Arabic text of the Qur'an according to the standards of European scholarship. Comparison of manuscripts should theoretically provide the means for weeding out any scribal errors that do exist and restoring the most likely original text, a task that traditional Muslim scholarship has also addressed.[19] That this has not yet occurred is partly because many reputedly ancient copies of the Qur'an are preserved in collections that are difficult to access. Indeed, the custodians of libraries in majority Muslim countries may be justifiably reluctant to make their treasures available to outsiders, given the history of negative European scholarship on Islam. There are many intrinsic difficulties in carrying out this project, so the 1924 Egyptian edition is certainly an impressive achievement, even if it does not adhere to the norms of European scholarship. It would be a mistake, however, to imagine that the existence of minor variations in the oldest manuscripts is likely to produce stunning new revelations that would overturn the entire edifice of the Islamic faith.

In the 1930s, two of Theodor Nöldeke's successors (Bergsträsser and Pretzl) in fact proposed an effort to collect microfilms of early manuscripts of the Qur'an to use as the basis for a critical edition. The collection of microfilms that they began was widely thought to have been destroyed by Allied bombing of Berlin during World War II, but recently it has become known that the collection of 450 rolls of film was actually preserved by another German scholar, Anton Spitaler, who died in 2003 at an advanced age. Journalistic accounts of this Qur'anic archive immediately took the sensational approach that has characterized the fitful interest in Islam and the short attention span that is so typical of the news/entertainment media today. A *Wall Street Journal* reporter published a lurid front-page account, strongly hinting that all the German scholars had been Nazis and suggesting that scholarly study of the Qur'an would provide shocking challenges to the Muslim faith in the authenticity of the Qur'an.[20] In response, Michael Marx, director of the Corpus Coranicum Research Centre (which is now undertaking a new project for editing manuscripts of the Qur'an), wrote a scathing reply, poking fun at the newspaper article. Marx argued that this article was an example of the modern tendency to believe in vast conspiracy theories like that in *The Da Vinci Code*, imagining fanciful scenarios of romantic historical research (à la Indiana Jones) that would call into question the entire history of a major religion, and which have certainly produced entire industries of publishing, film, and tourism. More seriously, Marx challenged the notion that all the German scholars were Nazis and also questioned the tendency of journalists to focus only on revisionist theories of the origins of Islam.[21] In truth, the Corpus Coranicum project has received reasonably positive responses in major Muslim academic circles, and it promises to make real advances toward what Marx calls "a vision of history in which Christian, Jewish and Muslim traditions refer to a shared Middle Eastern heritage."

What are the most recent scholarly perspectives on the history of the Qur'anic text and its origins? As mentioned previously, one of the objectives of Nöldeke's approach had been to refine on the basis of literary and historical criticism the chronological sequence of the 114 suras into which the Qur'an is divided. More radical proposals emerged at the hands of other European scholars, some of whom further revised the periodization of the Qur'an, such as H. Hirschfeld, who proposed five different Meccan periods, or William Muir, who considered several suras to have been composed before Muhammad's prophetic call. Richard Bell went even further. Noting that traditional Muslim scholarship identified quite a few verses from the Medinan period that occurred in suras that were otherwise Meccan (and vice versa), he argued that the leaves of the Qur'anic text had been hopelessly mixed up. The highly complex and idiosyncratic reordering of the sequence that Bell proposed to solve this problem has not proven to be persuasive.[22]

But the most revolutionary approach to the Qur'an in recent scholarship came in the work of John Wansbrough, a literary specialist, who argued that the text of the Qur'an could not have been compiled in its present form, as the traditional account has it, shortly after the death of the Prophet Muhammad. He proposed that the oral sayings on which the Qur'an is based were in circulation for as much as a couple of centuries before they were assembled as a book. The codification of the Qur'an, in his view, was part of a larger historical process in which an originally Jewish-Christian religious movement outside of Arabia eventually turned into an Arab-Islamic polity, which then retrospectively created a fictional account of its origins in Arabia.[23] Wansbrough's revisionist work (presented in two major publications of the late 1970s, *Qur'anic Studies* and *The Sectarian Milieu*) was an extremely learned and complicated argument that was, nevertheless, quite hypothetical, based on comparisons, and unsupported by direct external historical evidence. Parallel revisionist studies also emerged at the same time in the area of early Islamic history, in which Patricia Crone and Michael Cook argued that Muslim sources were completely unreliable and that therefore one can only reconstruct the early history of Islam through foreign sources.[24] A couple of even more radical studies then appeared, which maintained that the text of the Qur'an was originally a Christian work later revised along Islamic lines (G. Lüling) or that it was originally written in Syriac and then completely misunderstood as an Arabic text ("Christoph Luxenberg," a pseudonym). Both of these authors took the bold (and highly questionable) step of making significant alterations in the Arabic text of the Qur'an in order to make it fit their arguments. In literary terms, these last efforts overstate their case, by calling for the rejection of over a millennium of textual history and proposing completely new explanations previously unsuspected by anyone else. From a quite different perspective, John Burton also challenged the traditional account of the collection of the Qur'an, arguing that it was fully completed during the life of the Prophet.

It is remarkable that all these revisionist theories of the origins and history of the Qur'an share a strong confidence in overturning centuries of Islamic tradition yet offer dramatically different conclusions that clearly are in conflict among themselves. Although the questions raised by these studies have been seen as both infuriating and stimulating, the hypothetical character of these arguments means that they are essentially both unprovable and unfalsifiable. As Marco Schöller observes, they "negate the historicity of much of the traditional material on Islamic origins and thus constitute variants of conspiracy theories. . . . The general, somewhat paradoxical, effect upon many readers of their studies appears to be that much of what Burton and Wansbrough present in order to reach their respective conclusions is admitted by most to be sound and important for the course of future scholarship, yet their conclusions are not."[25] The preponderance of research over the past thirty years has not sustained revisionist hypotheses, and in fact it has tended to support an early date for the collection of the text. As one historian puts it, "What we can say is that the Qur'an text is demonstrably early."[26] Leaving aside the conspiracy theorists (who are chiefly supported by a handful of anti-Islamic activists),[27] the majority of scholars of Islamic studies today regard the traditional account of the historical context of the Qur'an, centered on the Prophet Muhammad in the Arabian Peninsula, to be the indispensable starting point for all research. Many scholars accept the idea that the Qur'an took on its present form by around 650 CE, and even comparative skeptics now assume that the text of the Qur'an was codified by the end of the seventh century.

History and Prophetic Biography in the Qur'an

To argue for a historical approach to the Qur'an raises the question of how the Qur'an itself testifies to history. To put it another way, what does the Qur'an say about events contemporaneous with its own composition? This also raises the question of how the Qur'an describes events in the life of the Prophet Muhammad, who is so intimately associated with the appearance of the Qur'an in history. Neither one of these questions admits of an easy or straightforward answer. In general, the style of the Qur'an is elliptical and allusive, and it seems to assume that its audience is already familiar with the characters and narratives to which it refers.

The Qur'an certainly has what may be called a historical perspective, looking back as it does on narratives dealing primarily with prophets, going all the way back to Adam. The complicated problem of the relationship of the Qur'an to earlier historical sources, including but not limited to biblical texts, can only be hinted at for the moment.[28] It may suffice for now to say that the Qur'an overlaps in many important respects with biblical accounts of the Israelites and their prophets, particularly Abraham, Moses, Noah, and Joseph, while according important roles to Jesus and John the Baptist as well. At the same time, this picture is integrated with narratives of Arabian prophets (Hud, Salih), who are unknown to the Bible (although some biblical prophets can be described as Arabian).[29] All these prophetic accounts share the characteristic of demonstrating what the Qur'an sees as the fundamental drama of human history, the appearance of prophets sent by God with divine warnings, which are invariably rejected, with disastrous consequences.[30]

The Qur'an is spare in providing historical detail, mentioning only a handful of geographical locations, including Mecca, Yathrib (identified with present-day Medina), and several other towns that are commonly located in the Arabian Peninsula. Some passages of the Qur'an may plausibly be connected to locations and incidents that would have taken place in Arabia during the century preceding the career of Muhammad.[31] The description of the flooding of the gardens of Sheba (34:15–17) most likely concerns the destruction of the Marib dam in Yemen, which sustained extensive irrigation and agriculture for over a millennium until it was abandoned in the middle of the sixth century; its ruins may still be observed today. The "people of the ditch," described (85:4–7) as perishing in fire, have been frequently identified with the Christian martyrs of Najran in South Arabia, put to death around 523 CE by the Jewish king Dhu Nuwas. Still, numerous other identifications of that episode have been found in commentaries (including the fiery punishment threatened by Nebuchadnezzar in Daniel 3:15). Another possible historical incident occurs in the sura of the Elephant (105:1–5), which appears to describe the frustration of a military invasion by miraculous divine intervention. Despite the absence of any names in this short sura, it is usually understood as describing an attack on Mecca (most likely dated between 540 and 547 CE) by the Ethiopian governor of Yemen.[32] These examples indicate how frequently it is necessary to go outside the text of the Qur'an to provide any kind of historical identification.

The Qur'an makes only a handful of references to contemporary individuals, though we read (106:1–3) of the Quraysh, the tribe to which Muhammad belonged, who are urged to "worship the Lord of this house," an apparent reference to the shrine of the Ka'ba in Mecca. An opponent of the Prophet is described with the nickname "father of flame" (Abu Lahab, 111:1), and there is a reference to the Prophet marrying the divorced wife of his adopted son Zayd (33:37). Yet these brief allusions, which presume an audience that is fully familiar with the individuals concerned, are far from providing a detailed historical context for the modern reader. That task was left to commentary and exegetical literature, which responded so enthusiastically to the need to identify each and every character hinted at in the Qur'an that modern scholars are often suspicious of attempts to "historicize" the text. As an example, one can take the detailed commentaries on the Companions of the Cave, whose story (18:9–26) bears close similarities with the Christian tale of the Seven Sleepers of Ephesus. In the Qur'anic version (discussed in detail in chapter 3), the heroes miraculously sleep in a cave for many years, with their dog at their feet, and when they awaken they find that they are saved from the persecutions of a tyrant. While there is much that may be said about this powerfully symbolic story, the fact that some commentators find it necessary to tell us the name of the dog (Qitmir, according to some) raises questions about the degree to which such details have been invented to fill the gaps in the narrative.

Much more consequential is the relationship of the Qur'an to the life of the Prophet Muhammad, since most modern scholarship explicitly accepts a correlation between the unfolding of the Qur'anic text and his prophetic career. Despite the existence of a chronological framework of Meccan and Medinan periods based on formal and stylistic considerations, there are relatively few internal markers where the Qur'an provides clear links to historical events. Suras from the Meccan period (traditionally regarded as covering the period from about 610 to 622 CE) highlight the first revelations and warnings that Muhammad transmitted to his people, and they allude to the opposition and persecution that he suffered, but with hardly any circumstantial detail. The Medinan suras (extending from the hijra, or immigration, to Medina in 622 to the Prophet's death in 632 CE) make fairly clear reference to a good dozen separate events marking the formation of the early Muslim community. These identifiable events include conflicts with the Jewish communities of Medina and battles with the pagans of Mecca.[33]

The Qur'an itself has much to say about the Prophet Muhammad, but mostly on a sublime plane that is unconcerned with the details of ordinary life. Within the text of the Qur'an, Muhammad is addressed three times by name (3:144, 33:40, 48:29), and he is clearly identified in those passages as the messenger of God. The dialogic form of address is present throughout the Qur'an, with numerous passages addressed to "you" in the singular; in most cases this form of discourse can be supposed to be aimed at Muhammad. There are over 300 passages that begin with the command, "Say!"; these messages unquestionably frame the warnings and exhortations that form the substance of the Qur'anic revelation. But the information that the Qur'an provides about Muhammad is primarily theological. It describes the nature of the prophetic communication that constitutes revelation and the mission of the Prophet to warn his people, in exactly the same manner as previous prophets have done. The Qur'an describes the Prophet's relation to his immediate community as well as to humanity at large, ranging from his role as a model for behavior to his exceptional apocalyptic importance. The most circumstantial references to Muhammad's life are a couple of stipulations about division of the spoils of war, plus a number of passages concerning the wives of the Prophet and how the believers should relate to them. Beyond that, there are extensive discussions of the resistance of unbelievers (whether pagan idolaters or monotheistic Jews and Christians), who mocked his message, persecuted him in Mecca, and debated him in Medina. The Qur'an frequently consoles Muhammad and defends him against his opponents.[34]

For any kind of detail on social or historical context or identification of individuals playing a part in the story, it is necessary to go outside of the Qur'an and consult other types of supplementary literature. The most directly relevant external source commenting upon the historical context of the Qur'an is the literature known as "occasions of revelation" (*asbab al-nuzul*). Texts on this topic typically contain short accounts from associates and followers of Muhammad, offering explanations of particular Qur'anic passages as responses to events occurring within the community. The "occasions of revelation" provided brief commentary on the meaning of the Qur'anic text, and they related who was present at the time or what it was that prompted a particular pronouncement. Thus we find a verse that strongly condemns drunkenness (4:43): "Do not approach prayer while you are intoxicated." The story is indeed told in the "occasions of revelation" that a particular companion of the Prophet had too much wine at dinner and was consequently unable to recite the Qur'an correctly at evening prayer, so therefore this verse was revealed that prohibited wine.[35] Attractive as this mode of explanation may have been, it had limited application, since the chief writings of this kind typically did not come close to discussing every verse in any sura, nor indeed all of the suras in the Qur'an, so it was a very selective and limited historical resource. Moreover, it is not at all clear how these reports were collected or what their historical value is. In this respect, they fall close to the category of the vast and uneven hadith literature, that is, the reports on the sayings and deeds of the Prophet Muhammad accumulated through oral tradition. This type of explanatory literature should be regarded with caution, although widely circulated reports are worth considering.

A much more extensive framework for the life of the Prophet Muhammad is found in the early Islamic biographical literature devoted to his life. This is usually referred to in Arabic by the word *sira*, also applied to some early political biographies but chiefly used in the sense of the exemplary life of the Prophet as a religious leader. The *sira* literature came into existence gradually, beginning with oral accounts that were elaborated into literary form over the course of a century or two. The two great surviving examples of this biographical phenomenon are *The Life of Muhammad* by Ibn Ishaq (d. 767) and *The Great Book of Generations* by Ibn Sa'd (d. 845).[36] The storytellers who first began to relate the Prophet's life were men like Wahb ibn Munabbih (d. 728), a Yemeni who was familiar with many biblical and pre-Islamic traditions and who was not at all reluctant to include miraculous stories and poetic digressions. Ibn Ishaq's work, which relied upon these early storytellers, has a strong narrative emphasis. It was quite different in style from the increasingly precise collections of prophetic hadith, which used extensively documented chains of transmission to support legal conclusions. This biography came about when the Caliph al-Mansur, of the newly installed 'Abbasid dynasty, asked Ibn Ishaq to write a universal history from the creation up to the present day. The resulting composition was divided into three parts: the first part treated the beginning of history and the careers of the prophets up to Jesus; part two described the mission of the Prophet Muhammad in the Meccan period; and part three was devoted to the expeditions and battles of the Medinan period. The first part is largely lost, except for portions preserved by the historian al-Tabari (d. 923). The second and third parts are most easily available in the version edited by Ibn Hisham (d. ca. 830), who evidently purged it of material that he considered theologically offensive.[37]

What might have been the problems with this earliest surviving biography of Muhammad? While Ibn Ishaq was suspected of Shi'i inclinations, the more likely issue was the frequent and unself-conscious reliance on biblical and pre-Islamic narratives that was typical of the early storytellers. Comparison indicates that earlier *sira* compositions frequently include biblical references and Arabic poetry, which in later versions were replaced by Qur'anic quotations that were felt to be more suitable. This transition indicates the formation of a theological barrier defining Islam as separate from Judaism and Christianity. These biographies also had an increasing tendency to historicize Qur'anic passages, functioning as a commentary that explained, paraphrased, and filled in the blanks. They also displayed a propensity to use Qur'anic language and quotations in order to impart a pious tone to the narrative. In short, the biographical tradition concerning Muhammad took shape in a milieu in which an emerging theological discourse played a dominant role. As one scholar summarizes it, "The *sira* as a whole is a vehicle of salvation history rather than scientific history."[38] While the religious function of this biographical literature is not surprising, it underlines the extent to which the historical traditions surrounding the Qur'an cannot be separated from the formation of early Islamic religious thought. Both with the "occasions of revelation" and with the biographies of the Prophet, there is a certain circularity involved in using these materials to situate the Qur'an historically. Since these texts function exegetically to interpret the religious meaning of the Qur'an, how can they at the same time stand as independent witnesses to the historical context of the Qur'an? This question cannot be resolved in a simple fashion. A historical understanding of the Qur'an will have to rely upon some external materials, but those materials themselves need to be analyzed for the perspectives and agendas that they bring to the subject.[39] Although it cannot be said that the biographical tradition is historically certain, I am taking the position here that the outlines of the Prophet Muhammad's biography, in terms of the Mecca-Medina paradigm, still provide a more compelling framework for understanding the Qur'an than any alternative yet proposed.

Form and Structure of the Qur'an
Form, Style, and Structure

The formal and stylistic features of the Qur'an are complicated and at first sight not easy for the reader to grasp. Fortunately, modern scholars have done much to advance the literary analysis of these aspects of the Qur'an. Following in the steps of Theodor Nöldeke, Angelika Neuwirth has carried out extensive investigations of the formal structure of the Qur'an, focusing particularly on the early Meccan suras. Her research has yielded important new insights into the way that the Qur'anic text unfolded as a communication orally performed for a community, which eventually took on a canonical literary form.[40]

The most obvious formal feature of the Qur'an is its division into 114 suras of unequal length, arranged roughly but unmistakably in descending order of size (although the first sura is quite short and although there are exceptions to the rule of declining length, the pattern is quite obvious). While this arrangement might seem at first an unusual formalistic approach, it is worth noting that biblical and para-biblical literature furnishes examples of texts organized according to length. The Pauline letters and the chapters of the Mishnah are arranged beginning with the longest and proceeding to the shortest.[41] The word *sura*, of unclear origin, occurs several times in the Qur'an, with the meaning of a section or portion of the revelation, and it has acquired a fixed meaning to denote the chapters or books into which the Qur'an is divided. Manuscript and printed copies of the Qur'an invariably include the word *sura*, followed by the distinctive Arabic name of the particular sura, in headings marking off the beginning of each of these units. During the earliest phases of the unfolding of the Qur'an, the first short suras appear to have been shaped for recitation in community. Others have extended to greater length, at times with insertions or additions over time, while some (particularly those longer suras dating from the Medinan period) seem to be composed of a number of discrete sections, to judge by the shifts of subject or style. Although these sections are not formally indicated in the text, some translators point to their existence by using paragraph divisions, subject headings, and other devices. The suras and their contents appear to have been fixed at a very early date, but the process by which they took the form we know today cannot presently be recovered from historical sources. That is, no one really knows how or why the fixed arrangement of suras took shape in this way.

Each of the suras has a characteristic name (in some cases, more than one name), by which Muslim readers identify them (see chart 1.1). The names of the suras typically are prominent words or phrases that occur early on in the sura, although occasionally the title comes from a later passage. Thus the names of the suras do not imitate the naming of the books of the Bible by describing the contents or transmitters of revelation. A sura's title may in fact be an oath formula or a brief reference that is not repeated or expanded upon. English translations of the Qur'an typically translate the names of the suras, but since there is no uniformity among different translations, there is no standard English nomenclature for the suras. While some authors use the Arabic names of the suras (for example, al-Baqara), others will cite it by an English translation ("The Cow") or simply use the number (sura 2). English translations of the Qur'an usually have an index listing the Arabic titles of suras.

Suras as chapters are further broken down into individual units of ex-

Chart 1.1. Numbers, Names, and Initial Letters of Suras of the Qur'an with Numbering in Chronologies of Nöldeke and the Egyptian Edition

Number	Arabic Name of Sura	Name in Arberry's Translation	Initial Letters	Nöldeke Chronology	Egyptian Chronology
1	al-Fatiha	The Opening		N48	E5
2	al-Baqara	The Cow	ALM	N91	E87
3	Al 'Imran	The House of Imran	ALM	N97	E89
4	al-Nisa'	Women		N100	E92
5	al-Ma'ida	The Table		N114	E112
6	al-An'am	Cattle		N89	E55
7	al-A'raf	The Battlements	ALMS	N87	E39
8	al-Anfal	The Spoils		N95	E88
9	al-Bara'a/ al-Tawba	Repentance		N113	E113
10	Yunus	Jonah	ALR	N84	E51
11	Hud	Hood	ALR	N75	E52
12	Yusuf	Joseph	ALR	N77	E53
13	al-Ra'd	Thunder	ALMR	N90	E96
14	Ibrahim	Abraham	ALR	N76	E72
15	al-Hijr	El-Hijr	ALR	N57	E54
16	al-Nahl	The Bee		N73	E70
17	Bani Isra'il/ al-Isra	The Night Journey		N67	E50
18	al-Kahf	The Cave		N69	E69
19	Maryam	Mary	KHY'S	N58	E44
20	Ta Ha	Ta Ha	TH	N55	E45
21	al-Anbiya'	The Prophets		N65	E73
22	al-Hajj	The Pilgrimage		N107	E103
23	al-Mu'minun	The Believers		N64	E74
24	al-Nur	Light		N105	E102
25	al-Furqan	Salvation		N66	E42
26	al-Shu'ara'	The Poets	TSM	N56	E47
27	al-Naml	The Ant	TS	N68	E48
28	al-Qasas	The Story	TSM	N79	E49
29	al-'Ankabut	The Spider	ALM	N81	E85
30	al-Rum	The Greeks	ALM	N74	E84
31	Luqman	Lokman	ALM	N82	E57
32	al-Sajda	Prostration	ALM	N70	E75
33	al-Ahzab	The Confederates		N103	E90
34	al-Saba'	Sheba		N85	E58
35	Fatir/ al-Mala'ika	The Angels		N86	E43
36	Ya Sin	Ya Sin	YS	N60	E41
37	al-Saffat	The Rangers		N50	E56

Chart 1.1. *Continued*

Number	Arabic Name of Sura	Name in Arberry's Translation	Initial Letters	Nöldeke Chro- nology	Egyptian Chro- nology
38	al-Ahzab/ al-Sad	Sad	S	N59	E38
39	al-Zumar	The Companies		N80	E59
40	al-Mu'min/ Ghafir	The Believer	HM	N78	E60
41	Ha Mim/ Fussilat	Distinguished	HM	N71	E61
42	al-Shura	Counsel	HM'SQ	N83	E62
43	al-Zukhruf	Ornaments	HM	N61	E63
44	al-Dukhan	Smoke	HM	N53	E64
45	al-Jathiya	Hobbling	HM	N72	E65
46	al-Ahqaf	The Sand-Dunes	HM	N88	E66
47	Muhammad	Muhammad		N96	E95
48	al-Fath	Victory		N108	E111
49	al-Hujurat	Apartments		N112	E106
50	Qaf	Qaf	Q	N54	E34
51	al-Dhariyyat	The Scatterers		N39	E67
52	al-Tur	The Mount		N40	E76
53	al-Najm	The Star		N28	E23
54	al-Qamar	The Moon		N49	E37
55	al-Rahman	The All-Merciful		N43	E97
56	al-Waqi'a	The Terror		N41	E46
57	al-Hadid	Iron		N99	E94
58	al-Mujadala	The Disputer		N106	E105
59	al-Hashr	The Mustering		N102	E101
60	al-Mumtahana	The Woman Tested		N110	E91
61	al-Saff	The Ranks		N98	E109
62	al-Jumu'a	Congregation		N94	E110
63	al-Munafiqun	Hypocrites		N104	E104
64	al-Taghabun	Mutual Fraud		N93	E108
65	al-Talaq	Divorce		N101	E99
66	al-Tahrim	The Forbidding		N109	E107
67	al-Mulk	The Kingdom		N63	E77
68	al-Qalam	The Pen	N	N18	E2
69	al-Haqqa	The Indubitable		N38	E78
70	al-Ma'arij	The Stairways		N42	E79
71	Nuh	Noah		N51	E71
72	al-Jinn	The Jinn		N62	E40
73	al-Muzammil	Enwrapped		N23	E3
74	al-Mudaththir	Shrouded		N2	E4
75	al-Qiyama	The Resurrection		N36	E31
76	al-Dahr/al-Insan	Man		N52	E98

Chart 1.1. *Continued*

Number	Arabic Name of Sura	Name in Arberry's Translation	Initial Letters	Nöldeke Chronology	Egyptian Chronology
77	al-Mursalat	The Loosed Ones		N32	E33
78	al-Naba'	The Tiding		N33	E80
79	al-Nazi'at	The Pluckers		N31	E81
80	'Abasa	He Frowned		N17	E24
81	al-Takwir	The Darkening		N27	E7
82	al-Infitar	The Splitting		N26	E82
83	al-Mutaffifin	The Stinters		N37	E86
84	al-Inshiqaq	The Rending		N29	E83
85	al-Buruj	The Constellations		N22	E27
86	al-Tariq	The Night-Star		N15	E36
87	al-A'la	The Most High		N19	E8
88	al-Ghashiya	The Enveloper		N34	E68
89	al-Fajr	The Dawn		N35	E10
90	al-Balad	The Land		N11	E35
91	al-Shams	The Sun		N16	E26
92	al-Layl	The Night		N10	E9
93	al-Duha	The Forenoon		N13	E9
94	al-Inshirah/ A-lam nashrah	The Expanding		N12	E11
95	al-Tin	The Fig		N20	E28
96	al-'Alaq	The Blood-Clot		N1	E1
97	al-Qadr	Power		N14	E25
98	al-Bayyina	The Clear Sign		N92	E100
99	al-Zilzal/ al-Zalzala	The Earthquake		N25	E93
100	al-'Adiyat	The Chargers		N30	E14
101	al-Qari'a	The Clatterer		N24	E30
102	al-Takathur	Rivalry		N8	E16
103	al-'Asr	Afternoon		N21	E13
104	al-Humaza	The Backbiter		N6	E32
105	al-Fil	The Elephant		N9	E19
106	Quraysh	Koraish		N4	E29
107	al-Ma'un	Charity		N7	E17
108	al-Kawthar	Abundance		N5	E15
109	al-Kafirun	The Unbelievers		N45	E18
110	al-Nasr	Help		N111	E114
111	al-Lahab/ al-Masad	Perish		N3	E6
112	al-Ikhlas	Sincere Religion		N44	E22
113	al-Falaq	Daybreak		N46	E20
114	al-Nas	Men		N47	E21

pression, or verses, commonly known by the Arabic term *aya* (plural *ayat*). The earliest instances of this term carry a generic sense of the signs of God's power manifest in nature, although one early Meccan sura (83:13) speaks of these signs being recited. Later the aya is referred to as part of the structure of revelation that has been expressed in a clear form. Ultimately the aya, endowed with the authority of divine communication, is synonymous with the numbered verses that constitute a sura. The characteristics of the aya or verse vary considerably from the earliest Meccan suras to the Medinan period. A sura may contain as few as three verses (suras 108 and 110) or as many as 286 (sura 2). Verses range from the short and simple hymnic lines of the early Meccan period to complex multipart arguments and descriptions in later suras. Thus the formal terms describing the units that make up the Qur'an cover materials that display a good deal of variety. For purposes of reference, the 286th verse of the sura entitled al-Baqara ("The Cow") is commonly cited as Qur'an 2:286. Almost all modern scholarship uses the verse numbering found in the 1924 Egyptian printed edition, which has become for all practical purposes the standard reference for the Qur'an.[42] There were, however, alternative verse divisions preserved in the different canonical readings of the Qur'an, which have allowed modern scholars to offer proposals for different verse divisions based on stylistic considerations, especially rhyme.[43]

Every sura of the Qur'an except one (sura 9) begins with a phrase that invokes the name and merciful characteristics of God: "In the name of God, the Merciful, the Compassionate" (*bismillah al-rahman al-rahim*).[44] This phrase of mercy, referred to as the *basmala*, is not normally counted as a verse except in sura 1, "The Opening," where it is the first aya. It is clear that this phrase invoking divine qualities took on the character of a respectful salutation and prayer in the early Muslim community; in practice, it is the most frequently recited Muslim religious formula, commonly repeated to initiate any new important affair. A similar ritual importance attaches to the whole of sura 1, "The Opening," which evidently was used as a communal prayer before it was formally included as a sura of the Qur'an.

The details of Qur'anic style and the variations that it displays are in fact the basis for the historical reconstruction of the chronology of the Qur'an. One of the salient characteristics of many Qur'anic passages is the use of rhyming prose—that is, the final syllables of a series of verses preserve the same end rhyme. While this feature bears an unmistakable resemblance to the rhyming found in poetry, the Qur'an as a text stands apart from the literary structure of pre-Islamic Arabic poetry, which deploys quantitative meters for verses of fixed length containing end rhymes that may be repeated for dozens of lines, or even over 100 lines in the longer odes. Although some of the shorter suras of the Qur'an do indeed preserve the same end rhyme throughout, the length of the lines is not fixed by regular meter as in poetry. More important, as soon as one moves past the shortest suras, it becomes clear that there are many cases where the rhyme shifts every few lines, sometimes obviously marking changes of subject. In addition, the emphatic use of rhyme is much more frequent in the earliest suras. The early Meccan suras feature at least eighty different kinds of rhyme, the middle Meccan suras display seventeen end rhymes, and the late Meccan feature only five. The Medinan suras, which include much longer descriptive, legal, and polemical passages, tend to a much more prosaic style, with lengthy verses featuring simple end rhymes based on the regular form of plural nouns and verbs and concluding formulaic phrases often consisting of a pair of divine attributes (for example, 4:148, "for God was the Hearer, the Knower"). Therefore the historical development of the sura shows striking changes, from an initial emphasis on oral recitation (*qur'an*) to the canonization of a written text (*kitab*, or book).

The mention of poetry raises an important question about the way at least some of the listeners of the Qur'an understood it. At several points, Muhammad must have been accused of being a poet, a soothsayer, and a madman, since the Qur'an adamantly refutes these accusations on more than one occasion. This means that at least some audiences observed significant similarities between the rhyming utterances of the Qur'an and the odes of the Arabian poets. It is also well known that the Arab soothsayer (*kahin*, similar to the Hebrew word for priest, *kohen*), like the poet, was typically inspired by a familiar spirit and would often utter strange oaths and obscure predictions of the future in a language composed of balanced rhyming phrases. The Qur'an (69:40–41, 52:29) is at pains, however, to deny any real similarity between its own form and inspiration and that of the tribal poets or spirit-channelers of Arabia. Indeed, the poet and the soothsayer were considered to be on the level of the madman (*majnun*), who was literally possessed by the spirits or genies known as the jinn. Given the theological consequences of aligning the Qur'an with those forms of writing, it is understandable that the Qur'an itself, and Muslim tradition in general, rejects any identification with the literature of poetry or soothsaying. And in terms of content, it is worth pointing out that the Qur'an's

Chart 1.2. Nöldeke's Qur'anic Chronology in Canonical Order

This chart follows the chronology of Theodor Nöldeke in dividing the 114 suras of the Qur'an into the first Meccan, second Meccan, third Meccan, and Medinan periods. Within each period, the suras are arranged in the standard canonical order as indicated by the numbers in the first column, while the numbers in the second column (preceded by the letter N) give the position of each sura in the chronology of Nöldeke.

48 Suras of the First Meccan Period (N1–N48)					
1	N48	81	N27	97	N14
51	N39	82	N26	99	N25
52	N40	83	N37	100	N30
53	N28	84	N29	101	N24
55	N43	85	N22	102	N8
56	N41	86	N15	103	N21
68	N18	87	N19	104	N6
69	N38	88	N34	105	N9
70	N42	89	N35	106	N4
73	N23	90	N11	107	N7
74	N2	91	N16	108	N5
75	N36	92	N10	109	N45
77	N32	93	N13	111	N3
78	N33	94	N12	112	N44
79	N31	95	N20	113	N46
80	N17	96	N1	114	N47

21 Suras of the Second Meccan Period (N49–N69)					
15	N57	25	N66	44	N53
17	N67	26	N56	50	N54
18	N69	27	N68	54	N49
19	N58	36	N60	67	N63
20	N55	37	N50	71	N51
21	N65	38	N59	72	N62
23	N64	43	N61	76	N52

21 Suras of the Third Meccan Period (N70–N90)					
6	N89	16	N73	35	N86
7	N87	28	N79	39	N80
10	N84	29	N81	40	N78
11	N75	30	N74	41	N71
12	N77	31	N82	42	N83
13	N90	32	N70	45	N72
14	N76	34	N85	46	N88

Chart 1.2. *Continued*

24 Suras of the Medinan Period (N91–N114)					
2	N91	33	N103	61	N98
3	N97	47	N96	62	N94
4	N100	48	N108	63	N104
5	N114	49	N112	64	N93
8	N95	57	N99	65	N101
9	N113	58	N106	66	N109
22	N107	59	N102	98	N92
24	N105	60	N110	110	N111

pronouncements refer to the apocalyptic events of Judgment Day and the resurrection rather than predicting mundane events; from a purely formal perspective, the horizon of reference in the Qur'an is transcendental. Moreover, it may be said that Qur'anic passages have more in common with Christian hymns or biblical psalms than with pre-Islamic Arabic poetry.[45] So despite its overt similarities to the pronouncements of poets and soothsayers in certain respects, there seem to be a number of reasons why the Arabic text of the Qur'an, in both distinctive style and scale, deserves to be treated on its own terms rather than as a subset of poetry or soothsaying.

To return to the question of the chronology of Qur'anic suras, it has already been mentioned that summations of traditional Muslim scholarship divide suras into two categories corresponding to the two major phases of the Prophet Muhammad's life, the Meccan (ca. 610–22 CE) and the Medinan (622–32 CE). Nöldeke's analysis further subdivides the Meccan period into early, middle, and late phases (see chart 1.2). In either case, it is assumed that one can trace a more or less clear chronological sequence of suras spanning the prophetic career from beginning to end, although the traditional Muslim and modern European systems have significant differences. The chronology of the 1924 Egyptian edition counts eighty-eight Meccan suras and twenty-six Medinan suras, while Nöldeke's chronology offers forty-eight suras in the first Meccan period, twenty-one in the second Meccan period, twenty-one in the third Meccan period (making ninety Meccan suras in all) plus twenty-four Medinan suras. Complicating this picture is the recognition (well established in Muslim scholarship) that there are a number of cases where a Meccan sura contains one or more verses that are Medinan, and likewise there are Meccan insertions in Medinan suras. Nöldeke also argues that there are later Meccan additions to earlier Meccan suras. No early manuscripts containing alternate versions of suras have survived, which could shed light on the editorial process by which this final result came about. Textual variations recorded in commentaries and preserved in a few older manuscripts (notably those found recently in Yemen) occasionally include slight variations in the sequence of suras, but within suras the textual differences are restricted to the level of spelling and occasional substitution of alternate words or phrasing, rather than being major structural changes. In other words, while it is widely accepted that there is a general chronological trend that may be applied to the suras of the Qur'an, there are passages that will need to be read against the grain, so to speak, of the suras where they occur.

A notable example of the phenomenon of apparent textual addition is the early Meccan sura 74, al-Mudaththir ("Wrapped in a Cloak"), which Nöldeke considers to be the second sura in the chronological sequence; it is number four in the Egyptian chronology. While lengthy for a Meccan sura (containing fifty-six verses), this text displays an unmistakable pattern of short verses generally consisting of no more than four or five words, with a strong emphasis on rhyme that shifts several times into a different pattern. This sura takes the form of a consolation address to the Prophet, whose message has been scornfully rejected by the pagans of Mecca. Halfway through the sura (74:26–29), attention shifts to the painful doom of hellfire that awaits the rejecters of revelation, and this depiction of hell is surrounded in typical style with an aura of mystery that enhances the dreadfulness of the scene:

> I shall cast him into the burning.
> And how do you know what the burning is?
> It does not save or leave anything,
> Consuming the man.

The next verse (74:30) adds an enigmatic comment: "And over it are nineteen."

Countless explanations have been provided for this statement, generally (following hints in the next verse, 74:31) identifying the nineteen as angelic powers. It is easy to imagine that this verse raised questions among listeners concerning the nature and purpose of these mysterious nineteen. Indeed, one can suppose that verse 31 was added later on, precisely as an explanation and auto-commentary on a passage that was admittedly obscure. Here is the complete text of 74:31:

We have only set angels as guardians of the fire, and we only set
their number as a trial for those who reject, so that those who have
received the Book may seek certainty, and those who believe will be
increased in faith, and those who have received the Book and the believers will not question, and those who have sickness in their hearts
and the rejecters will say, "What does God mean by this parable?"
Thus God misleads whom He wills and guides whom He wills; none
knows the armies of your Lord but He—and this is nothing but a reminder for humanity.

This long paragraph is then followed by twenty-five more brief rhyming
verses. In the midst of the short, powerful rhymes of sura 74, this lengthy
and explanatory passage in verse 31 stands out in remarkably high contrast.
Here, the language of 74:31 echoes language from several later suras, in
passages that discuss number symbolism and the objections of unbelievers.[46] This verse also seems to presuppose a mixed audience of People of
the Book (that is, Jews and Christians) as well as the new Muslim community, which is more easily envisaged in Medina than in Mecca. The closing
phrase in this verse ("this is nothing but a reminder for humanity"), while
technically following the rhyme, is repeated frequently in the Qur'an. It
could be argued that insistence on remembrance would be unexpected in
a sura occurring at the very beginning of the Prophet's career, before the
audience has become familiar with the matter of revelation. In short, there
is good reason to think that 74:31 is a Medinan addition to an early Meccan
sura. So whether due to stylistic considerations, as in the case just mentioned, or because of other data recorded in traditional sources, the suras
considered in chronological perspective should also be examined for verses
that may plausibly belong to a different time period.

While there is agreement that the Qur'anic text has a chronological aspect, the question of the precise order of the appearance of the suras of
the Qur'an is the subject of debate.[47] On the one hand, the 1924 Egyptian printed edition of the Qur'an canonizes a particular chronological sequence of the Meccan and Medinan suras that is widely accepted today
among Muslims (although early Muslim sources in fact contain a number
of different chronologies).[48] On the other hand, European scholars established a rather different chronology of the order of the suras and indeed of
individual verses. Or rather, one may say that there is a scholarly debate
about this chronology that takes Nöldeke as a starting point.[49] The main

outlines of Nöldeke's chronology in terms of three Meccan periods and one Medinan period are widely accepted, though we do not have a convincing demonstration of an exact sequence of individual suras within those main divisions. While it is essential to discuss the problems in the European scholarship on Qur'anic chronology, from Nöldeke to Bell, one should note the comment of Neal Robinson: "I am bound to conclude that for all its faults, the Nöldeke-Schwally sura classification, occasionally modified in the light of Bell's insights, is a better working hypothesis than the standard Egyptian chronology."[50] I take this not as an authoritative conclusion but as a good indication that there is evidence and argument in the Nöldeke-Schwally hypothesis that can be debated.

This chronological principle should be employed in reading selections from the Qur'an, just as if one were attempting to read the entire text sequentially (for suggestions on a chronological approach to reading selections from the Qur'an, see appendix C). Certainly such a selective reading cannot be exhaustive (and let us admit that it is not likely that all readers will finish the entire text of the Qur'an), but one can nevertheless track particular circumscribed topics according to both the Nöldeke and the Egyptian chronologies, by using subject indexes and chronological charts, to demonstrate the consequences of both hypotheses.[51] Such a developmental approach can be an agenda for scholarly research, as in the example of the maidens of paradise (the *hur* or *houris*). According to Nöldeke's chronology, these maidens are gradually transformed into purified spouses in Medinan suras, suggesting a shift of emphasis to address a more mature community. This particular case offers support for the explanatory value of Nöldeke's system, since the Egyptian chronology does not demonstrate any such obvious historical development.[52] Another example is the prominent genre of the punishment stories, widely represented in Meccan suras but almost entirely absent from Medinan suras. These narratives of the destruction of unbelieving peoples, aimed at encouraging the faithful in the difficult situation of Mecca, are replaced in Medinan suras with the much more immediate problem of battles with the Meccan pagans (see chapter 4). There is no reason that this developmental method cannot also be followed by individual readers to track other topics.

While the sura is in effect the most obvious structure in the Qur'an, in practice over the centuries it has been more common to consider the verses individually, rather than as elements that combine together to create a sura as a harmonious whole. The approach that highlights individual verses is displayed in the most famous commentaries on the Qur'an, such as the great hadith-based commentary of al-Tabari (d. 923), which proceeds to explain one verse at a time without pausing to reflect on interpretation of the sura as a whole.[53] It was not until the twentieth century that Muslim modernists and reformists like Rashid Rida' (d. 1935) and Sayyid Qutb (d. 1966) began to employ a form of commentary in their Arabic writings that stressed the notion of the sura as a literary unit focused on a particular central point or pivot. This approach received a parallel and more extensive development at the hands of two South Asian scholars, Hamid al-Din Farahi (d. 1930) and his student Amin Ahsan Islahi (d. 1997), who elaborated a theory of suras as complementary pairs, further dividing suras into seven groups dealing with major themes.[54] While it is undeniable that many suras exhibit a composite structure, including passages from different periods in the same sura, it is nevertheless attractive to consider each sura as a literary whole, especially since the structure of the suras seems to be unchanged throughout the history of the Qur'anic text. It is particularly noteworthy to see the promising results from the symmetrical or ring structure exhibited in some suras, where the beginning and ending of a sura, and sometimes intermediate sections as well, reflect each other. This inverse parallelism or symmetry, also known as chiasmus, is well attested in the Hebrew Bible and other ancient Near Eastern texts.[55] In the Qur'an, symmetrical structure occurs notably in the story of Joseph in sura 12, but recent research has revealed that ring structure is much more pervasive, in both the Meccan and the Medinan suras, than had previously been noticed.[56] This particular feature of Qur'anic style will be explored in more detail for the Medinan suras, in chapter 4.

Another major and distinctive feature of the Qur'an is the fundamental question of the voice of the speaker. In a text commonly regarded as being the speech of God, it is not surprising that there are many passages where the speaker is "I," in the first-person singular. As one scholar has observed, when the speaker is "I," this usage strikes a note of intimacy when God relates narratives of sacred history or describes the end-times.[57] On the other hand, it is surprising and even disconcerting to see how frequently the principal speaker is expressed in the first-person plural as "We" or in the third-person singular as "He." Some scholars have even suggested that the use of "We" implies a plurality of speakers, that is, the angels alongside of God, but on closer examination this proves to be a weak argument loosely based on biblical analogies. The Qur'an does not provide any example of angelic participation in the creation.[58] Instead of overlaying such a simplistic theological interpretation onto the text, a literary approach will take seriously the different contexts and forms of expression of the different voices and personas found throughout the Qur'an. The shift from "I" to "We" for the principal speaker is very characteristic of Qur'anic discourse, and the use of the plural is widely accepted as an example of the "plural of majesty" or the "royal we," where the plural is used for respect.[59] Likewise, the Qur'an displays frequent shifts of voice or person, without any announcement, which first-time readers may experience as abrupt and even confusing.

Arabic literary scholars refer to this sudden change of voice by the term *iltifat*, meaning literally "turning to one side," as one does when shifting attention from one person in the conversation to another. This phenomenon can be summarized as "dynamic style."[60] Such a shift of voice is well known in Near Eastern literatures, such as in the opening lines of the Song of Songs: "Let him kiss me with the kisses of his mouth, for your love is sweeter than wine." This rhetorical shift of person is also common in biblical texts.[61] The shift from "him" to "you" is a dramatic device that brings the reader into the conversation abruptly and even with a sense of shock. In a sense, dynamic style overlaps with the strongly dialogical aspect of the Qur'an contained in the very frequent addresses to an implied audience in the second-person singular. Usually this "you" in the singular is assumed to be the Prophet Muhammad, and some translators insert his name into the text in parentheses, or add an identification in a footnote, to underline this point, since modern English does not distinguish between the singular and plural "you." The point is that in all these cases the reader of the Qur'an internalizes an intensely conversational dialogue, echoing its reverberations in every recitation. There are literally hundreds of such cases of shifts of dynamic style to be found in the Qur'an, including changes in person, number, and other grammatical features. Arabic literary critics see this device as a way of conveying emphasis and dramatic effect by making unexpected moves. Unfortunately, while this type of dynamic style is highly admired in Arabic literature, it loses much of its force in translation, since foreign readers have not formed the conventional expectations needed for this experience of pleasurable surprise. As a result, the first-time reader can experience many dramatic passages in the Qur'an almost as though reading a Shakespeare play that has been deprived of the stage directions containing the names of the characters—and that can be a baffling experi-

ence. Translators need to resort to various devices, such as prefaces, paren-
thetical remarks, and footnotes, in order to keep the reader from going too
far astray. James Morris has provided an instructive example of plotting
the voices of the story of Joseph in sura 12 into four columns identified as
different voices: the frame narrator, the divine "We," various actors, and
inner asides. The result is a sensitive portrayal of the dynamic potential
of the Qur'anic text, with a multiplicity of voices that recalls the Greek
chorus.[62]

Literary Genres of the Qur'an

Scholars have broken down the types of material that appear within the
suras into "building blocks" of various types, which could be considered
the basic literary genres or forms of composition within the Qur'an.[63] It is
helpful to have an overview of these elements before undertaking closer
readings. It is also worth keeping in mind that the Qur'an exhibits definite
changes in the kinds of building blocks employed as one moves from the
early Meccan suras to the Medinan period. In addition, some early Meccan
suras strike a single note, while others demonstrate a twofold or threefold
structure containing exhortation, debate with opponents, and affirmation
of the Qur'an, with significant reference to the holy places of Mecca. Later
Meccan suras evoke forms of worship, including Qur'anic scripture, but
Mecca is replaced by the land of the earlier prophets, including Jerusalem.
The Medinan suras do not so obviously have the three-part scheme. Some
of these later suras are rhetorical sermons to the people, which also address the Prophet either alone or together with God. Their structure is very
difficult to decode.[64]

Many suras, particularly the early Meccan ones, begin with emphatic
formulas of assertion in the form of oaths, which call to witness various extraordinary entities, both natural and supernatural, to underline the truth
of the revelation. The beings called upon in these oaths include the day-
break (89:1), the fig and olive trees (95:1), the star that sets (53:1), and
others, even including God. Sometimes the oath begins with the simple
word "By . . . ," and other times it starts with the formal assertion, "I swear
by. . . ." A number of these, called "rider oaths" (found in 51:1–4, 77:1–6,
79:1–4, and 100:1–5), invoke the powers of nature as partially personi-
fied entities, in grammatical forms that are obviously plural. They have
the characteristics of galloping riders, winds, or angels, expressed in short,

terse lines with strong metrical emphasis, with rich, yet elusive language.[65] These beings are called upon, in effect, to testify to the reality of revelation, particularly the afterlife. To take one example (77:1–7), which evokes the sense of raging winds, with a touch of horse imagery:

> By the sent ones, tightly maned,
> By the stormers in storm,
> By the scatterers of scattering,
> By the dividers of division,
> By the casters of reminder,
> In excuse and in warning—
> The very thing you are promised [i.e, Judgment Day] is surely
>   happening!

Here the language is partially abstract and impersonal, an effect that is heightened by three consecutive verses, each repeating a single linguistic root first as subject and then as modifier (77:2–4). Yet these examples of oath clusters with rider imagery also create the impression of a violent desert raid, giving a gripping sense of impending doom to the promised judgment in the afterlife.[66] In this way, these Qur'anic oaths draw vividly on the social reality of pre-Islamic Arabia, even as they shift from heroic battle imagery to the ethical consciousness responding to the reminder of revelation.

These earliest suras of the Qur'an convey the definite sense of introducing new and powerful ideas to the audience, using words that are clearly novel. One characteristic formula, repeated a dozen times, is a teaching question that theatrically demands of the listener, "How do you know of (*wa-ma adraka min*) . . . ?" The question has an ironic tone; it might be more literally translated as, "What has made you know . . . ?" Like the partial personification found in oath formulas, these question formulas create an aura of mystery, which is intensified by the intimacy of the first-person singular dialogue form. On several occasions the question is repeated for emphasis, as in this example (82:17–19) leading up to the partial disclosure of an awe-inspiring feature of the end-time:

> And what do you know of the Day of Judgment?
> Then, what do you know of the Day of Judgment?
> It is a day when no soul controls anything for another, for that
>   day the command belongs to God!

By framing these intimations of the afterlife in unfamiliar terms, the Qur'an heightens the feeling of mystery and conveys a sense of being given glimpses of a transcendental realm.[67]

Another prominent building block or genre in the Qur'an is the depiction of the end-times—the Judgment Day and the afterlife of the soul in heaven or hell—in vivid and dramatic portraits. This kind of eschatology, which shares important themes with ancient Iranian and biblical literature, takes on a particular stylistic form in the Qur'an. The language is factored by time, with a series of verses introduced by "when . . ." or "on the day when . . ."; the powerful images displayed in these clauses build up to a climax of revelation, when one realizes that judgment is inevitable. One example is 82:1–5:

> When heaven splits
> And when the planets are scattered
> And when the oceans are poured out
> And when the tombs are overturned—
> A soul shall know what it has prepared for and what it has
> neglected.

These end-time depictions share with the oath formulas the rhythmic and poetic form of rhyming prose. Frequently, they are presented in the form of double portraits that balance heaven and hell, the garden and the fire, or the righteous and the damned. Scholars call these double portraits "diptychs," since these verbal descriptions recall the double panels of that name that were commonly used to illustrate heaven and hell in medieval Christian art. Some of the judgment scenes accentuate the sense of pathos by showing the virtuous and the sinner reflecting aloud on the good or evil deeds that brought them to this final moment, and the sinner may lament his unfortunate situation, although it is too late to change it.

One of the most typical forms of Qur'anic expression is the description of the "signs" of God (*ayat*, also used for the verses of the Qur'an), which are manifest both in nature and in human history. Although depiction of nature was a prominent feature in pre-Islamic Arabic poetry, it served as a theater for heroic action, and it presented a dialectic between transitory human culture and the permanence of nature.[68] In the Qur'an, nature is treated as the abundantly manifest display of divine blessing through the gifts of water, plants, animals, and abodes ideally designed for human habitation. Recognition of God's signs in nature brings forth the appropriate response of gratitude and obedience to the divine will. Thus God's creation of the natural universe is itself a form of revelation, and God's creative power is therefore a proof of God's ability to resurrect the dead on Judgment Day. An example of this treatment of nature is found in 50:6–11:

> Have they not looked to the sky above them, how We adorned
>   its construction, with no rifts in it?
> And the earth that We spread out, when We cast mountains
>   upon it, and We planted on it every delightful variety —
> It is an insight and a reminder for every trusting worshiper.
> And We send them blessed water from heaven, by which We
>   grew gardens and crops,
> And tall date palms layered in fruit,
> Sustenance for worshipers; by it We bring life to a dead land —
>   the resurrection will be like that.

Many readers familiar with biblical texts will see in such verses a similarity with the hymns of praise found in the Psalms.

For the Qur'an, human history is also the stage for the display of God's signs. Divine power manifested in history is illustrated in numerous accounts focusing on the prophets. The earliest suras in the Qur'an include short narrations relating to the Arabian Peninsula (particularly the stories of the people of 'Ad and Thamud) as well as the prophets Abraham, Moses, and Noah. Some of these take on the form of "punishment stories," in which divinely appointed messengers deliver revelation and warning, only to be rejected and harassed, leading to God's punishment or annihilation of the offending parties. The existence of abandoned ancient cities like al-Hijr (a Nabatean center known today as Mada'in Salih in the north of Saudi Arabia, dating from the first century CE) was taken to be clear evidence of the punishment of the people of Thamud for their rejection of the prophet Salih, as described in sura 15 (entitled al-Hijr). The pre-Islamic Arabic odes often began with a focus on the traces of abandoned habitations but generally served as a springboard for reminiscences of adventures or romantic encounters. Reflection on ancient ruins takes on a greater urgency in these Qur'anic accounts, going beyond the ephemeral quality of human life to stress the disastrous consequences of opposing the omnipotent God.[69] In any case, the basic outline of the punishment story (archetypally demonstrated in sura 36, Ya Sin, without any names or location) serves as another important building block of Qur'anic composition. In a briefer fashion, the Qur'an also contains parables (*mathal*) illustrating the consequences of obedience or disobedience to God, through images like the grateful and ungrateful gardeners (18:28–44).

The existence of significant narratives in the Qur'an that overlap with accounts of biblical figures creates a complicated literary problem. In the past, the overriding tendency has been to view this connection between the Qur'an and the Bible from a position of theological one-upmanship. Christian and Jewish writers have often viewed the Qur'anic stories as derivative from and dependent on the canonical source in the Bible; thus any variance from biblical accounts was proof of the defective character of Islamic revelation. In turn, later Muslim writers took the position that the Christian and Jewish scriptures have been corrupted and are no longer reliable, a position that relieved them of the responsibility to know the earlier texts. Although early Muslim scholars were eager to draw upon pre-Islamic narrative materials (the so-called Isra'iliyyat) to flesh out details of stories sketchily told in the Qur'an, it soon became common to discard them as tainted sources that might contaminate the true revelation. The theological wall erected between these different interpretative communities has not been helpful for the understanding of the relationship between the Qur'an and earlier traditions such as the biblical texts. Recent studies suggest that the Qur'an assumes as an audience listeners who were quite familiar with texts from the Hebrew Bible, New Testament, and even the Talmud and the Mishnah.[70] The "full knowing reader" may detect direct allusions and subtler echoes of earlier texts, not as simple sources that are pillaged in an uncomprehending fashion, but as an ongoing colloquy and intertextual debate within the larger Irano-Semitic prophetic tradition. A full-scale investigation of connections between the Qur'an and the Bible is beyond the scope of this book, but it is important to realize that this is a literary problem that can be tackled.[71]

To return to the immediate task, one can take a literary approach that does not depend upon these theological exercises of exclusion. The narratives of biblical prophets, beginning in the second Meccan period, take on the character of scriptural texts that can be recited orally during a worship service, as was indeed common in the monotheistic communities of Jews and Christians. In sura 19, which is devoted to the story of Mary, the text repeatedly and explicitly instructs the listener to "remember [or mention] in the book" the figures of Mary, Abraham, Moses, Ishmael, and Idris (the latter is often identified with Enoch). A process of canonization is taking place here, in which the oral revelation is calling upon the notion of a previous sacred text while it itself becomes the new sacred text. This was obviously a complicated phenomenon, and we can only reconstruct it by extrapolating the persona of the implied audience from the structure communicated in the text. But by the time of the later Meccan and Medinan suras, it is evident that the stories of prophets are well enough known that they can be evoked by brief references that listeners are expected to understand thoroughly.

One of the most prominent forms of expression in the Qur'an is debate, which occurs in numerous passages that imply a strong resistance to the prophetic message. Muhammad's proclamation of judgment and resurrection seems to have been met with incredulity, ridicule, and disdain. In direct address to disbelieving listeners, the Qur'an observes their bewilderment and their laughter. Doom is predicted for the naysayers and the sinners who scoff at the thought that they will be held to account. Earlier passages are content with arguing against the disbelievers, but later passages include the adversaries' replies, so that the dialogue performs a debate, perhaps as a model for the strategies recommended to the beleaguered believers and, indeed, to the Prophet. Thus, when the Prophet's opponents challenged him to produce a revelation, the Qur'an advises him to counsel patience without trying to predict the future (10:20): "And they will say, 'If only a sign had descended to him from his Lord!' You say, 'The hidden [future] only belongs to God. So wait, for I am one of those who waits with you.'" Some debate statements argue the privileged status of the Qur'an as revelation, consoling the Prophet and the believers and urging them to be steadfast. It is noteworthy that many suras begin with prominent assertions of the authority of revelation, particularly in the later suras that manifest more completely the process of canonization.

There is another phenomenon that one finds as a feature of Qur'anic texts, which defies easy categorization. Twenty-nine suras in the Qur'an open with isolated or detached letters of the Arabic alphabet, occasionally with a single letter (suras 38, 50, 68) but generally with a combination of anywhere from two to five letters (see chart 1.1). Some suras are entitled by the letters they begin with (suras 20, 36, 38, 41, 50). Countless solutions have been proposed for these "mysterious letters," with many adventures in cabalism and numerology, but it is difficult to resolve the issue. Some traditional commentators have suggested that the letters are abbreviations for persons or subjects discussed in the Qur'anic texts, but it is difficult to find a way to apply the abbreviations consistently. European scholars have suggested several documentary hypotheses, according to which individual letters stand for scribes entrusted with the preservation of particular sections of the Qur'an.[72] Attempts have also been made to link the letters to the ordering of the suras according to size.[73] Given the fact that many of the suras that begin with the isolated letters also immediately declare the authenticity of the revelation, it is tempting to accord the letters the status of revelation, as the primal elements that compose the language of divine communication. Nevertheless, this remains an elusive question, which is perhaps essentially insoluble.

While it has been frequently observed that legislation forms a relatively small portion of the Qur'anic corpus, it nevertheless remains true that there is a significant amount of regulation that takes place in the text.[74] Much of this pertains to ritual, particularly the performance of prayer, fasting, alms, and pilgrimage, but there are also lengthy prosaic sections pertaining to property, marriage, inheritance, and criminal law, which seem to have been inserted into certain suras without strong connections to the surrounding content. These prescriptions are particularly prominent in the Medinan suras, which is not surprising in view of the role of arbitration that the Prophet undertook there. The regulations for Muslims occupied a position comparable to that of the legal authority of the Torah or the Gospel for Jews and Christians, despite the rejection of the law in certain portions of the New Testament. Indeed, the document known as the "Constitution of Medina" clearly makes the analogy between the law of the Jews and the law of the Arab submitters (*muslimun*), both of which were accepted within the city for their respective communities.[75] This insistence on ethical norms clearly formed an essential portion of the Qur'anic message. The elaboration of legal passages from the Qur'an into the system of Islamic law is a later development that lies outside of this discussion, but readers will definitely notice the presence of legal material in the Qur'anic text.

Finally, it is important to observe the presence of certain Qur'anic references to contemporary events of significance to the early Muslim community. These contemporary references are almost entirely missing from the early Meccan suras, which elliptically avoid referring to individuals and events for the most part (the doom pronounced on an early opponent of the Prophet in sura 111 only uses an epithet, "father of flame," to refer to him). In that respect, the Meccan suras retain a focus on the cosmic and universal aspects of the revelation, with little detail on current history. Notable events of the Medinan period noticed in the Qur'an include the battles of Badr (624 CE) and Uhud (625 CE), the struggle against the Banu Nadir tribe (625 CE), the events leading up to the treaty with the Meccans at Hudaybiyya (628 CE), the military expedition to Tabuk (630 CE), and the farewell sermon of the Prophet at the time of the pilgrimage of 631 CE. Although these historical references are still brief and require elaboration from external sources whose use needs to be justified, it is clear that these later portions of the Qur'an plausibly contain a fair amount of material relating to important events of those times.

Ways of Reading the Qur'an
Ritual Reading of the Qur'an

The Arabic word *qur'an*, as we have seen, means both to read and to recite aloud. For most Muslims, it is not helpful to separate these two meanings of the term, since reading the Qur'an is generally an activity carried out aloud. In this respect, reading the Qur'an resembles the way that most reading has been done until relatively recently. In Roman times, it was considered remarkable that Julius Caesar read a letter silently in public, when he was reluctant to reveal its contents to bystanders. Likewise, St. Augustine was struck by the way that St. Ambrose would read the Bible silently without moving his lips. In Christian monasteries, it was normally assumed that the reading of the Bible and other texts would be done aloud as a matter of course. There is a considerable literature on the role of orality in connection with reading in European culture as well as in comparative contexts.[76] And the reading of biblical passages aloud continues to play a significant role in both Christian and Jewish worship. Yet modern practices of reading scripture, at least in largely Protestant circles, tend to focus on the private, individual, and silent reading of the text for purposes of understanding and spiritual insight. This view of reading often assumes a context of criticism of both legal interpretation and ritual performance of the text, which are condemned as the reprehensible habits of Pharisees and Catholics.[77] Such habits of silent reading (which are not limited to Protestants) may get in the way of understanding the extent to which the vast majority of readers of the Qur'an (that is, Muslims) normally engage with the text, in what may be called a ritual fashion. Although the aim of this book is to offer a nontheological model for literary study of the Qur'anic text, it will be useful to offer a brief overview of ritual aspects of reading the Qur'an, if only to sharpen the notion of a nontheological approach by way of contrast with these other readings.

The definition of ritual is notoriously slippery, but anthropologists usually consider it to consist of the performance of more or less fixed actions, often repeated at particular times. To be qualified as religious, ritual needs to center on reverence for the divine. One scholar divides Islamic rituals into seven categories: rites of communication; rites of passage and life cycle; calendrical rituals; rites of exchange and communion; rites of affliction; rites of feasting, fasting, and festivals; and political rituals.[78] In nearly all of these rituals, the Qur'an is recited. Another theorist has in a more detailed fashion described ten kinds of ritual in which the Qur'an plays a significant role: transformative rituals; rituals of purification; rituals fulfilling an obligation; rites of passage; rituals required in the Qur'an; rituals of abstinence; rituals of sustenance; protective rituals; rituals inflicting harm; and rituals of social cohesion and solidarity.[79] Although these two approaches to Islamic ritual differ in their conceptual arrangement, both emphasize the extent to which reciting the Qur'an plays a leading role in many important aspects of Islamic religious life. Just in terms of rites of passage, it is important to note the crucial role of Qur'an recitation throughout life, beginning with birth rituals and extending to circumcision, marriage, and funerals.

Perhaps the most notable way in which the Qur'an functions in Muslim religious life is in the five required daily ritual prayers. Since each of the five daily prayers consists of a different number of cycles or units of prostration (two at dawn, four at noon, four in the afternoon, three at sunset, and four in the evening), there are in all seventeen daily cycles of prayer, and in each of them one must recite the first sura of the Qur'an (al-Fatiha, "The Opening") and other Qur'anic verses. This requirement applies to all Muslims, whether or not they are native speakers of Arabic. Since fewer than 20 percent of Muslims are Arabic speakers, this means that the vast majority of Muslims learn these required Qur'anic passages as a sacred liturgy to be memorized, rather than as an ordinary text to be read, studied, and understood in a particular fashion. As a form of expression, Muslim ritual prayer is structured along the lines of major Qur'anic themes relating to magnification, recollection, praise, glorification, and supplication of God.[80] Thus the recitation of the Qur'an is essentially a method of communicating with God. This is intensified in numerous particular instances, such as the month of Ramadan, when Qur'anic recitation throughout the day plays an extraordinary role in many Muslim-majority countries. As another sign of ritual engagement, passages in the Qur'an that contain the command to prostrate are generally marked in the margins, and the reader/reciter at that point is expected to perform the same prostration required in ritual prayer.

It may make more sense to understand the profound importance of reciting the Qur'an if one highlights the definition of the Qur'an as the word of God, in terms both of listening and recitation. More than one author has observed that recitation of the Qur'an is comparable to the Christian ritual of the Eucharist, as a process of internalizing the word of God.[81] Yet it is essential that this word should not only be heard but also recited. A common Muslim understanding of the process of revelation is that the angel Gabriel was the medium for divine communication between God and the Prophet. What is normally viewed as the very first portion of the Qur'an revealed to the Prophet (sura 96) begins with the command, "recite!" (*iqra'*), held to be Gabriel's direction to the Prophet. Shocked by this unexpected experience, Muhammad is said to have responded three times with incomprehension, "What shall I recite?" It then dawned on him that he first needed to listen to the divine word conveyed to him by the angel and then repeat it himself. This understanding is enlarged upon in another early sura (75:18), where it is said, "And when we recite it, follow our recitation." That is, after hearing the revelation, the Prophet would recite the text itself, making the recitation an integral part of the revelatory process. The Prophet himself is reported to have said that if a reciter is to experience the Qur'an as if it had been revealed directly, it is necessary to be aware of the fact that one is listening to the recitation of God's speech.[82] In a similar fashion, early Muslim mystics emphasized that one could listen to the Qur'an on different levels of intensity: "The first kind of listening is to hear the Qur'an as though the Prophet is reciting it to you. Then you go beyond that, and it is as though you hear it from Gabriel. . . . Then you go beyond that and it is as though you hear it from God."[83] So it will be helpful to take seriously the sacredness with which the word of God is invested in Islamic religious practice. Reading or reciting the Qur'an is a direct engagement with the divine speech, not to be confused with ordinary acts of reading, nor to be dismissed as a meaningless repetition. This means that one can understand Muslim memorization and recitation of the Qur'an outside of the polemical framework of the Protestant critique of "mechanical" Catholic rituals.

Thus it should not be surprising to find that Muslim religious practice treats the Qur'an, as a physical object, with great reverence and respect. To pick up and handle the Qur'an requires that one should be in a state of ritual purity, that is, one should have performed the same washing by ablutions required for ritual prayer. Many pious Muslims express their respect by kissing the Qur'an, and it is customary to keep it in an elevated position, above other books, and certainly never touching the ground. The sanctity of the Qur'an as a religious object may be compared to other religious traditions, such as the reverential treatment of the Torah in Orthodox Judaism. Popular religious practice preserves doctrines, dating from times when literacy was rare, ascribing extraordinary virtues to particular passages from the Qur'an. Major hadith collections generally contain a section on "the virtues of the Qur'an" enumerating the benefits that may accrue from repeating a particular sura or passage a fixed number of times. And there are many other magical and talismanic uses of the Qur'an that are historically widespread, including healing practices using vessels containing Qur'anic inscriptions.[84] While some of these practices have become controversial in recent reformist critique, they nonetheless attest to a broad range of ritualistic reading practices beyond what is usually understood by reading today.

One of the most typical examples of the ritual structuring of the reading of the Qur'an is the division of the text into equal parts to facilitate recitation. It is very common to find manuscripts and printed editions of the Qur'an that have been bound in thirty equal portions (*juz'*) for daily recitation during the course of a month. Since this division into thirty portions obviously will not coincide with the literary units of the 114 suras, it is clear that the point is to have recited the entire Qur'an aloud in a deliberate ritual fashion in the course of a month rather than to have pondered particular issues that are discussed in the text. This emphasis on recitation of the Qur'an as a sacred practice has led to the elaboration of a complex and demanding discipline of correctly pronouncing and embellishing the text, sometimes with considerable musical effect.[85] It is very common for Muslims from all classes of society to devote considerable effort to learning the art of Qur'anic recitation, which involves a high degree of memorization. Famous reciters of the Qur'an are celebrities in their own right, and since the 1960s the spread of cassette recordings of the Qur'an and, later, digital recordings available on the Internet have made these high-quality recitations available for countless listeners to appreciate and imitate.

Interpretation of the Qur'an

It is commonplace to hear Muslim authors assert that the Qur'an is the literal word of God. This statement should probably be taken as an assertion that the words of God as revealed to Muhammad are indeed the words of God. That is, the Arabic text of the Qur'an is regarded as divine speech. From here, it would seem a short step to assume that Muslims inevitably interpret the Qur'an literally, but that would be far from the truth. Such a judgment employs language that overlaps with the notion of biblical literalism, which is associated with conservative Christian groups such as evangelicals and fundamentalists. Reference to literal interpretation often carries with it the pejorative overtones that customarily accompany journalistic discussions of fundamentalism. This negative aura is enhanced in discussions of Islam, since Qur'anic literalism is associated with terrorist violence, which many Americans assume is both a natural and a typical product of reading the Qur'an. The atmosphere of anxiety about the Qur'an that has dominated public discussion since 2001 obscures the significant and wide-ranging debates about the interpretation of the Qur'an that have characterized Muslim religious thinking for over 1,000 years.

There is a considerable gap between the deep suspicion of many non-Muslims toward the Qur'an and the emotional impact that the text actually has on believers who engage with it. Just to give one example, how do most readers of the Qur'an experience its overall tone, the voice of its expression? Despite its numerous warnings of the perils of hellfire, the mood of the Qur'an is not experienced by most listeners as primarily one of anger or wrath. As one sensitive observer has pointed out,

> Qur'anic reciters and commentators characterize the tone of the Qur'anic recitation as one of sadness (*huzn*). Indeed, the sadness is at its most telling in those passages in which the world's mystery and splendor are evoked. Yet there is a sense that somehow the splendor and mystery are too great for the human to encompass—or that the human heart has somehow forgotten it actually has the capacity to encompass splendor and mystery. At this moment of reminder, the text expresses not fear but the sadness that comes with a personal realization of a loss that is part of the human condition.[86]

This is a thoughtful comment that highlights Muslim scholars' reports about what it feels like to recite the Qur'an, though it may surprise those who are new to the text. The distance that separates an insider's experience from alarming journalistic reports of outsiders is a good indication that the phenomenon is more complex than commonly assumed. In any case, it is useful to recognize here the predominant emotional depiction of the tone of the Qur'an.

To return to the question of interpretation, a crucial observation was made on this topic by the fourth caliph, 'Ali ibn Abi Talib (d. 661), who is regarded as one of the most astute members of the early Muslim community: "The Qur'an is only lines inscribed between two covers; it does not speak; people only utter it."[87] In another version of this saying, he says, "This Qur'an is only lines inscribed between two covers; it does not speak with the tongue, but it certainly needs an interpreter (*tarjuman*), for people only speak about it."[88] This remark has been rightly called "a classic statement of the need for the interpretation of Scripture."[89] The point here is one that would easily be acknowledged by anyone who has attempted to wrestle with the difficulties of the text of the Qur'an: it is not simple, and in order to make sense of it one inevitably has to bring to it an apparatus for interpretation based on considerations outside of the text itself, such as history, comparison, or the characteristics of the Arabic language. Of course, theology is another resource one can draw upon to interpret the Qur'an, although we are specifically bracketing that out from the present enterprise.

Nevertheless, the history of Islamic religious thought is marked by a number of quite diverse yet compelling strands of interpretation of the Qur'anic revelation.[90] Several of the associates of the Prophet Muhammad, in addition to 'Ali, were regarded as authoritative sources for the interpretation of the Qur'an (for example, Ibn Mas'ud and Ibn 'Abbas), although their opinions are only known from later sources. The enterprise of interpreting the Qur'an was known under two somewhat overlapping Arabic terms, *tafsir* and *ta'wil* (the latter generally implying a more esoteric form of interpretation). Early interpretations of the Qur'an took the form of paraphrase, focusing on the aspects of words with multiple meanings, and narrative explanation that filled in the gaps in stories by referring to biblical and other Near Eastern sources (*Isra'iliyyat*). Some of this early material has been questioned in terms of later theological consensus positions. Early commentators also used topical approaches that lent themselves to legal issues, by organizing material under the headings of questions such as prayer, fasting, and so on. Attention was paid to issues of Arabic vocabulary and grammar, which became highly developed disciplines in connection with the understanding of the Qur'an. The commentary of al-Tabari (d. 923) is a milestone in the detailed explanation of the Qur'an in terms of the sayings of the Prophet Muhammad.[91] Another important early interpreter is al-Tha'labi (d. 1035), whose (still unpublished) commentary has drawn recent attention as a masterful achievement of intellectual synthesis.[92] Other major commentaries were produced by theologians such as al-Razi (d. 1210), from a Sunni perspective, and al-Tabarsi (d. 1153), from a Shi'i point of view.[93] An important esoteric commentary from the perspective of the Isma'ili school of Shi'ism by the eminent theologian al-Shahrastani (d. 1153) has recently been translated.[94] Sufi mystics such as al-Sulami (d. 1021) compiled spiritual insights into the mysteries of the Qur'an.[95] Philosophers since the time of Ibn Sina (d. 1037) also offered their reflections on the possible meanings of Qur'anic verses.[96] In recent years, a number of important commentaries have been translated into English; translations are available on websites, so that one can compare different interpretations of a particular verse.[97] Reading an entire commentary by one of these authors might be an intimidating task, but there are some useful publications that include a wide range of different commentators on a particular verse, in this way making it easy to compare different perspectives on understanding a given Qur'anic text.[98] Like any other text with a global impact, the Qur'an has appealed to readers in different times and places for different reasons, which has given rise to distinctive modes of interpretation.[99]

In modern times, in part under the impact of European colonial conquest, new trends have developed in the interpretation of the Qur'an.[100] Some of these have a defensive character, as nineteenth-century Muslim intellectuals grappled with the seeming superiority of European civilization, with its claim to mastery of science and technology. This challenge inspired figures such as Indian scholar Sir Sayyid Ahmad Khan (d. 1898), who founded the Aligarh Muslim University, and Egyptian reformist Muhammad 'Abduh (d. 1905). To varying degrees, both of these commentators relied upon rationalistic interpretations to highlight the harmony between the Qur'an and the laws of science. They were succeeded by interpreters who developed a full-fledged "scientific" exegesis of the Qur'an, which argues that the Qur'an anticipated the discoveries of modern science, a miraculous achievement that offers proof of its divine inspiration; proponents of this approach seem not to be bothered by the way in which it subordinates divine revelation to the authority of contemporary science. Another modern emphasis was the development of literary studies of the Qur'an in its historical context, particularly among Egyptian scholars in the school of Amin al-Khuli (d. 1967). Some of these scholars have encountered stiff opposition and even outright persecution, as in the case of Nasr Hamid Abu Zayd.[101] Especially noteworthy is the approach of Algerian scholar Mohammed Arkoun, who has developed an anthropological and semiotic interpretation of the Qur'an, with a strongly antiauthoritarian emphasis.[102] A quite different and much more conservative direction was taken by activist scholars such as Sayyid Qutb (d. 1966), a leader of the Muslim Brotherhood in Egypt, and Abul 'Ala Maudoodi (d. 1979), founder of the Jama'at-i Islami in Pakistan,[103] who saw the Qur'an as the source of divine instructions about the system or method that must be followed strictly by humanity today, just as in the time of the Prophet. Thus there is a considerable diversity still to be found today in the approaches that Muslim thinkers take to understanding the Qur'an.[104]

Serious readers of any major scripture sooner or later run into the problem of how to deal with apparent inconsistencies in the text. From both theoretical and practical points of view, it is hard to resist the challenge of reconciling different passages that evidently are in conflict with each other. The Qur'an is certainly no exception to this situation. Interpreters gravitated to the notion of abrogation (*naskh*), a word which in different forms is repeated four times in the Qur'an, as a way to solve this problem. The development of the doctrine of abrogation is complicated and even confusing, but it is generally understood as the replacement of one authoritative text by another.[105] The larger analogy recognized by Muslim scholars was the replacement of the Jewish and Christian scriptures with the Qur'an as the recognized divine message. Although that particular substitution may not have caused Muslims any concern, the doctrine of abrogation as applied to the Qur'an itself inevitably raised questions, such as why God would change his mind about anything, if indeed he is omniscient. Some theologians resisted the notion of abrogation, pointing out that one passage in which it is mentioned (2:106) offered variant readings that undercut the theory to some extent, and there is a significant debate about the extent to which there are passages from the Qur'an that abrogate others. Perhaps the most influential version of the theory of abrogation was proposed by legal scholar al-Shafi'i, in close connection with his doctrine that the example (*sunna*) of the Prophet was the second-most-authoritative source of law after the Qur'an. By linking the Qur'anic text to the biography of the Prophet Muhammad (as detailed, for instance, in the "occasions of revelation" literature), one could in theory establish which were the later revelations that would have the authority to abrogate any earlier ones with which they were in conflict.

Instances of abrogation were held to include, first, the overruling of the legal force of an earlier text by a later one, while the earlier text continues to exist in letter only. Examples of this would include the change of nighttime vigil from an obligatory practice to an optional one, in sura 73. It was also held that certain verses of the Qur'an had been revealed to the Prophet but subsequently withdrawn by God, in the process disappearing without leaving any trace of their existence (although several cases are cited). A third form of abrogation was also recognized, in which a phrase or verse of revelation has disappeared from the final text of the Qur'an but its legal ruling continues to apply. Thus it was believed by many that the Prophet had received a revelation concerning the punishment of adultery by stoning, which was also thought to be decreed in the Torah. A number of legal scholars appealed to this alleged revelation to overrule the punishment by lashing, which is prescribed in the Qur'an. This was done despite the fact that the so-called stoning verse does not actually occur in the Qur'an. In all these cases, what we see is an interpretive mechanism developed by legal scholars and scriptural interpreters in an effort to iron out inconsistencies in the text. From a literary point of view, the somewhat artificial character of this exercise is indicated by the fact that it not only makes certain actual portions of the text irrelevant but even supposes the authority of verses that do not exist.

The most notorious example of abrogation in the Qur'an concerns verses on warfare, particularly the so-called sword verse (9:5).[106] It is well known that the Qur'an contains a wide range of positions on how Muslims should respond to opponents, ranging from avoiding confrontation to restricted conflict to outright war. By using the model of abrogation offered by legal scholars, one could suppose that the early verses counseling quietism and moderation were suited to the weak condition of the early Muslim community in Mecca. Likewise, the increasingly belligerent tone of later verses could be seen as a reflection of the growing strength of the movement in Medina. Enthusiastic legal scholars have applied the theory of abrogation to argue that the sword verse effectively abrogates over one hundred earlier verses containing peace treaties or counsels of tolerance.[107] There are several problems with this interpretation, beyond the fact that it makes a significant number of Qur'anic passages irrelevant. As pointed out earlier, relying on the biography of the Prophet and the supposed "occasions of revelation" to provide the interpretive context for the Qur'an is ultimately a circular exercise. This is because the standard narrative of the biography of the Prophet Muhammad has been constructed in part in order to solve the problems of Qur'anic chronology. It is circular because the biography is used to frame the Qur'anic text, but then the Qur'anic text is cited as the basis of the biography. As one alternative explanation, it is quite possible that the conflicting verses on warfare reflect the palpable disagreement that existed within the early Muslim community on the question of conflict and that this disagreement was unresolved.[108] Another possible interpretation is provided by ring composition, according to which conflict verses are generally external frames for central affirmations of religious pluralism. According to this view (see chapter 4 for examples), the general principles of the central points have lasting implications, in contrast to the more limited historical circumstances of conflict in the framing verses.

The emergence of a dominant interpretation of jihad stressing militancy took place in the ninth century, in an atmosphere of imperial expansion defined by the empire of the caliphate, where the ethical struggle of jihad was redefined as world conquest. From the long view of history, we know that other interpretations have been offered for the notion of jihad, including the defensive theories proposed by Muslim thinkers and anticolonial leaders of the nineteenth and twentieth centuries.[109] An intriguing example is the theory of the controversial Sudanese thinker Mahmud Muhammad Taha (executed in 1985), who viewed the Meccan suras as having a universal validity that trumped the particular political significance of the Medinan suras. He thus, in effect, turned the classical theory of abrogation upside down, by arguing that the earlier portions of the Qur'an were more authoritative than the later ones.[110] In any case, abrogation stands as a prominent example of an external interpretive model that is brought to bear upon the text of the Qur'an in order to achieve certain results.

In any consideration of interpretation of a sacred text, another of the major questions concerns its translation into other languages.[111] It is often asserted that, unlike the Bible, the Qur'an is untranslatable. On the face of it, such an assertion may be hard to understand, given that there are today hundreds if not thousands of translations of the Qur'an into many different languages. The notion that the Qur'an really exists only in its Arabic form has several aspects. One may be considered the ritual perspective, since most schools of law regard the recitation of the accepted Arabic text of the Qur'an as a requirement for a valid ritual prayer. There is a notable exception, however, in the Hanafi school of law going back to its founder, Abu Hanifah (d. 765), who approved the recitation of translations of the Qur'an and ritual prayer in local languages such as Persian, for the sake of comprehension. But it is largely the case that only the recitation of the Arabic Qur'an counts as a religious act, regardless of whether the reciter understands the text or not.

A second aspect of the concept of untranslatability relates to the doctrine that the Qur'an is inimitable (*i'jaz*) and that it demonstrates an eloquence that is beyond human power.[112] This argument arises from passages where the Qur'an challenges those who reject Muhammad's prophecy, demanding that they try to compose something equal to the Qur'an (with the strong implication that this is impossible). This was originally a theological position, in which the revelation of the Qur'an was proved to be a miracle (and, according to some, the only miracle performed by Muhammad). Later on, scholars defined the nature of this miracle as aesthetic, something that could be confirmed by anyone capable of recognizing its beauty.[113] Thus a special power was attached to the word of God as revealed in the original Arabic. Even though in practice it may have been common for preachers to explain the meaning of Qur'anic passages in local languages, there is a tendency to consider this as "explanation" or "commentary" (*tafsir*), as opposed to a translation that could replace the original text. As early as the tenth century, the massive Arabic Qur'an commentary of al-Tabari was translated into Persian, and then into Turkish, necessarily including the verbal translation of the Qur'anic text into those languages. Countless manuscripts of the Qur'an include interlinear glosses, expressing the meaning of the text in a word-by-word fashion, in Persian and Turkish. Although those early interlinear versions technically did not constitute independent translations, they certainly indicate that the act of translation was taking place (see figure 1.2). This ambivalence about the concept of Qur'anic translation was demonstrated by the title of the 1930 English translation by Muhammad Marmaduke Pickthall, which he entitled *The Meaning of the Glorious Qur'an*, carefully referring to it in the subtitle as "an explanatory translation."[114] The point of this title was that this English "translation" only explained the meanings of the text, without actually replacing the Arabic original. Nevertheless, today there are easily available

Figure 1.2. Qur'an leaf with interlinear Persian translation. Ackland Art Museum, University of North Carolina at Chapel Hill; gift of the Ackland Associates.

translations of the Qur'an into all major European languages as well as the languages of Africa and Asia, and their dissemination has been considerably speeded by print technology and now the Internet.

The concept of the untranslatable Qur'an is clearly theological, although the argument is often made in terms of the distinctive linguistic and literary properties of the text.[115] From a strictly literary perspective, however, there does not seem to be any good reason why the Qur'an should be privileged among all other texts in the world as being only accessible in the original language. From a hyper-literalistic position, one could make the same argument about the Greek epics of Homer, or the Chinese writings of Confucius—each of these has unique characteristics that cannot be duplicated in another language. Translation is, moreover, a constantly shifting target—in each generation, skillful literary scholars have created new translations suitable in style and mood to their own age. In this way, the seventeenth century saw Chapman's English version of Homer as a great achievement of Elizabethan style, while the rhyming couplets of Alexander Pope's *Iliad* satisfied the taste of the eighteenth century, and so on. In terms of style, it may be said that ambivalence about the validity of translating the Qur'an has not been conducive to the achievement of notable literary success. Many English translations clearly agonize over dictionary-style word-for-word renderings, and frequently they make the unwise choice of emulating the archaic style of the King James Bible, complete with "thee" and "thou." The results of these translations are all too often scarcely readable productions that contribute to the general impression that the Qur'an is an impenetrable work.

The issue of translating the Qur'an into European languages is also complicated by the long history of hostile use of these translations in anti-Islamic arguments.[116] As mentioned previously, from the time of the first major Latin translation of the Qur'an in 1143 by Robert of Ketton until fairly modern times, nearly all translations of the Qur'an into European languages had the aim of refuting and casting doubt upon the credibility of the Islamic revelation, from an explicitly Christian perspective. It was common for many Christian intellectuals to write not only treatises against Islam and the Prophet Muhammad but also in particular attacks on the Qur'an. These attacks were generally carried out with the clear presumption that translating the Qur'an would expose its manifest errors and falsity for all to see. An example is the remark of Martin Luther on the usefulness of translating the Qur'an for this polemical purpose:

It has struck me that one is able to do nothing more grievous to Mohammad or the Turks, nor more to bring them to harm (more than with all weaponry) than to bring their Koran to Christians in the light of day, that they may see therein, how entirely cursed, abominable, and desperate a book it is, full of lies, fables and all abominations that the Turks conceal and gloss over. They are reluctant to see the Koran translated into other languages, for they probably feel that it would bring about apostasy in all sensible hearts.[117]

Ironically, European critics of the Qur'an often relied on translations that were quite faulty, so that their criticism of the alleged incoherence of the Qur'an was itself the result of a flawed process of translation. Given this hostile approach to Qur'anic translation by European Christians, one can understand why some modern Muslim reformist thinkers like Rashid Rida' (d. 1935) opposed translation and encouraged non-Arab Muslims to read the text in the original Arabic, in order to preserve religious unity against the onslaught of colonialism.[118] More recently, the missionary attack on the Qur'an has been joined by nominally secularist critics, who see the Qur'an as the inspiration for terrorism and the source of an irreconcilable divide between Muslims and European culture. As I have pointed out elsewhere, these opponents of Islam are themselves wedded to a fundamentalist-style notion of literal interpretation, which seizes upon the most extreme interpretation and identifies that as being "true" Islam; any Muslims who engage in broader mainstream interpretive strategies can then be safely dismissed as not being real Muslims.[119] Ironically, these anti-Muslim ideologues place themselves in the position of being the ultimate judges of who is qualified to interpret the Qur'an.

The modern era has seen extensive dissemination of the Qur'an on an unprecedented scale, both as an Arabic text and in translation, thanks to new technologies of communication. Although print technology had an impact on Christianity by the end of the fifteenth century through printed editions of the Bible, the printing of the Qur'an by Muslim authorities did not take place on a large scale until the mid-nineteenth century, initially in Persia and India. Before printing, manuscripts of the Qur'an were expensive and hard to come by, and literacy was not widespread. Muslim jurists also had concerns about whether the printing process would violate rules of purity or treat the Qur'an with disrespect. In the Ottoman realms, printing of the Qur'an was at first prohibited, but eventually it was embraced by the state as a way of consolidating its authority. The translation of the Qur'an into Turkish in the early 1900s was a state project opposed by traditional religious scholars, who correctly saw that their own authority would be undermined by the wide availability of the Qur'an among the population.[120] The official Egyptian printed edition of the Qur'an published in 1924 was a landmark that until today has served as the standard. Nowadays, in every country with majority Muslim population, it is easy to obtain printed copies of the Qur'an.

A new chapter has opened up with the availability of the Qur'an on the Internet, both in digitized recordings of oral recitation and in hypertext markup versions of the Arabic text.[121] There is even a dispute about whether it is appropriate to create ring tones from Qur'an recitation for use on cell phones. Beginning in the 1980s, Muslim college students in American universities began to put Islamic texts online, creating new questions about how one approaches the text. Any reservations about the issue of translation were left aside as new digital resources were created. These websites devoted to the Qur'an often feature numerous translations into European and Asian languages, sometimes including multiple English versions side-by-side as well as commentaries. Although it is certainly significant to see the widespread availability of these texts on the Internet, it has also been remarked that the textual sensibility underlining these websites is basically that of an engineer toward an instruction manual, which can only be understood in one way. That is, the people responsible for creating these websites are not trained in the humanities nor in the traditional Islamic religious disciplines, so their concept of textual interpretation tends to be one-dimensional and authoritarian.[122] That being said, it is hard to deny that the creation of "cyber-Islamic environments" has introduced a new era in the study of texts like the Qur'an.

Toward a Chronological Reading: The Qur'an as an Unfolding Text

The problem addressed by this book is the impasse created by rival theological and ideological readings of the Qur'an. Although these interpretations certainly serve the interests of those already committed to such positions, they are surprisingly ineffective and irrelevant for those who are simply interested in an open-minded and fair reading of the text—and not interested in embracing or rejecting it as a matter of faith. For those readers who seek a humanistic understanding of the Qur'an as a literary work, which is not a negligible goal, a chronological reading recommends itself as a productive strategy.

This kind of historical approach to the Qur'an as a literary text has not been undertaken often. Nevertheless, according to a tradition preserved by the Egyptian scholar al-Suyuti (d. 1505), no less a person than 'Ali had in his possession a copy of the Qur'an with the suras organized in chronological order of revelation.[123] A few modern translators have actually published their versions by putting the suras in some kind of chronological order different from the canonical sequence. A Christian clergyman named J. M. Rodwell adopted this strategy in his 1861 translation, which drew upon the first edition of Theodor Nöldeke's study of the Qur'an. Yet the sequence that he presented was idiosyncratic, due to decisions he made on a thematic basis, and reference was difficult because he numbered only every tenth line.[124] Nevertheless, this translation received new popularity in its 1909 reprint in Everyman's Library and is still available today, though it has been criticized for its theological bias. The scholarly French translator Régis Blachère used Nöldeke's chronological arrangement of suras in the 1947 edition of his widely admired French version, but in subsequent editions he returned to the standard order because of its convenience for locating particular verses.[125] Likewise, N. J. Dawood in his 1956 English translation of the Qur'an for Penguin Classics offered an idiosyncratic, partly chronological sequence chosen for aesthetic appeal, but subsequent editions returned to the traditional order, again for largely practical reasons.[126] From these less than successful experiments, it appears that printing the suras of the Qur'an according to a chronological order is not likely to be welcomed by readers. What is proposed here instead is a strategy for reading the suras in a sequence that approximates the historical chronology, as far as scholarship can determine it. Everyone can still use their favorite Qur'an translations, but if they follow the recommended strategy, they will not be simply starting with page one.

As far as reading practice is concerned, the standard order of the 114 suras of the Qur'an may be considered as the ritual order of the recitation of the text. The late Medinan suras so prominent at the beginning of the Qur'an (that is, suras 2, 3, 4, 5, 8, and 9) were revealed to a predominantly Muslim society, unlike the Meccan suras, which were revealed earlier in a largely non-Muslim context. Therefore it may be said that the canonical sequence of suras is indeed aimed at a Muslim readership.[127] There is consequently no apparent necessity for reading the text of the Qur'an according to the traditional order in an academic context, unless one has in mind its ritual performance or its theological reception by a Muslim community. Thus in principle it is attractive to propose a reading of the Qur'an that follows its presumed historical sequence. If the academic study of the Qur'an does not aim to imitate the theological approach of the madrasa, I see no reason not to use the Nöldeke sequence as a baseline. The principle I appeal to here is that the academic study of religion does not simply replicate the views of any particular group of believers, though it certainly takes those views into account as an important consideration. Nevertheless, what distinguishes the academic study of religion is the impartial use of theoretical approaches, without privileging one theological position over another.

To reiterate, the method proposed here for reading the Qur'an is both literary and historical, and it pays special attention to the rhetorical structure of the text itself. Rhetoricians have pointed out how one can distinguish the implied audience, or "second persona," which is addressed in any given text; at the same time, one can extrapolate unspoken contexts that are not mentioned, or are implicitly negated, which constitute a "third persona" that stands in the background of the text.[128] In addition, there are all the features of literary genre, form, and structure that have been sketched out above. By applying such tools to the understanding of the Qur'an as an unfolding text, one can interrogate the sequence of delivery and its introduction of new terms and topics, and one can see how the text addressed intended audiences and implicitly commented on its own context. One does not have to take a theological position in order to understand that the structure of the Qur'an implies a sender and an audience, by the very choice of the pronouns and verbs that are used. In this way, the reader has the opportunity to understand the Qur'an as a literary problem (understanding the word "problem" in its primary sense of a question that is raised for inquiry and solution rather than as a difficulty or source of distress). This is an enormous opportunity for readers. After all, if the Qur'an remains a mystery, it is insoluble and inscrutable, and not much more can be said. But if it is a problem, that is, a question to which we seek a solution, we may indeed ask how it is constructed, to whom it is addressed, and how it unfolds over the period of its articulation. In short, we may approach the Qur'an as a fascinating literary text, which presents rich challenges—and, one hopes, rich rewards—for its readers. Of course, no single reading carried out in such a spirit will be final. What is offered here as a demonstration is simply one example of how one may read the Qur'an, using the modern scholarly equipment that has been created with so much labor and ingenuity. This approach has as its aim understanding, rather than preaching or refutation. And the test of such a method will have to be judged from the results that follow. I invite the reader to join me in this reading of selected suras of the Qur'an, pursued in a fair-minded manner with the tools of literary and historical scholarship.

2

Early Meccan Suras

Our literary investigation of the early Meccan suras begins with an overview of the structural composition and principal themes of these texts.
This includes close analysis of several suras that are translated in full and
broken down into their components or building blocks. Then follows a
critical survey of a particularly important literary form that is prominent
from the first stage of the Qur'an's unfoldment: apocalyptic or end-times
scenarios. It will then be possible to consider the question of later additions to the early Meccan suras, with a detailed focus on sura 53, "The Star,"
in relation to the notorious question of the "Satanic verses."

Structures and Themes

From a stylistic perspective, the early Meccan suras demonstrate considerable variety. Not only do they employ a far greater number of different
rhymes than later sections of the Qur'an, but they also display a remarkable range of structural composition. There are five very short suras consisting of five verses or less (97, 103, 105, 108, 111), and another ten suras that
are relatively short, with small clusters of verse groups (93, 94, 95, 99, 100,
101, 102, 104, 106, 107). On the level of somewhat greater complexity, one
can distinguish suras in which the verses are organized primarily in clusters of two (81, 91), three (82, 84, 86, 90, 92), or four (85, 89) verses. There
are several suras, traditionally considered to be the earliest, which exhibit
a tightly structured organization (73, 74, 87, 96). Two suras (55, 77) con-

tain what appear undeniably to be refrains that are repeated periodically throughout the sura. Several of the longer suras (51, 53, 68, 79, 80) seem to be rather neatly divided into three symmetrical sections, while other longer suras (52, 56, 69, 70, 75, 78, 83, 88) show no such obvious organization.[1] So the notion of the sura as a literary structure is quite flexible, from the very beginning of its development.

The structure and thematic organization of these early Qur'anic suras are in reality inseparable, since the sections that may be detected within a sura are most clearly evident when marked by both separate stylistic features (such as change of rhyme) and shifts of subject.[2] For that reason, it is crucial to the understanding of any sura to be able to divide it into its natural constituent parts, as a guide to understanding its meaning. The major themes of the early suras are strongly delineated and well known, and they may be summarized as follows: their cosmic significance is underlined by the use of many oath formulas invoking the powers of nature. God is declared to be the Creator of heaven and earth, and the Qur'an emphasizes gratitude as the appropriate response of humanity to the gift of life and existence. The Qur'an presents numerous examples of God's generosity in the abundant signs of nature, including the bounty of water and the life displayed in growing things and animals. So complete is the genuine acknowledgment of God's creation that men and women should never harbor the fantasy that they themselves are independent and self-sufficient. The regrettable human habit of hoarding wealth comes under special condemnation in many passages, and the duty to share one's good fortune with the poor and the stranger is stressed again and again. Humanity's forgetfulness, or deliberate heedlessness, of its fundamental debt to God is the pretext for God to communicate a message that reminds humanity of its duty and the consequences of neglecting it. That message—that Reminder, to give scripture one of its Qur'anic names—is prophecy.

It is in such a cosmic context that the Qur'an takes on its distinctive tone. At this point, regardless of one's attitude toward the status of the Qur'an as a divine revelation, it cannot be denied that the Qur'an is in large part a discourse about divine revelation. Most of the narratives of the Qur'an revolve around a single storyline, which with few variations is played out in the careers of the prophets. Each prophet addresses his people, warning them of the dire punishments awaiting the unfaithful in hellfire, while at the same time promising the rewards that the virtuous will experience in paradise. God's power to resurrect the dead cannot be doubted if one realizes that it is God who gives life to all beings in creation. Numerous passages juxtapose these dual outcomes of Judgment Day as contrastive double portraits of the fire and the garden. Unfortunately, in spite of the manifest truth of the message that the prophet delivers, in this scenario the people nearly always respond with mockery and insults, rejecting the revelation altogether (the one exception is the people of Jonah, who repent). Refusal to heed the warning of punishment in the afterlife ironically leads to destruction in this life. Proud and arrogant leaders, like Pharaoh, who cast aside the admonitions of prophets like Moses, are doomed to a catastrophic end. The evidence for these punishment stories, which will be discussed in further detail below, is on display in the ruins of past civilizations scattered across the Near Eastern landscape.

The interweaving of structure and theme can be seen from an examination of several of the most symmetrically structured longer suras from the early Meccan period (51, 68, 79, 80). For example, sura 51, "The Scatterers," consists of sixty verses that can be divided into three major parts (consisting of 23 + 23 + 14 verses). The first part (twenty-three verses) devotes nine verses to rhyming oaths sworn by the forces of nature, promising the truth of judgment in spite of doubts (51:1–9); then follow fourteen verses (51:10–23) providing double portraits of doom and reward in the afterlife, signs of nature, and a closing oath. The second part (also twenty-three verses) relates stories of grace and punishment, mirroring the 14 + 9 verse division of the first part by devoting the first fourteen verses to Abraham (51:24–37) and then nine verses to four other prophets (51:38–46). The third part (fourteen verses) concludes with an enumeration of the consequences of the second part, with the first seven verses devoted to signs, monotheism, and previous prophets (51:47–53). The last seven verses console Muhammad, prove the Creator, and promise doom to opponents (51:54–60).[3]

To illustrate the symmetrical deployment of structure and theme more concretely, one may consider the case of sura 79, which at first glance does not display such a neat structure. The symmetry of this sura becomes clear when one reconsiders it by removing a later addition (79:33) and dividing two verses (79:40–41) into three, based on the internal rhyme. This reconsideration reveals a tight original symmetrical verse structure, as indicated below.[4] The following translation is organized in paragraphs, with numbered headings added in italics indicating the original articulation of the sura into three symmetrical parts (I: 5 + 9 verses; II: 6 + 6 + 6 verses; III: 9 + 5 verses):

I. Rider oaths (5 verses) and end-times (9 verses)

(1–5) By the pullers to the limit, yanking on ropes, plunging in, rushing ahead, running a situation — 5

(5–14) On the day when the quaking quakes, and the next one follows it — On that day hearts will be throbbing, their glances humble; they will say, "Shall we be restored to our first state, when we have become rotten bones?" They will say, "This would be a lost effort, then!" But it only takes a single shout, and they will be awakened.

II. Punishment story of Moses' call (6 verses), Pharaoh's rejection (6 verses), and God's power (6 verses)

(15–20) Has the story of Moses reached you? When his Lord called him to the sacred valley of Tuwa: "Go to Pharaoh, who has rebelled! And say, 'Do you wish to become pure? So I will guide you to your Lord, and you will fear.'" Then he showed him the greatest sign.

(21–26) But he [Pharaoh] called it a lie and disobeyed. Then he turned back quickly, till he summoned and called, saying, "I am your highest lord!" So God took him, as an example in the next world and the last; so there is a warning in this for those who fear.

(27–33) Are you harder to create, or is the heaven that He made? He raised its roof and righted it, darkening its night and bringing out its morning light, and after that He spread the earth, bringing out from it water and pasture, and fixing the hills, as a sustenance for you and your herds.[6]

III. End-times with double portraits (9 verses) and consolation regarding an unknown hour (5 verses)

(34–41) But when the greatest calamity comes, on the day when man recalls what he has attempted, and hell will be displayed to one who sees — then, the one who rebelled, and took the earthly life, will have hell for his abode! But one who fears standing before his Lord, and denies the soul its desire, will have the garden for his abode.[7]

(42–46) They will ask you about the hour: "When is its arrival?" What do you recall of it? Your Lord is its goal. You are only a warner to one who fears. On that day when they see it, it will be as though they only lingered an afternoon, or its morning.

Seen in the light of this striking symmetry, this sura looks to be a balanced and deliberate composition, quite similar in structure to other early Meccan suras.

Another example of a tightly structured early Meccan sura is sura 80, "He Frowned." This sura is noteworthy for evidently criticizing the Prophet Muhammad (in the third person in 80:1-2, shifting to the second person in 80:3-4) for treating a blind man with indifference. Once again, this sura may be divided into three sections containing 16 + 16 + 10 verses. Sura 80 has numerous verbal echoes of another early Meccan text, sura 74, "Wrapped in a Cloak."[8] It neatly demonstrates the typical feature of dynamic style (*iltifat*), not only in the shift from third to second person in the opening (80:1-4), but also in the dramatic shift to "We" in 80:25.

I. Encounter with a blind man, the arrogance of the wealthy, and confirmation of Revelation (16 verses)

(1-4) He frowned and turned back, because the blind man came to him.—And how do you know? Perhaps he purifies himself, or is reminded and the Reminder benefits him.

(5-10) But the one who thinks himself rich—you pay attention to him, though it's nothing to you that he fails to purify himself. But the one who came hurrying to you, who is humble, him you have neglected.

(11-16) No! It is a Reminder; let him who wishes remember it. It is on honored pages, sublime, purified, by the hands of scribes noble and virtuous.

II. Doom of the ungrateful (16 verses)

(17-23) The man is cursed; how ungrateful he is! From what did He create him? From a drop He created him, and measured him, making the way easy for him. Then He caused him to die, and buried him. Then, when He wished, He raised him up. No—he does not perform what He ordered.

(24-32) Let the man look on his food: We made the rain fall, then We split the earth in cracks, so We made the seed sprout in it, and grapes and plants, olives and palms, dense gardens, fruit and grass, sustenance for you and your herds.

III. End-times scene and double portrait (10 verses in two equal parts)

(33-37) But when the crack of doom comes, on the day when a man flees from his brother, his mother, father, wife, and children, on that day every man will have business to occupy him!

(38-42) There are faces that will shine that day, laughing and joyful; and there are faces with dust on them that day, covered in dirt. They are the vicious unbelievers.

The balance and order of this sura demonstrate the rhythms of measured delivery with which the earliest audience of the Qur'an must have become familiar through frequent repetition. The original symmetry of the sura demonstrates the balanced structures of oral composition. Opposites complement each other, from the juxtaposition of the blind man and the willful rich man to the shining faces and the dirty faces of the blest and the damned. The principal theme of revelation is clarified in terms of the awesome power of divine creativity and generosity. All of this is presented in a structure of harmonious proportion that facilitates the reception of the message.

One final example will suffice to demonstrate the propensity for balanced composition in the early Meccan suras. This is sura 68, "The Pen," which also displays, at greater length, the familiar tripartite organization seen in other early Meccan suras. The oath that opens this sura invokes one of the Arabic letters and the apparatus of writing, as images of revelation. What follows is noteworthy for its extended address in second-person singular, evidently to the Prophet, encouraging him to remain steadfast in spite of opposition. There is considerable evidence here of the kind of language used by the rejecters of the revelation, who dismiss it as madness and fable. This sura also makes an explicit connection between its punishment story and the retribution of Judgment Day (68:33). In a debate sequence marked by heavy irony, it is also evident that the assumed detractors (who are addressed in the plural) must be quite familiar with the concept of a written revelation (68:37).

I. Address to Prophet: oath and consolation (7 verses) and debate with critics (9 verses)

(1–7) N, by the pen, and what they write! By God's bounty, you are not mad, and yours will be a well-earned reward. You are indeed of great character; so you shall see, and they will see, which of you is derailed. Your Lord is the one who knows best who has strayed from His path, and He knows best who is guided rightly.

(8–16) So do not obey the deniers, who would love you to be slick, so they could be slick. And do not obey everyone who is an oath-breaker, slanderer, spreader of lies, obstacle of good, transgressor, criminal, brute, and on top of that an upstart, just because he has money and children. When Our signs were recited to him, he said, "Fairy tales of the ancients!" We shall brand him on the snout!

II. Punishment story of garden, with end-time conclusion (18 verses in two equal parts)

(17–25) We tried them as We tried the owners of the garden, when they swore they would reap it in the morning, though they reserved nothing (for the poor). But a visitation from your Lord came round to it while they were sleeping, and when morning came it was like a field stripped bare. Yet they cried out to each other that morning, "Hurry to the field, if you are one of the reapers!" So they headed off, whispering to each other, "No poor gleaner will enter it today, to your loss!" So they hurried off, prepared for their resolve.

(26–34) When they saw it, they said, "We're lost! No, we're destitute!" The more moderate of them said, "Didn't I say to you, 'Why don't you praise God?'" They said, "Glory be to our Lord! We were really sinners." Then some of them approached others, blaming each other. They said, "It's too bad for us that we were arrogant. Perhaps our Lord will replace it for us with something better; we are begging our Lord!" Their punishment was like that, and the punishment of the next world is greater, if you only knew. Truly the God-conscious will have gardens of bliss.

III. Revelation debate (18 verses in two equal parts, with asides on end-times and Jonah)

(35–43) Shall We treat those who submit (*al-muslimin*) like criminals? What's wrong with you? How can you judge? — Or do you have a book, from which you deduce that you will find there whatever you think best? — Or do you have promises from Us, reaching to the day of resurrection, that you will have whatever you decide? Ask them which of them can guarantee that! — Or do they have (divine) partners? Let them bring their partners, if they're telling the truth. On the day when things become serious, they will be called to bow down, but they will be incapable — their eyes cast down, overcome by humility. For they had been called to bow down while they were safe and sound.

(44–52) So leave to Me those who call this story a lie. We shall lead them on, from where they will not know. But I give them a reprieve, since my stratagem is firm. — Or do you ask them for a fee, so they are weighed down with debt? — Or does the unseen belong to them, so they can write about it? So be patient with the command of your Lord, and don't be like the man in the fish (Jonah), who cried out while he was confined. If it were not that he was reached by favor from his Lord, he would have been thrown in the wasteland as one condemned. But his Lord chose him and made him one of the virtuous. Even if the disbelievers nearly make you stumble with their stares, when they hear the Reminder, and they say, "He is crazy" — it is nothing but a Reminder for the creation.

Even a moderately long sura like this one exhibits a variety of themes, and the often abrupt and dramatic shifts of point of view can prove confusing at first glance unless there is some framework to break up the text and provide entryways. That interpretive framework is provided by comparison with other early Meccan suras that exhibit the same kind of structure as this one. Although this particular kind of symmetry only describes a portion of the early Meccan suras, it nonetheless demonstrates that structure is present in these texts, a structure that is reinforced by the frequent use of rhyme change to designate new subjects.

Apocalypse and Meditation on the Ruined Cities

One may point to a number of important thematic emphases that take the form of discrete building blocks in the Qur'an. Notable are the hymns of praise, whether they focus on God himself, apart from human dependence and gratitude, or whether they hint at divine power and deeds as a warning against human self-centeredness. There are also frequent passages of consolation to the Prophet during his trials. There are numerous confrontations with opponents through debate and denunciation, ranging from outright curses to rebukes of human folly and threats against the ungrateful and arrogant, particularly those who reject the Qur'an and its revelation.[9] But perhaps the most prominent theme in the early Qur'anic suras is the description of the end-times.

The afterlife, the resurrection of the dead, and Judgment Day are topics of great importance throughout the Qur'an, and they received memorable treatment, particularly in the early Meccan suras. How were these scenarios understood by those who were first exposed to the Qur'anic revelation? One of the perplexing issues concerning the implied audience for the

Qur'an is the question of belief in the afterlife among pre-Islamic Arabs. It is often asserted that Arab paganism was a superficial form of polytheism, which authorized a hedonistic and devil-may-care attitude toward life, with no thought for tomorrow. This impression seems to be primarily gained from a reading of pre-Islamic bardic poetry, with its heroic boasting over love affairs and battles, seeing it as a comprehensive portrait of the religious lives of Arabs before the rise of Islam. Such was the opinion expressed a century ago by British Orientalist R. A. Nicholson:

> Religion had so little influence on the lives of the Pre-Islamic Arabs that we cannot expect to find much trace of it in their poetry. They believed vaguely in the supreme God, Allah, and more definitely in his three daughters—al-Lat, Manat, and al-ʿUzza—who were venerated all over Arabia and whose intercession was graciously accepted by Allah. There were also numerous idols enjoying high favor while they continue to bring good luck to their worshipers. Of real piety the ordinary Bedouin knew nothing. He felt no call to pray to his gods, although he often found them convenient to swear by. He might invoke Allah in the hour of need, as a drowning man will clutch at a straw; but his faith in superstitious ceremonies was stronger. He did not take his religion too seriously.[10]

Similar views are widely repeated in later literature. The emphatic tone of the Qur'an, moreover, paints a picture of arrogant Meccan pagans who seem to demonstrate an almost Epicurean rejection of the notion of resurrection and Judgment Day. Yet at the same time, the Qur'an's references to biblical and other Near Eastern prophetic traditions are so frequent and so allusive that they presuppose an audience in Mecca that was quite familiar with those religious narratives. Is it likely that Arabia was largely populated by religiously well-informed skeptics?

There is an unspoken context or third persona that deserves some consideration here, namely, the evidence of archaeology regarding belief in the afterlife in the Arabian regions. Unfortunately, archaeological research is still relatively undeveloped in the territories of Saudi Arabia, because of political and religious sensitivities. A highly conservative religious establishment sees no reason why the traces of Judaism and Christianity should be celebrated in the homeland of Islam, and it views digging up and displaying pagan idols as even more repugnant. Nevertheless, there are significant indications that burial in elaborate tombs was practiced on a surprisingly large scale throughout Arabia and adjoining regions. Just in the island of Bahrain, there are thought to have been over 80,000 ancient mounded tombs (of which about 6,000 remain intact), making up the largest single funerary complex of the ancient world. Some of these (in A'ali and Sar) are impressive royal mausoleums recalling the funerary constructions of Mesopotamia and Egypt.[11] In Saudi Arabia itself, recent explorations have been proceeding discreetly, in spite of contrary sentiments, and discoveries in the regions of Harrat Khaybar and al-Hayit include what appear to be thousands of tombs, along with low-walled structures creating gigantic kite shapes visible from satellite photographs.[12] In al-Ula, excavations of Nabatean and Dedanian sites have drawn attention to tombs comparable to the majestic Nabatean sites of Mada'in Salih (in northwestern Arabia) and Petra (in Jordan), incidentally yielding mummies from 2,000 years ago.[13] All of this suggests that the afterlife was in fact a major obsession of the ancient Arabians. It can be added that, despite the Qur'an's devastating critique of the iniquitous cities that were subjected to divine punishment, the advent of Islam did not by any means put a stop to either the creation of cities or the building and visitation of tombs in Arabia, especially tombs of the prophets.[14] It seems that one must probe further into the significance of the Qur'an's emphasis on the rejection of the afterlife by Muhammad's critics, beyond the superficial assertion that the pagan Arabs did not believe in an afterlife.

One possible clue lies in the inscriptions found in the tombs of the Nabateans in Mada'in Salih (figure 2.1). The eighty monumental burial sites there provide considerable evidence of the respect paid to the royal dead and the practice of ritual meals and drinking parties in the tombs. To some degree, these burial practices of the Nabateans have much in common with the customs of the Mesopotamians, the Syrians, the Aramaeans, and the Israelites. What is distinctive about the tomb inscriptions from a religious perspective is a focus on the particular deities of the Nabateans (the supreme god Dushara, plus the goddesses al-Lat, al-'Uzza, and Manat and the gods Qaysha and Hubal). But from a social point of view, it is also informative to observe the aristocratic and exclusive tone of the inscriptions, something not surprising in monuments that were primarily constructed by a wealthy elite. Thus, not only do the tombs feature the customary Near Eastern curses for anyone who disturbs the dead, but the inscriptions repeatedly condemn the burial in the tomb of anyone who is not related to the builders.[15] This rejection of strangers and unapproved relatives from

Figure 2.1. Twin Nabatean tombs at Mada'in Salih. © Jane Taylor
(www.janetaylorphotos.com).

the precincts of the sacred dead certainly confers a sense of exclusion and privilege on this ancient necropolis. While these tombs predate the rise of Islam by over 500 years, the identification of Mada'in Salih with the city of al-Hijr (known as Hegra to the Romans) clearly links this Arabian site with the prophetic history of the Qur'an—al-Hijr is, after all, the title and a principal subject of sura 15. The drama of the prophet Salih and the punishment of the unbelieving people of Thamud in that very location form one of the standard narratives in the Qur'anic repertoire, though it exists in a fragmentary form.[16] It is entirely plausible to assume that the Nabatean deification of kings, with the aristocratic monopoly on monuments and rituals of immortality, was one of the provocations underlying the Qur'an's harsh critique of the vanity of earthly wealth. From a more positive perspective, one can also imagine that the portrayal of the delights of paradise in the Qur'an draws upon the imagination of the afterlife as practiced in the ritual feasts carried out in the tombs of the Nabateans.

The prominence of tombs among ancient monuments meant that ruins of ancient cities could serve as symbolic reminders of the wrath of God, which was delivered to unjust peoples when they rejected the calls of their prophets. Presumably it would be easy to make a historical connection between these narratives and observable sites like Mada'in Salih or Petra, which had indeed suffered periodic earthquakes that echoed in collective memory, though impressive monuments had survived (figure 2.2). But from the early Meccan period onward, this symbolism of the ruined cities of Arabia was also extended to include biblical narratives of the mythic past, in the complex of narratives commonly known as punishment stories. Biblical characters could be juxtaposed effortlessly with figures of Arabian lore, as in this brief comment: "Has the story reached you of the armies of Pharaoh, and Thamud? Rather, those who reject are in denial" (85:17–18). Another example adds the tribe of 'Ad, believed to have created a city in Yemen called Iram: "Have you seen how your Lord acted with 'Ad, with Iram of the many pillars, the like of which was not created in the lands? And Thamud, who hollowed out the rocks in the valley, and mighty Pharaoh, who rebelled in the lands and increased corruption in it—your Lord poured upon them the portion of punishment" (89:6–13). The lists of prophets whose opponents were destroyed went on to include more detailed accounts of Abraham and Moses (51:24–56). But historical specificity is not the hallmark of the Qur'anic punishment stories. Even at the earliest appearance of this motif, the generic narrative of prophecy, rejection,

Figure 2.2. Nabatean monument at Petra (usually called "the monastery" [*al-Dayr*]). © Jane Taylor (www.janetaylorphotos.com).

and punishment is told repeatedly without any particular name or location (77:16–28, 83:29–36, 85:1–6, 88:21–26). These punishment stories take on even greater importance in the second Meccan and late Meccan periods, only to vanish from the Qur'an in the Medinan period. The reason for that shift of emphasis will be discussed later.

Readers familiar with other forms of religious literature of the Near

East will notice the overlap between these punishment stories and the genre of apocalyptic literature, the revelation of things to come. Apocalyptic literature, in turn, can be considered as a literary subset of eschatology, the doctrine of last things, whether for an individual in the afterlife or for the cosmos at the end of time. But the sight of abandoned ancient cities does not necessarily lead every observer to the conclusion that God has punished those people for their rejection of prophecy. Such a moralizing conclusion requires an already established belief in the power of God to transform the nature of the world in a drastic fashion. The Qur'anic punishment stories presuppose, on a more limited scale, the vision of the end-times, including scenarios of resurrection and judgment of the dead, which have played out in many of the cultures of the ancient Near East and the Mediterranean. There is something irresistible about extrapolating from the finite lifetime of a human being to the birth and death of the cosmos, yet of course no one has ever experienced the beginning or the end of the world. Philosopher of history Eric Voegelin referred to this complex of expressions, in the context of the Israelite prophets, as "metastatic vision," by which he meant "the vision of a world that will change its nature without ceasing to be the world in which we live concretely."[17] Such a cosmic transformation, although it lies outside of the realm of living human experience, exerts a powerful pull over the imagination. This was what Paul invoked when he wrote, "We will be changed, in a moment, in the twinkling of an eye, at the last trumpet" (1 Corinthians 15:51–52). This vision of transformation is even echoed in the secular apocalypse of Karl Marx and Friedrich Engels: "All that is solid melts into air." The early Meccan suras use such a vision to masterfully display not only a transforming vision of divine punishment of the iniquitous cities of the past but also the pure vision of reward and punishment in the events at the end of time.

The images in which the Qur'an describes the end of the world are powerful and picturesque. Although they occur in a more or less consistent fashion in many different passages, it has been a challenge for later commentators to formulate a systematic scenario that would include all of the dramatic sequences clearly.[18] One scholar has nicely summarized the impact of the Qur'anic end-times descriptions:

The earth begins to move violently. It staggers, quakes and is crushed and flattened. It brings forth what is inside of it and empties itself. Like a mirage the mountains assume variable forms. They collapse, are like teased wool and disintegrate into sand and dust. Heaven will be like molten metal and be rent asunder, split open and full of gaping holes. The sun will be coiled up. The moon will darken. The sun and moon will be brought together. The stars will go out and tumble down (or become dull), etc. It would be pointless to try to patch together a coherent and comprehensive account of the events on the last day from the different statements. The individual suras must be taken separately, just as they originally were recited. Indeed, the images of the events on the last day are not intended to, as it were, depict objective reality or to foretell the future exactly in all its details. They have been designed and formulated with the intention to shock the audience, to foreshadow the terror that, at some time in the future, on the last day, will seize all of creation.[19]

Some of the details of the Qur'anic apocalyptic descriptions would be familiar to readers of biblical and other Near Eastern texts, such as the depiction of the heavens being rolled up like a scroll, an image found in the Hebrew Bible (Isaiah 34:4) and the New Testament (Revelation 6:14) and possibly even in Plato.[20] Other images, like the pregnant camels that are neglected at the hour of the apocalypse (81:4), are distinctive to the Arabian ecology of the Qur'an. Nevertheless, the overlap in apocalyptic concepts across the eastern Mediterranean is so significant that it clearly indicates the widespread presence of the same type of visionary literature.

The structure of end-times accounts in the early Meccan suras exhibits clear characteristics. As Angelika Neuwirth points out, depictions of the end-times, whether expressed by a few verses in short suras or in more substantial blocks in the longer suras, can be divided into three separate groups: the scenery of judgment; the actual process; and a description of the fates of the judged, usually in dual portraits of heaven and hell. More than half the suras of the early Meccan period display these three divisions, and even when all three groups do not occur together, their recurrence is otherwise unmistakable.[21]

To take these three aspects of end-times stories in sequence, first of all, the scenery of judgment is typically introduced in the language of time, with the expressions "on the day when . . ." (*yawma*) or simply "when . . ." (*idha*). Examples include the following:

> On the day when people will be like scattered moths, and the mountains will be like teased wool. (101:4–5)

On the day when the quaking quakes, and the next one follows it. (79:6–7)

On the day when the heavens will shake, and the mountains will shift. (52:9–10)

When the earth is shaken with her tremor, and the earth expels her burdens, and men say, "What's wrong with her?" (99:1–3)

When heaven splits, and listens to her Lord and submits, and when the earth is spread, and casts out what was in her, and is empty, and listens to her Lord and submits. (84:1–5)

What is distinctive about this formula is the way in which it relates a series of extraordinary and shocking events that no one has ever experienced, while at the same time it makes them seem recognizable, inevitable, and present by the simple use of time-factored expression. This is not put into a conditional formula, using the language of "if." Instead, the confident "when" is followed by verbs that are technically in the past tense, but in terms of narrative logic they have to be translated in a present or future tense, in this way dramatically enhancing the vividness of the scene.

Next, accounts of the actual process of judgment often follow an account of the scenery of judgment and are introduced by the more specific temporal phrase "on that day . . ." (*yawma'idhan*). Thus, in sura 99, the sequel to the three verses quoted above is: "On that day, she (the earth) will relate her news. . . . On that day, people will go forth in groups to see their deeds" (99:4, 99:6). Likewise, the continuation of sura 79 is: "On that day, hearts will be throbbing" (79:8). In other cases, an untranslatable particle of emphasis (*inna*) introduces this account of the process: "Their Lord, on that day, will truly know them" (100:11). Occasionally, the process of judgment has no verbal introduction: "A soul knows what she has prepared" (81:14).

Finally, the fate of the judged in the afterlife has been mentioned several times already. The double portraits of the blest and the damned use a balanced antithesis to contrast rewards and punishments as sharply as possible. This contrast can be achieved by a simple alternation: "Then one whose weighed good deeds are heavy will be in a pleasing life, but one whose weighed good deeds are light—his mother is devastated!" (101:6–9). Likewise, the judgment is depicted as the presentation of the "book" containing the register of one's deeds, in ways that symbolically indicate reward or punishment: "Then one who is given his book in his right hand will reckon with an easy account, and he will return happily to his family. But one who is given his book behind his back will cry out his ruin" (84:7-12). At other times, the contrast pivots around a single feature, like the face: "There are faces that will shine that day, laughing and joyful; and there are faces with dust on them that day, covered in dirt. They are the vicious unbelievers" (80:38-42). The double portraits of reward and punishment, which can be encountered at every turn, are complemented by dramatic flashbacks, in which the description of the afterlife turns back to contemplate earthly life, either to single out opponents of the Prophet or to provide descriptions of reprehensible or exemplary behavior. Thus the description of a malefactor is converted into a warning: "For he did not trust, nor did he pray, but he rejected and turned away. Then he went arrogantly to his family. It is closer to you, and closer! Again, it is closer to you, and closer!" (85:31-35). The moral calculus of the Qur'an çlearly revolves around these prominent deployments of narratives of the afterlife and end-times.

Later Insertions in Early Meccan Suras

The forty-eight suras of the first Meccan period are nearly all clustered in the latter half of the Qur'an. It is noteworthy that, from a ritual perspective, the majority of these early Meccan suras (thirty-five out of forty-eight) occur within the last thirtieth portion (*juz'*) of the Qur'an.[22] And within this final thirtieth section, which contains thirty-seven relatively short suras, all are from the first Meccan period except for two (98 and 110), which are Medinan. Thus the earliest Meccan suras predominate in the final ritual portion of the Qur'an, and they constitute the most commonly memorized and recited passages of the sacred book in Muslim religious practice.[23] The prominent role of the early Meccan suras in the religious practice of the early Muslim community is indeed one of the chief characteristics of this portion of the Qur'an, and their repeated use in worship service also had distinctive effects that are visible in the later insertions to these suras.

The use of the early Meccan suras in liturgy or worship service is evident from a number of specific references to ritual practice occurring in these passages, frequently placed prominently at the beginning or end of the sura. The most typical examples of such ritual actions are remembering and praising God, prostrating in prayer, and keeping awake to meditate on God during the night. At the end of sura 93, following injunctions to avoid mistreating orphans or turning away beggars, the Qur'an instructs the listener to relate the blessings of his Lord (93:11), that is, to recite the specific gifts of God. Likewise, the listener is told, "Praise the name of your highest Lord" (87:1), and the same sura goes on to tell the listener to remind others of God's blessings, adding that one who remembers also prays (87:9, 87:15). A more overt reference to religious practice is found at the end of sura 96, which instructs the Prophet to prostrate himself before God and draw near (96:19). Other early Meccan passages conclude with the instruction to prostrate before God as part of a nighttime vigil at which the praises of God are also recited (76:26), or else passages simply call for praising God at night and when the stars set (52:49). These examples are generally framed as orders to a single individual, presumably the Prophet Muhammad, but by extension these acts of prostration and worship become religious duties for the entire community. (As previously indicated, certain Qur'anic passages, some fourteen in all, contain the command to prostrate in worship; these are marked in the margins of copies of the Qur'an as requiring prostration when recited.)[24] This communal application of worship commands is explicit in the closing line of sura 53, which instructs members of the community in the plural to prostrate themselves before God and serve him (53:62). These commands for communal prostration in worship proliferate in the second Meccan period (17:61, 18:50, 20:116, 25:60), a likely indication of the increasingly firm establishment of worship services among the early Muslim community. Paradoxically, the importance of the early Meccan suras to religious practice is also evident from the fact that the first sura and the last two suras have occasionally been considered as not being a part of the Qur'an at all, primarily because of their prominent role as often-repeated prayers. All this indicates that the texts of the early Meccan suras were repeatedly recited in both individual and communal worship, so it is not surprising that difficult words or passages could easily have become the occasions for questions and discussions leading to subsequent clarifications, in the form of Qur'anic revelations inserted into the sura at a later date. It is widely acknowledged in traditional Muslim scholarship that there are many suras of the Qur'an that contain passages from both the Meccan and the Medinan periods. What is distinctive about the literary and historical interpretation of the Qur'an is the appeal to reader-oriented explanations of unusual stylistic features that suggest later additions.

The text of the Qur'an clearly indicates expectation of the need to explain new and unusual phrases. This is evident from a dozen early Meccan passages that introduce mysterious terms, often in the context of the afterlife.[25] In each of these cases, the novel word is followed by a rhetorical challenge, asking how the addressee could possibly know the meaning of the term: "And how do you know what X is?" The effect of this formula highlights the unknown character of the new term; even though a dramatic explanation immediately follows with the answer, the question itself accentuates the mysterious and transcendental quality of the events of revelation. One example has already been mentioned, which contains the term "burning" (*saqar*, 74:26–29):

> I shall cast him into the burning.
> And how do you know what the burning is?
> It does not save or leave anything,
> Consuming the man.

Once the term has been introduced and explained, it can be assumed that readers will become familiar with it. Thus, later in the same sura, the term "burning" is used again: "In gardens, they ask of the sinners, 'What brought you to the burning?'" (74:40–42).

The same tension-inducing question, "And how do you know what X is," introduces other new terms that later become normalized in Qur'anic usage. These unusual terms include "the calamity" (*qari'a*, 101:1–3, repeated at 13:31 and 69:4), "the day of separation" (*yawm al-fasl*, 77:14, repeated at 37:21, 44:40, and 78:17), and the very common expression "the day of judgment" (*yawm al-din*, 82:17–18, where the introductory question is repeated for emphasis). On the other hand, certain new terms introduced by this formula occur nowhere else in the Qur'an, and so they retain an air of particular mystery. These include "the smasher" (*hutama*, 104:4), "the happening" (*haqqa*, 69:1–3), "the night of power" (*laylat al-qadr*, 97:2), "the night visitor" (*tariq*, 86:2), "devastated" (*hawiya*, 101:10), and "the mountain pass" (*'aqaba*, 90:12). In the case of the two new terms of sura 83, *sijjin* (83:8) and *'illiyin* (83:18), which denote the "inscribed books" that record the deeds of the wicked and the virtuous, many translators leave these unique words untranslated, as a sign of their enigmatic character. In any case, these examples of difficult new words, which are framed by questions and explanations, establish the principle that the Qur'an can explicate its own more difficult passages. From this point it is not difficult to imagine that questions arising from the first reception of certain Qur'anic verses could lead to explanations being inserted later on into some of the earlier revelations.

How can one detect a later insertion into the early Meccan suras? The most obvious indication is the occurrence of a long prose section that appears out of place in a series of very short rhyming verses. This was the case in the verse concerning the nineteen angels (74:31), discussed in chapter 1. In addition, the need to provide exceptions to a general statement or rule can plausibly be seen as the occasion for a later addition to a Qur'anic text. Such additions are particularly likely in the form of passages beginning "except for. . . ." There are also passages in which an extended debate appears to be added on to a previously symmetrical composition or in which a moralizing conclusion is inserted to draw a lesson.

One example of later insertion by way of exception is the case of the night vigil, mentioned in the short opening verses of sura 73, which suggest a regular practice of lengthy nighttime meditations: "You, wrapped in a cloak! Stand by night, except a little; half of it, or reduce it by a little; or add to it, and set forth the recitation (*qur'an*) in order" (73:1–4). Here Muhammad, as exemplar for the community, is evidently required to spend much of the night in prayer and meditation. The first nineteen short verses of this sura are all characterized by a strong end rhyme, but they are followed by a lengthy and prosaic twentieth verse (nearly ten times as long as any preceding verse) that relates how this kind of demanding nighttime exercise may be relaxed for the community. This verse (73:20) has all the appearances of a later Medinan addition, placed here as an explanatory legal appendix. It clarifies that the rigorous practice of night vigil can be reduced for certain classes of people, including the sick, travelers, and fighters. In a similar fashion, the final section of sura 84, in short and strongly rhymed lines, paints a gloomy portrait of the fate that awaits those who reject the Qur'an, with this conclusion: "So give them the news of a painful doom" (84:24). It appears that the next line (84:25), which makes an exception for the believers, was added as a prose postscript to clarify that this is not universal: "Except for those who have faith and perform good works—theirs is a reward rightly earned." The exact duplicate of that verse has also been inserted as an exception in 95:6, where it stands out against a series of short rhyming verses. It may even be said that the very short sura 103, consisting of only three verses, was expanded by the addition of the third verse with a similar exception: "By the afternoon! Truly humanity is in a crisis—except for those who have faith, and perform good deeds, counseling one another with truth and counseling one another with patience" (103:1–3).

Other passages have been proposed as later insertions on the grounds that they appear to be moralizing comments added to an original composition that could stand on its own. In the opening hymnic lines of sura 55, "The Merciful," two moralizing verses (marked below in bold) appear to be inserted as a commentary in the midst of a poetic celebration of signs of God in heaven and on earth:

> And heaven He has lifted up, and He has placed the balance—
> **so that you don't exceed the balance,**
> **but set the measure with justice, and do not stint on the**
>   **balance—**
> And the earth, He has placed it for creatures . . . (55:7–10)

In the midst of a sura celebrated for its poetic enumeration of the bounties of God, these two verses (55:8–9) have an oddly prosaic explanatory effect. Later in the same sura, an unusually long verse (55:33) inserts a challenge to humans and jinn, challenging them to penetrate the mysteries of creation. This also is placed somewhat inconsistently in the short rhyming lines of this sura.[26] Another example of a moralizing addition is 52:21 (marked in bold), which interrupts a beautiful description of the blessed in paradise:

> Those who are God-conscious are in gardens and in bliss,
> Cheerful with what their Lord has brought them, for their Lord
>   has protected them from the punishment of hellfire.
> "Eat and drink the good stuff, for what you have done!"
> They are reclining on seats in rows, and we have wedded them
>   to the ones with beautiful eyes.
> **And those who have faith, and whose offspring follow them**
>   **in faith, We have joined their offspring to them, and We**
>   **have not shorted them at all for their work. Every man is**
>   **a pledge for what he has acquired.**
> And We supply them with fruit and meat as they desire.
> There they pass around a cup which holds no nonsense or
>   temptation.
> Encircling them are the youths that belong to them, as though
>   they were hidden pearls. (52:17–24)

The rhapsodic quality of this depiction of heaven is interrupted by the intrusion of a seemingly unrelated moral reflection (the ending is a partial repetition of 74:38), which is considerably longer than the surrounding verses. When read without verse 21, this passage exhibits much tighter unity. In fact, the last twenty-one verses of this sura (52:29–49) shift away from a cosmic portrait to a debate with opponents, laden with irony, which exhibits phrases more commonly found in later suras. This last section of sura 52 may thus be a later addition.[27]

A similar observation may be made about the composite character of sura 56, "The Event," which is noteworthy for its depiction of the judged as divided into three groups: the front-runners, the companions of the right, and the companions of the left. After an opening end-time scene (56:1–6) and the initial mention of these three categories, the sura carefully describes the destiny of each group in the afterlife: the front-runners (56:10–26), the companions of the right (56:27–40), and the companions of the left (56:41–56). This group of three is an interesting variation on the usual double portrait; while the companions of the right and left are clearly the inhabitants of paradise and hell, the front-runners appear to be an especially favored group of the blessed.[28] Then follows a description of the signs of God that demonstrate the truth of revelation (56:57–73), concluding with a verse commanding the receiver of the message (presumably Muhammad) to praise the name of his Lord (56:74). That ritual conclusion, so common as the beginning or the ending of a sura, might lead the reader to suppose that the sura has come to an end. Surprisingly, the sura resumes with a new topic, undertaking a lengthy defense of the revelation (56:75–95), marked by strongly argumentative rhetoric. At that point, the sura closes with a command to ritual praise (56:96), which is identical with the first apparent ending of the sura (56:74). Given the different subject of this last section and the repetition of an apparent closing verse, it seems likely that in this sura as well there has been a later addition.[29]

Obviously the notion that the Qur'an has gone through stages of revision raises questions about how, and under whose authority, later additions could be made to the text. Admittedly, this observation is speculative, since it is based entirely on internal stylistic evidence rather than on any external proof; there are no manuscripts that contain any earlier versions of these Qur'anic texts. The two factors that make this hypothesis attractive are, first, the dialogical character of the text, which displays a clear recognition of the audience's questions about mysterious terms and sweeping statements; and, second, the strong presence of symmetrical composition throughout the Qur'an, which highlights by contrast any unusual departures from the style and structure that a particular passage displays. From this perspective, it is plausible to assume that the process of revision could indeed have taken place with the explicit involvement of the Prophet Muhammad. Insertions of lengthy explanatory passages, or exceptions to broad statements, or moralizing commentary, could well have taken place as natural extensions of the communication process that is embodied in the Qur'an. Just as many suras of greater length seem to have been delivered in sections, so too it is possible that individual verses may have been introduced to previously recited suras, to guide the audience to the appropriate understanding of the text in question. Indeed, it would be far more likely for this revision process to have taken place under the supervision of the Prophet Muhammad than at some later time, if it is correct to link the chronology of the Qur'an's unfolding to his career in Mecca and Medina. Any interruption of the symmetry of the Qur'an's composition would have been justified, for at least some portion of its audience had failed to grasp the intended message from the earlier version. Since there is no external evidence that clearly supports the notion of revision of the Qur'an after the death of Muhammad, I see no reason not to suppose that any insertion of later passages was done by the Prophet himself, as part of the ongoing process of the delivery of revelation. On top of these general considerations, a recent analysis of one of the Yemen manuscripts, which carbon-dating techniques identify as from the mid- to late seventh century, provides support for the contention that "the sequences of verses and sentences were fixed already in the Prophetic prototype," that is, during the lifetime and presumably with the approval of the Prophet Muhammad.[30]

Sura 53 and the "Satanic Verses"

One of the most challenging problems in interpreting the early Meccan suras revolves around the text of sura 53, "The Star," or to be more precise, it revolves around both the existing text and certain nonexistent verses that allegedly once formed part of the text. In terms of the development of Islamic religious thought, the opening lines of this sura (53:1–18) are extremely important as being the main location for describing the ascension (*mi'raj*) of the Prophet into paradise and his encounter with God. In later Muslim tradition, this event is celebrated as an important devotional holiday, observed on 27 Rajab in the Muslim lunar calendar. It has been the subject of lavishly illustrated manuscripts produced in the artistic workshops of central Asia, Iran, and the Ottoman regions.[31] There are numerous elaborations of the ascension story in hadith and biographical literature as well.[32] Yet in a sense, this remarkable narrative apparatus rests primarily on these verses from sura 53, which are also juxtaposed with a couple of other passages that solidify the context of the ascension (17:1, interpreted as describing the *isra'* or night journey to Jerusalem prior to the heavenly ascension, and 81:19–25, a brief account of the messenger's encounter with God). The question of a prophetic ascension is primarily related to the development of the interpretation of the Qur'an, and this portion of sura 53 does not involve any issues of later insertions in the text.

The other extratextual issue in sura 53 is the notorious question of the so-called "Satanic verses," a topic that was sensationalized if not clarified by Salman Rushdie's controversial 1988 novel by that name. To summarize briefly, this refers to a report concerning the Meccan career of the Prophet, usually dated by commentators to the fifth year of his mission, when Muhammad was in a weak position and a number of his followers had fled to Ethiopia to avoid persecution in Mecca. According to the story, he was so keen to soften the opposition of the hostile Meccans that in the midst of reciting the revelation of sura 53, when he reached a section denouncing the goddesses worshiped by the pagan Arabs, he inadvertently succumbed to an insinuation coming from Satan, in the form of two verses approving the adoration and the intercession of the goddesses. The two verses in question are said to have read as follows: "These are the lofty cranes; indeed, their intercession is to be hoped for." For this reason, Muslim tradition refers to this incident as "the story of the cranes," since that term for elegant birds (or possibly maidens) was used to designate the goddesses al-Lat, al-'Uzza, and Manat. Then, according to tradition, at a later date the Prophet was warned by God that intrusion had taken place, and the questionable verses were replaced with what is now the text of 53:21–22.

Many questions have been raised about the story. Is it conceivable that the Prophet Muhammad, who devoted his career to establishing monotheism, would embrace polytheistic worship for the sake of momentary political gain? Is it possible that such a flagrant reconciliation with idolatry would occur in the same sura with the most sublime account of the Prophet's spiritual encounter with God? Much of the debate centers on issues outside the text of the Qur'an itself. Evidently the vast majority of early commentators on the Qur'an and biographers of the Prophet until relatively recent times accepted the authenticity of the story.[33] It seems likely that, with the confidence of an emerging religious community in a period of expansive empire-building, these early Muslim interpreters never considered the story of the cranes as casting any blemish on the prophetic credentials of Muhammad. On the contrary, the story was appreciated as a dramatic example of how God could rescue his followers and his Prophet even from the wiles of the devil. Later on, however, Muslim scholars gravitated toward the view that genuine prophets would be protected by God from any error, and such a notion of infallibility gradually led to the complete rejection of the story of the cranes as an impossible fiction.

To make things more complicated, European Orientalists almost without exception considered the story of the "Satanic verses" to be true, on the grounds that it was so damaging to Muhammad's reputation that it could not conceivably have been fabricated; in other words, they embraced it because it confirmed their worst suspicions about Islam. This hostile reading was hardly a recommendation, as far as Muslims were concerned. In such a situation, it is not surprising to find that contemporary Muslim scholars universally condemn the story of the "Satanic verses" as false.

What can a structural literary analysis tell us about the nature of sura 53 in relation to these extra-Qur'anic discussions? First, it is evident that this sura of sixty-two verses consists primarily of short rhyming lines typical of the first Meccan period. The exceptions are eight verses (53:23, 53:26–32) that consist of lengthy and prosaic debates with opponents and consolation of the messenger. Modern scholarship identifies these eight verses as later additions.[34] Not counting those additional verses, sura 53 exhibits a markedly symmetrical composition of fifty-four verses, in three groups consisting of 24 + 24 + 6 verses, with several subgroupings. It therefore falls into a recognizable pattern familiar in the early Meccan suras. In the following translation, where the verses are separated by slashes, those verses identified as later additions are bracketed and marked in bold, while the two verses that supposedly replaced the "Satanic verses" are underlined.

I. Oath (1 verse) and affirmation of revelation (4.5 verses), two visions (6.5 + 6 verses), debate over goddesses (6 verses), [and additional debates (1 + 7 verses)][35]

(1–6.5) By the star, when it sets! / Your companion is not mistaken or astray, / nor does he speak from desire. / This is nothing but inspired revelation, / which the All-powerful taught him, / the Mighty one.

(6.5–12) And He stood erect, / while on the highest horizon. / Then He drew near and descended, / so He was two bows' lengths distant, or nearer, / and He revealed to His slave what He revealed. / The heart did not lie about what it saw. / Will you then cast doubt on him about his vision?

(13–18) And he saw Him on another descent, / by the lotus tree of the end, / near which is the garden of refuge, / when the lotus tree was enshrouded. / The eye did not flinch or swagger; / he saw one of the greatest signs of his Lord.

(19–25) Have you thought about al-Lat, al-ʿUzza, / and Manat, the third one? / <u>Do you have the males, while He has the females? / This would be an unfair division!</u> / **[They are only names invented by you and your fathers; God revealed no proof about them. They (you and your fathers) only follow conjecture, and what they themselves desire, but now guidance has come to them from their God!]** / Or shall man have whatever he wishes? / But the next life and this one belong to God!

(26–32) **[How many angels are there in the heavens whose intercession does not suffice at all, except after their Lord permits those whom He wishes and is pleased with? / Those who do not have faith in the afterlife have called the angels by female names. / They have no knowledge of it; they only follow conjecture. And conjecture avails nothing against the truth. / So avoid whoever turns away from Our Reminder and desires only the life of this world. / That is what their knowledge amounts to. Truly your Lord knows best those who stray from His path, and He knows best those who are guided. / To God belongs whatever is in the heavens and the earth, so He may reward those who do evil with what they have done, and reward those who do good with goodness. / Those who turn away from major sins and outrages, except for misdemeanors,—your Lord is enormously forgiving. He knows you best, since He created you from embryos in your mothers' wombs. So don't claim that you are pure; He knows best who is God-conscious.]**

II. Debate over revelation: misers ignorant of scripture (5 verses), the economy of judgment (5 verses), God's creation (7 verses), punishment stories (5 verses), and affirmation of Qurʾan (2 verses)

(33–37) Have you thought about the one who turned away, / and gave a little, but was stingy? / Does he have knowledge of the hidden, so he can see it? / Or hasn't he been told what is in the books of Moses / and Abraham, who paid his dues: /

(38–42) that no one bears the burden of another; / and that a man only owns what he strives for; / and that his effort will be seen, / and then he will receive full payment; / and that your destiny is toward your Lord;

(43–49) and that He is the one who brings laughter and tears; / and that He is the one who gives life and death; / and that He creates mates male and female, / from the seed when it is poured forth; / and that the next creation is up to Him; / and that He is the one who brings wealth and contentment; / and that He is the Lord of Sirius;

(50–54) and that He destroyed the 'Ad of old, / nor did He leave Thamud, / and Noah's people before them, for they were truly more unjust and extreme, / and He smashed the overturned cities (of Lot) / so they were enshrouded.

(55–56) So which of the signs of your Lord will you cast doubt upon?[36] / This one (Muhammad) is one of the warners of old!

III. End-times (2 verses) and debate with opponents (3 verses), concluding with ritual command (1 verse)

(57–58) That which is drawing near is approaching. / There is no one except God who can reveal it.

(59–61) So are you amazed at this account? / You laugh and weep, / since you are carefree.

(62) So all of you bow down to God and worship Him.

Viewed in its entirety, this early Meccan sura, when divided into its original structure, shows clearly the relationship between the initial composition and the later additions.

The relationship between the opening visions of sura 53 and the debate about the goddesses in the first section revolves around a powerful affirmation of prophecy and a rejection of alternative theology. The Qur'an places special emphasis on the truth of Muhammad's inspiration by linking it with two extraordinary visionary experiences. The rejection of the goddesses, apart from the eight later verses, is a terse and heavily ironic argument. The two verses (53:21–22) allegedly taking the place of the "Satanic verses" actually fit very well here; they repeat an ironic remark appealing to the patriarchal sensibility of the Arabs, ridiculing the notion that the

Arabs would be honored with sons while God would have only daughters. Similar statements appear throughout the early, middle, and late Meccan suras (16:57–58, 37:149–53, 43:16, 52:39). The prosaic later additions to sura 53, which are stylistically out of sync with the sura as a whole, develop the debate in line with the theological articulations that appeared in the later unfolding of the Qur'an. They offer a critique of other gods or goddesses as mere names, presenting an explanation of goddess worship as a mistaken adoration of angels. The closing consolation in these additions to the first section conveys the sense of resignation common to other Meccan suras, in which the messenger is advised to trust in God and ignore those who reject the revelation.

Section II of sura 53 continues to emphasize the theme of revelation, starting out by condemning the miser for his ignorance of the scriptures given to Moses and Abraham. There follows a series of topics that are revealed in those scriptures, as a kind of catechism or list of beliefs, constituting a theodicy or affirmation of divine justice. The opponent is taunted for his lack of knowledge of the nature of moral responsibility, God's creative power, and punishment stories. The section ends with another ringing affirmation of the prophetic authority of Muhammad. The six verses of section III form a fitting coda to conclude the sura. The end-times description in 53:57–58 has obvious stylistic similarities with the opening sections of five other early Meccan suras (51:5–6, 52:7–8, 56:1–3, 70:1–3, 77:7). Overall, the last half of the sura demonstrates a carefully crafted series of verbal echoes of ten key terms from the first half of the sura.[37] When the community of listeners is commanded to ritual prostration in the final line, this puts an effective closure to a composition marked by strong thematic and stylistic unity.

Seen from this internal stylistic perspective, the story of the cranes does not seem at all likely as part of the composition history of sura 53. Because of the rarity and extraordinary character of the visions at the beginning of sura 53, which portrayed the Prophet in intimate direct contact with God, it might even be said that this is the least likely place in the Qur'an for the intrusion of a polytheistic concession to the Meccan pagans.[38] Everything about the sura is focused on the authenticity of the revelation from the one true God, and it is difficult to conceive how the two "Satanic verses" could have been accepted even momentarily by the audience of the Qur'an. The circumstances of the commentators' account of the revocation of the "Satanic verses" is also suspicious. God is said to have revealed the passage that describes the possibility of Satanic temptation of the prophets (22:52–54) in order to show Muhammad that he had to recant the verses about the cranes. Since that passage is from a Medinan sura, the story presupposes that the two "Satanic verses" were in circulation in the accepted Qur'an for a number of years, a possibility that seems incredible. It is also noteworthy that all of the accounts of the story of the cranes come from commentary literature and biography, but there are no examples of this story in the principal collections of prophetic hadith, so its historical connection appears weak. In other words, this is essentially a matter of narrative, and it is well known that early Muslim Qur'an commentators and biographers were especially prone to fall back on creative fictions to fill in the gaps in sacred texts or to provide examples for general principles. Popular storytellers were noted for their tendency to embroider and fabricate exciting tales that would keep their audiences on tenterhooks.[39] It has even been suggested that the "Satanic verses" incident was fabricated by scholars seeking to provide a plausible example of the doctrine of abrogation—for if ever a passage of the Qur'an deserved to be abrogated, it would surely be in the case of a Satanic insinuation.[40] In this respect, the story of the cranes resembles the so-called stoning verse, discussed above. In both cases, the alleged text is not found in the Qur'an at all, yet it has taken on a life of its own, for reasons that lie outside the sacred book itself.

*   *   *

The readings of the early suras of the Qur'an presented so far describe a repertoire of rhetorical gestures clearly preserved in literary structures. The major forms of exposition contained in end-times accounts and other literary forms crystallized into the flexible multipart divisions found in many of these suras. The later insertions to these texts—and there are other passages, believed to be later additions, that have not been explored here—offer the reader the opportunity to consider the sura as a literary unit, both before and after its revision.[41] The increasing insertion of theological argument and explication into the dense poetic structure of the earliest versions provides an important key to the urgent questions that governed the later development of the Qur'an. That development during the middle and late Meccan periods is the subject of the next chapter.

3

Middle and Later Meccan Suras

Structural and Stylistic Approaches

The forty-eight suras of the early Meccan period are followed by the twenty-one suras of the middle Meccan period and the twenty-one additional suras of the late Meccan period. What is the stylistic or literary basis for distinguishing these groups? To be sure, there are overlaps and continuities, but certain trends unmistakably appear. Comparison strongly suggests a shift away from short and powerful oath formulations of the early Meccan suras to lengthier affirmations of revelation.[1] The terse and distinctively memorable rhyming structures of the early suras yield to the simplified and repetitive use of formulas with plural nouns and verbs at the ends of verses, creating simple and predictable rhymes with long vowels ending in -*in* and -*un*. On average, suras of the middle Meccan period are over six times as long as early Meccan suras; in turn, suras of the later Meccan period are nearly 50 percent longer than the middle Meccan suras.[2] Debates become more pronounced and are featured more prominently, particularly in the middle Meccan suras. Scripture itself becomes a notable theme in the later Meccan suras, typically in the mode of self-affirmation, and prophetic narratives (both biblical and extrabiblical) take on increasing importance as they are narrated in greater detail. The basic unit of the sura, the verse, becomes longer and more complex, so that the verse itself needs to be broken down into its components; sometimes verses demonstrate complex reference and demanding grammatical connections to surrounding verses. What is perhaps the most notable structural feature is a clear emergence of the tripartite division, already present among some early Meccan suras but now becoming the norm for most of the middle and later Meccan suras.

This triple structure calls for some comparative analysis. There are two notable precedents for the tripartite organization of the Qur'anic sura in bodies of literature characterized by ritual practice and oral performance. One is the pre-Islamic Arabic ode, and the other is the worship service of monotheistic communities of the Near East.[3] The pre-Islamic Arabic poem is famous for its threefold structure: first, the opening description of an abandoned campsite and memories of a romantic encounter there; second, the poet's journey and encounter with nature; and third, a closing boast, which might also become a satire of opponents or, in later times, praise of a ruler, in either case affirming heroic tribal values. This well-established structure can be understood in terms of ritual and rites of passage.[4] It is the poet who stands at the center of this structure, using the conventions of verse and the story of his life to comment on the limits that frame human existence. Likewise, the middle and later Meccan suras generally have three parts. Many exhibit a ring structure, beginning and ending with parallel sections that praise God, list virtues and vices, debate unbelievers, and affirm the revelation; the third section normally concludes with a flourish, containing a powerful affirmation of revelation.[5] The second part, in the middle of the sura, is typically a narrative of prophecy and struggle that highlights the crucial choices facing the messenger's audience. Like the poet in the journey section of the Arabic ode, the Prophet is (implicitly or explicitly) both the main character in the narrative and at the same time the storyteller.

This connection between poetry and prophecy is demonstrated by carryover of key terms from the pre-Islamic period into a new world of religious meaning. One example of this transformation would be the ode of Labid, in which the poet describes "a clan whose fathers set for them their law (*sunna*) — / For each tribe has its leader (*imam*) and its law (*sunna*)."[6] Needless to say, the Islamic concepts of religious leadership and law differed considerably from tribal ways. In the Muslim cosmos, the terms *imam* and *sunna* take on new meanings relating to ritual (*imam* as prayer leader) and ethics (*sunna* as prophetic norms). This comparison of the structural roles of poet and prophet does not by any means erase the Qur'anic critique of tribal morality and the role of the poet as its exemplar and spokesperson. Nevertheless, Suzanne Pinckney Stetkevych points out that "the role of the

Qur'an in Islamic times was perceived as equatable with that of poetry, and
. . . the Qur'an played, as it were, the 'New Testament' to the pre-Islamic
poetic 'Old Testament,' at once abrogating and fulfilling it."[7]

There is another dimension to the comparison of the structures of
the Qur'anic sura and the pre-Islamic poem. It was stereotypical for pre-
Islamic odes to begin with the evocation of a ruined habitation, the meaning of which might or might not be interrogated successfully. Consider
again the case of Labid, from the beginning section of his famous Mu'allaqa
ode:

> The torrents have exposed the ruins,
>   as if they were
> Writings whose texts pens have
>   inscribed anew
> Or like the tattooer sprinkling lampblack
>   again and yet again
> Over hands on which
>   tattoos appear.
> Then I stopped and questioned them,
>   but how do we question
> Mute immortals whose speech
>   is indistinct?[8]

For this pre-Islamic poet, the message conveyed by these half-effaced
vestiges of the past is primarily that nature endures permanently, while
human culture cannot last. The Qur'anic punishment stories, in contrast,
read these ruins as testimony to God's wrathful punishment of fatal human
error. So the mood of the pre-Islamic poem in its opening sections is lyric,
nostalgic, and melancholic in its confrontation with the traces of vanished
civilization. In the Qur'anic punishment story, however, the scene of ruined
cities has become the sign of a moral tragedy.[9]

To return to the threefold structure of the sura, its other ritual precedent is the worship service, whose features would have been observable in
Jewish and Christian religious practice in Arabia. The threefold formula of
an introductory section, a reading of the scriptures, and a closing section
offers a tantalizing similarity to the tripartite Qur'anic sura of the middle
and later Meccan periods. The majority of these suras (twenty-seven out
of forty-two) contain strong narratives occupying the second of the three
sections.[10] These narratives are often framed by announcement formulas

reminiscent of the words used to mark the reading of scripture (as in the Christian formula, "This is the word of the Lord"). So the middle section of sura 20 announces, "Has the story (*hadith*) of Moses reached you?" (20:9). And it concludes this narration by saying, "In this way We tell you the story of news of what has gone before, and we have brought you a Reminder from Us" (20:99). The use of terms like "story" and "Reminder" self-consciously highlights and sets apart a sacred narrative as the center of the sura. The threefold structure of the middle and later Meccan suras in this way furnishes evidence of increasing liturgical use in worship service as a formal principle behind the composition of the suras.

The question of Qur'anic appropriation of biblical narratives deserves further comment. As previously indicated, this issue has been largely framed around competing arguments concerning authenticity, in which religious loyalties have constructed walls to prevent open-minded consideration of the literary connections between Qur'anic texts and biblical texts. Christian and Jewish authors have tended to dismiss Qur'anic narratives as derivative borrowings, while Muslim authors have resolutely rejected biblical accounts as corrupted by human error. The dogmatic concept of a fixed and unchanging scriptural text, so prominent in modern fundamentalist interpretations, plays an important role in supporting the contention that one or the other scripture is a timeless revelation that is impervious to change, and indeed, to analysis. Yet the historical and literary approach to the Qur'an proposed here has already demonstrated significant evidence of internal revision of the text of the Qur'an over time, very likely in response to reader reactions. Leaving aside the theological debates in defense of particular holy books, how can one understand the notion of literary adaptation of earlier texts as part of a process of revelation?

In reality, the reinterpretation and reframing of previous revelations has always been the hallmark of prophecy. The most prominent example of this phenomenon is the wholesale adoption of Hebrew biblical texts in early Christianity, but with a radically new theological interpretation, renaming the former scriptures as the "Old Testament." This terminology simultaneously sanctifies the Hebrew Bible as the word of God, while relegating it to a secondary and inferior position in relation to the New Testament. As is well known, numerous Hebrew biblical texts received specific new interpretations relating to Christian theology, such as the identification of the "suffering servant" mentioned by the prophet Isaiah, now seen as a clear reference to the career of Jesus Christ. This interpretation is so powerfully developed in Christian thought that to its exponents it seems entirely natural and inevitable, although from Jewish perspectives it appears to be a high-handed intrusion of a foreign idea. Muslim interpreters have gone one step further by seeing a prophecy of Muhammad in the text of Isaiah, alongside that of Jesus.[11] It is worth pointing out that one of the chief mechanisms for this kind of reinterpretation of previous scriptures is to regard them retroactively as predictions of the future. That is one reason why prophecy, which literally means being a "spokesperson," the one who "speaks for" God, has so often been understood as foretelling a particular future.

The idea that future events can be decoded from an ancient biblical text (or from a divinatory source like Nostradamus or the Mayan calendar) exerts an enormous and undeniable attraction over the human imagination, despite the mutually incompatible applications of the same prophetic texts to a practically endless series of different events over the centuries.[12] If, however, one does not wish to engage in scriptural futurology, prophecy can be much more clearly understood as a movement in the reverse direction of time. That is, prophecy always looks back toward earlier manifestations of prophecy, yet it does so by making a rhetorical claim to be the true meaning of earlier proclamations. Thus, the claim to be the "fulfillment of prophecy" is in reality a literary move to reinterpret an earlier text in a new way. This is one of the most characteristic features of the history of religion, that by introducing new interpretations of texts from a previous age, one keeps them relevant to changing situations. The revision of earlier scriptures by the rhetoric of fulfillment ironically reinforces the authority of the past by claiming it as a witness for a new stage of prophecy or interpretation (as in the allegorical readings of the Song of Songs as a depiction of the Church and Christ rather than as a Near Eastern love song). Yet the net effect of new prophetic readings is that they inevitably transform older texts in ways that were never conceived by previous readers. Seen in this light, the Qur'anic appropriation of biblical and other pre-Islamic narratives, oftentimes with new emphases and differing conclusions, is a logical extension of the same literary processes of prophecy that have been practiced over the centuries. And the ongoing revision of earlier Qur'anic suras through intensive ritual readings is simply a subset of the same prophetic activity of literary reframing.

Apart from the larger question of the threefold structure of the sura, on a more detailed level the verse itself requires further explanation. Simple verses with a single clause, so typical of the early Meccan suras, in later texts are accompanied and replaced by verses with two or three individual phrases or clauses, extending over several lines, amounting almost to a paragraph. The contrast can be vividly illustrated by juxtaposing a short passage of six verses from an early Meccan sura alongside a single long verse from the later Meccan period; these two passages are comparable insofar as both are essentially lists. The first of these (53:50–55) is a sequence listing punishment stories:

> 50 and that He destroyed the ʿAd of old,
> 51 nor did He leave Thamud,
> 52 and Noah's people before them,
>   for they were truly more unjust and extreme,
> 53 and He smashed the overturned cities (of Lot)
> 54 so they were enshrouded.
> 55 So which of the signs of your Lord will you cast doubt upon?

The second passage (6:84) is a single verse containing a list of Abrahamic prophets sent by God, which can be subdivided into half a dozen simple phrases:

> We gave him Isaac and Jacob, guiding them all,
> and Noah We guided before,
> and from his seed there were David and Solomon,
> and Job and Joseph,
> and Moses and Aaron;
> in this way We reward the virtuous.

The increasing complexity of Qurʾanic style is evident from the fact that the individual clauses of this long single verse are more or less equivalent in length to the six separate verses of the earlier sura. While these six verses from sura 53 may be said to constitute a building block within the second section of this sura (see the complete translation of the sura in chapter 1), the lengthier verse, 6:84, itself plays a comparable role as a building block composed of separate parts.[13] This comparison—and many other examples can be supplied—illustrates the extent to which the notion and function of the Qurʾanic verse has undergone transformation between the early and middle Meccan periods.

Internal Qur'anic Reference in the Middle Meccan Suras:
The Case of Sura 15 (al-Hijr)

Periodization of the Qur'an's chronology has already been demonstrated through the phenomenon of later insertion, for which there are a number of clear instances in the early Meccan suras. Interestingly, the middle Meccan period is less touched by this particular type of textual development, and later insertions are rare among these suras.[14] There is, however, another type of temporal textual relationship created through the phenomenon of reference or allusion, in which a later passage refers to and presupposes familiarity with an earlier one. An outstanding example of this kind of referentiality is provided by sura 15, al-Hijr, which contains numerous echoes of earlier suras. These would have been immediately obvious to those members of the community exposed to frequent repetitions of these verses in worship service. It is instructive to see how many references sura 15 makes to the resonant language found just in the first sura of the Qur'an, "The Opening." This can be illustrated by laying out the verses of sura 1, with the echoing lines from sura 15 indicated within parentheses, highlighting the echoing phrases with underlining:

1 In the name of God, the Merciful, the Compassionate.

2 Praise be to God, the Lord of creation,
   ("Glorify the praise of your Lord," 15:98)

3 The Merciful, the Compassionate,
   ("Announce to My servants that I am the Forgiving, the
      Merciful," 15:49)

4 The Master of the Day of Judgment.
   ("The curse is upon you until the Day of Judgment," 15:35)

5 It is You who we worship, and You whose aid we seek.
   ("And worship your Lord until the sure [victory] comes to you,"
      15:99)[15]

6 Guide us on the straight path,
   ("This is a path that is straight for Me," 15:41)

7 The path of those who receive Your grace, not those who have
      angered You nor those who go astray.
   ("Who despairs of his Lord's mercy except those who go
      astray?" 15:56)

This series of echoes neatly demonstrates how sura 15 at multiple stages invokes key phrases and vocabulary terms that have been established in the early Meccan suras, particularly in this most important Opening.

The further reliance of sura 15 on other early Meccan suras[16] can be seen in the context of a full translation of al-Hijr, again laying out the echo passages within parentheses, highlighting the similar phrases with underlining:

I.A. Introduction (3 verses) and debate on revelation (12 verses)

   1 A.L.R. These are the signs of the Book, and of a clear Recitation (*qur'an*).

      ("It is a glorious Recitation on a preserved tablet," 85:21–22; "It is truly a noble Recitation in a hidden Book," 56:77–78).

   2 Perhaps those who have rejected wish that they had been submitters.

      ("Doomed are those who have rejected," 51:60; "Give a respite to those who have rejected," 86:17; "We only found one house there of submitters," 51:36)

   3 Let them eat and enjoy, and their hope will distract them—but they will know!

      ("So let them be, until they encounter their Day, when they will be struck by lightning," 52:45; "So let them chat and play, until they encounter their Day, which they are promised," 70:42; "Eat and enjoy a little, you criminals!" 77:46)

   4 We only have destroyed a town when it had a known decree.

      ("We have destroyed your comrades," 54:51)

   5 No people outstrips its destiny, nor can they delay it.

   6 They said, "You, to whom the Reminder is revealed! You are crazy!

      ("And your companion is not crazy," 81:22; "When they hear the Reminder, and they say, 'He is crazy,'" 68:51)

   7 "Why don't you bring us some angels, if you are one of the sincere?"

      ("Your Lord comes, and the angels are file upon file," 89:22)

   8 We only send down angels on the [Day of] Truth; these people will not be considered then.[17]

      ("And the angels will be on the rim of [heaven], eight of them carrying your Lord's throne above them on that day," 69:17)

9　It is We who send down the Reminder, and it is We who guard it.

10　Any messenger who came to them, they mocked.

11　We sent messengers before you to the factions of the ancients.

12　That is how We send it [revelation] to the hearts of criminals.

13　They do not believe in it, even though the law of the ancients has passed away.

14　And even if we opened up for them a gate from heaven, and they kept ascending through it,

15　They would have said, "Our vision has just been intoxicated, or else we are people under a spell."

　　("This is nothing but magic handed down," 74:24)

B. *Signs of God in creation (10 verses)*

16　We have placed fortresses [constellations] in the heavens and adorned them for the beholders,

　　("By heaven, which holds the fortresses [constellations]!" 85:1)

17　Protecting them from every accursed demon,

　　("Nor is he [inspired] with the word of an accursed demon," 81:25)

18　Except for one who sneaks and eavesdrops—but an obvious shooting star chases him.

19　We spread out the earth and placed mountaintops upon her, and We grew upon her everything in due proportion.

　　("We spread out the earth and placed mountaintops upon her," 50:7)

20　We have given to you livelihoods upon her, and to those whom you do not support.

21　We have the treasures of everything, and We only send it down in a deliberate amount.

22　And We send the humid winds, so We bring down water from heaven, then We give it to you to drink; you are not the ones who store it!

　　("And We bring down from the rain clouds torrents of water," 78:14)

23　It is We who give life and death, and it is We who inherit.

　　("It is We who give life and death, and the destination is Ours," 50:43)

24　And We know which of you will precede [in their doom], and We know those who will come later.

25 Your Lord is the one who assembles them; He is the Wise, the
    Knowing.

C. Story of Iblis (23 verses)

26 We created humanity from raw clay, from smoothed mud.

27 And the jinn we created from the fire of hot wind.
    ("He created humanity from raw clay, like the potter, and created
    the jinn from a mixture of fire," 55:14–15)

28 And when your Lord said to the angels, "I'm creating a human
    from raw clay, from smoothed mud,

29 "So when I have formed him and breathed into him from My
    spirit, then you fall down, prostrating before him!"

30 And the angels prostrated, all of them together,

31 Except Iblis; he refused to be with those who prostrated.

32 [God] said, "Iblis! What's wrong with you, that you won't be with
    those who prostrated?"

33 He replied, "I'm not one to prostrate to a human You created from
    raw clay, from smoothed mud."

34 He said, "Then get out of here! You are accursed!

35 "The curse is upon you until the Day of Judgment."

36 He replied, "My Lord, give me a respite until the day they are
    raised up."
    ("Don't they think that they will be raised up on a mighty day?"
    83:4–5)

37 He said, "You are one of those given a respite,

38 "Until the day of the predicted time."

39 He replied, "My Lord! By the fact that You misled me! I'll
    glamorize things on earth, and I'll mislead them all,

40 "Except for Your sincere servants."

41 He said, "This is a path that is straight for Me:

42 "You have no authority over My servants, except for those
    misguided ones who follow you.

43 "Hell is the destination for them all."

44 It has seven gates, each of which has an assigned portion.

45 And those who are God-conscious are in gardens and springs,
    ("And those who are God-conscious are in gardens and springs,"
    51:15)

46 [Being told,] "Enter it in peace and safety!"

47 We remove the bitterness from their breasts; they are as brothers,
    facing one another on couches.

48 No hardship affects them there, nor will they be exiled from it.

II. Punishment stories (36 verses)

Abraham

49 [Muhammad], tell My servants that I am the Forgiving, the
Compassionate,

50 And that My punishment is the painful punishment,
("So God will punish him with the greatest punishment," 88:24)

51 And tell them of the guests of Abraham,

52 When they entered his house and said, "Peace!" He replied, "We
are afraid of you!"

53 They said, "Don't be afraid! We give good news of a wise son."

54 He said, "Do you bring me good news, though I've reached old
age? So what are you giving me good news of?"

55 They said, "We bring good news in truth, so don't be one of those
who despair!"

56 He said, "Who despairs of his Lord's mercy except those who go
astray?"

57 He said, "So what is your concern, messengers?"

58 They said, "We were sent to a criminal people,

59 "Except for the family of Lot; we shall save them all together,

60 "Except for his wife; we have decreed that she is one of those left
behind."

Lot

61 And when the messengers came to the family of Lot,

62 He said, "You people are strangers."

63 They said, "No; we came to you with [the warning] that they
doubted,

64 "And we bring you the truth, for we are sincere.

65 "So travel with your people in a section of the night, and follow
behind them; but let none of them turn around, and go where
you are ordered."

66 And We decided that matter for him, that the last of them should
be cut off in the morning.

67 And the people of the city came, rejoicing.

68 He [Lot] said, "These are my guests, so don't disgrace me,

69 "Be wary of God, and don't humiliate me!"

70 They said, "Did we not forbid you [to give hospitality to]
anyone?"

71 He said, "These are my daughters, if you do [what I ask]."

72 —By your life, [Muhammad]! They were blinded in their
   intoxication!

73 But the Shout seized them at dawn,

74 We turned the city upside down, and rained down upon them
   stones of hot clay.
   ("And He smashed the overturned cities [of Lot]," 53:53;
   "Throwing at them stones of hot clay," 105:4; "That We may
   send upon them stones of clay," 51:33)

75 In that there are signs for those who read the signs,

76 And they are in an established path,

77 And in that there is a sign for those who believe.

The People of the Woods

78 The people of the woods were unjust,

79 So We took vengeance on them. Both of them [Lot and the
   Woods] are a clear model.

al-Hijr

80 And the people of al-Hijr called the messengers liars.

81 And We gave them Our signs, but they turned away from them.

82 They used to carve out houses from the mountains to be secure.

83 But the Shout seized them at dawn,

84 And that which they acquired was no use to them.
   ("His wealth is of no use to him, nor what he acquired," 111:2)

III. Revelation and consolation (15 verses)

85 We only created the heavens and the earth, and what lies between
   them, in Truth; and the Hour is coming, so forgive graciously.

86 Your Lord is the Creator, the Knower.

87 We have given you seven of the repeated [verses], and the great
   Recitation.

88 Don't cast your eyes towards what We have allowed some couples
   to enjoy, and don't be sad for them, but spread your wings over
   the believers.

89 Say, "I am the clear warner!"
   ("I am a clear warner to you from Him!" 51:50, 51:51)

90 But We did not send it down to those who would divide [the
   revelation] among themselves,[18]

91 Who treat the Recitation as lies.

92 By your Lord! We will question them all together,

93 About what they used to do.

94 So proclaim what you are commanded, and turn away from the
    idolaters.

95 We are guard enough for you against the scoffers,

96 Who put another god alongside God. But they shall know!

97 We know that you are depressed ["your breast is constricted"] by
    what they say.

   ("Did We not bring you relief ['expand your breast']?" 94:1)

98 So glorify the praise of your Lord, and be one of those who
    prostrate,

   ("Glorify the name of your highest Lord," 87:1; "Prostrate and
      draw near," 96:19; "When the Recitation is recited to them, they
      do not prostrate," 84:21)

99 And worship your Lord until the sure [victory] comes to you.

   ("So let them worship the Lord of this house," 106:3)

The level of intertextual reference in this sura is remarkable. In the samples
quoted above, over one-quarter of the verses (twenty-seven of ninety-nine)
echo words, phrases, or whole verses of earlier suras; in all, there are references to at least forty earlier passages cited in sura 15. The evocation
of other Qur'anic passages is deliberate reference rather than mechanical
repetition, even in the cases of the quotation of entire verses. Listeners
are called upon to recognize the obvious references to earlier texts, to be
"those who read the signs" (15:75), by discerning references to the biblical
story of Lot (53:53) and to the local Arabian tale of the Ethiopian invasion,
found in the sura of the Elephant (105:4). This list of correspondences
could be expanded further by taking a more exhaustive approach to the
echoes of vocabulary in the Qur'an.

The intricate composition of sura 15 is further enhanced by ring structure. A number of passages from the beginning and ending sections play
upon the same vocabulary and themes, in a way that brings the reader back
full circle. The temporary enjoyment of the unbelievers (15:3) is balanced
by the enjoyment of couples who have offspring (15:88). The unbelievers
will come to know on Judgment Day not only the vanity of their pleasures
(15:3) but also the falseness of their idolatry (15:96). The mocking accusation that the Prophet is crazy (15:6) is outweighed by the consolation
offered for these insults (15:97). The prostration of the angels before Adam,
except for Iblis (15:29–33), finds its counterpart in the prostration of God's
worshipers (15:98).

What does the complex internal and external referentiality of sura 15 say about the development of the Qur'an at the time of this sura's delivery? A key may be provided by two crucial terms that appear repeatedly in the course of this sura, namely, oral recitation (*qur'an*) and written book (*kitab*). These terms admittedly have a flexible range of application. In the early Meccan suras, the word *qur'an* often has a very generic sense of "recitation," rather than describing a fixed body of materials (Arkoun's "closed official corpus"). In 15:4 above, the phrase *kitab ma'lum* is translated as "a known decree," to reflect another aspect of the subject field of "the book," the widespread ancient notion of the destinies of humanity as written in the heavenly scrolls. But the two terms converge in the opening verse of sura 15: "These are the signs of the Book (*kitab*), and of a clear Recitation (*qur'an*)." Parallel early Meccan verses that link recitation with writing still highlight the book as a mysterious cosmic archetype rather than as a physical text ("It is a glorious Recitation on a preserved tablet," 85:21–22; "It is truly a noble Recitation in a hidden Book," 56:77–78). Sura 15 seems to mark an important stage in the canonization process of the Qur'an, that is, the process by which a series of oral recitations gradually became concretized as a separate scripture. In the historical and chronological perspective, at the time when sura 15 was delivered this process was obviously only partially complete. On the three occasions where sura 15 mentions the word *qur'an* (15:1, 15:87, 15:91), the word does not signify the completed canonical text of the Qur'an as it is known today, "between two covers," since the unfolding of revelation would continue for a number of years after this middle Meccan sura. Nevertheless, there is reason to think that sura 15 illustrates a self-conscious notion of scriptural authority by the way it references earlier Meccan suras as authoritative texts employed in divine service.

If indeed the middle Meccan suras parallel the worship services of monotheistic communities in their tripartite organization, this would seem to be confirmed by dialogical address to the messenger, who is consoled in the opening and closing sections of the sura (15:6–11, 15:85–96) for the humiliations inflicted upon him by his hostile opponents. Such a dialogue, responding even to the messenger's thoughts, parallels the interaction between religious leader and community in worship service. Even more important as an index of the ritual importance of early Qur'anic texts is the frequent reference to the first sura, "The Opening," as indicated above. Most authorities indeed identify sura 1 with the seven repeated verses (*al-sab' al-mathani*) mentioned in parallel with "the great Recitation" as a divine gift (15:87). It is also likely that the text of sura 1, "The Opening," is what is meant by "the praise of your Lord," enjoined in 15:98, since sura 1 begins with the phrase "Praise be to God" (1:1). The same formula, "glorify the praise of your Lord," has also been announced in early Meccan (52:48) and middle Meccan texts (50:39), probably as an instruction to recite sura 1. The placement of this phrase toward the end of those suras suggests the employment of "The Opening" as a key text in worship service, so that its recitation may have immediately followed upon that instruction. In this way, sura 15 clearly builds upon the ritual sanctity of earlier Qur'anic texts as it moves further toward scripturalization.

Finally, sura 15 also demonstrates the development of the audience of the Qur'an's listeners into a community defined by both earlier prophetic narratives and the primordial myth of the satanic figure known as Iblis. This communal dimension is a significant expansion of the explicit audience of the Qur'anic message. Here in sura 15, the phrases "Your servants" (addressed to God by Iblis, 15:40) and "My servants" (addressed by God to the messenger, 15:49) create the notion of a transhistorical community of worshippers/servants linked by loyalty to God and enmity from demonic forces.

Up until this point in the Qur'an's chronology, the dialogical format of communication has stressed the intimate relationship between the messenger and his divine interlocutor; the phrase "your Lord," clearly addressed in Arabic to a singular "you," has been the dominant characterization of Muhammad as the direct recipient of revelation (and it continues to be used here in sura 15 as well). The nascent community of believers has been an implied third person rather than the direct addressee. Now, for the first time in the chronological sequence of the Qur'an, there is an emphatic definition of the servants/slaves/devotees (*'ibad*) of God as a religious community.[19] It is noteworthy that this new self-conscious notion of community is articulated in the context of a creation story, in which Iblis plays the role of the recalcitrant opponent and the model both for the resistance to the prophets of old and for the opponents of the Prophet Muhammad. Thus the faithful recipients of the Qur'an are in solidarity of monotheistic worship along with the obedient angels and the bearers of revelation in earlier ages. The cosmic character of this struggle is underlined by a description of the fortresses (*buruj*) of the heavenly constellations as a line of defense against demonic spies. Ironically, the opponents of Muhammad have attempted to cast him as the recipient of devilish inspiration, since the insult they continually hurl at him is that he is crazy or insane, literally, "possessed by the jinn" (*majnun*). But in an interesting recapitulation of well-known Near Eastern creation motifs, the Qur'an depicts God creating humanity like clay pots thrown on a potter's wheel, while the jinn (spirits intermediate between humanity and the angels) are simply another subordinate race created from a different elemental construction, fire. This narrative ties up theological loose ends while simultaneously creating a space for the listening audience. So as a distinct expression of the middle Meccan period, sura 15 plays an important role in the increasing literary canonization of Qur'anic texts, in their ritual deployment in worship service, and in the articulation of a communal religious identity.

External Narratives and Literary Structures in Sura 18 ("The Cave")

Sura 18, "The Cave," has been called the most mythical section of the Qur'an.[20] It contains three brief and enigmatic tales that later interpreters have connected to pre-Islamic legends: the Seven Sleepers of Ephesus, the encounter of Moses and the enigmatic figure known as al-Khidr, and the deeds of Alexander the Great. There may be no better example than sura 18 of the Qur'an's ability to capture and reinterpret compelling narrative traditions of the ancient world in the context of a new form of revelation. It is also noteworthy that, despite the presence of Moses in one of the stories, none of these appears to relate directly to biblical sources. Yet, as indicated above, the central section of the middle Meccan suras typically plays a decisive role, both as a narrative of prophetic struggle analogous to the journey section of the pre-Islamic ode and as a formal recital comparable to the scriptural reading of a monotheistic worship service. Thus a key question will be how sura 18 reinterprets and reframes the narratives it invokes, in terms of the ongoing process of prophecy. Because of its length and complexity, in the remarks that follow, sura 18 is addressed one section at a time to clarify its literary structure. At the same time, because of the strong referentiality of this sura to earlier texts, in this particular case reference will regularly be made to the pre-Islamic writings that were evidently addressed by the Qur'anic revelation.

Building upon the analysis already established, it is apparent that sura 18 exhibits an overall tripartite structure, with an introduction and conclusion symmetrically balancing each other, with eight verses each. The middle section, consisting of stories and parables, constitutes the bulk of the sura, containing four major sections of comparable length distributed over ninety-six verses. In addition to the three pre-Islamic narratives just mentioned, it also includes a couple of generic moral parables as a second section, immediately following the story of the Seven Sleepers. The rhetorical delivery of this sura has a strongly dialogical element; there are seven verses addressed to "you" in the singular (18:9, 18:17–18, 18:23–24, 18:57, 18:83), and one can count seven more passages (18:24, 18:26, 18:29, 18:83, 18:103–4, 18:109, 18:110) that contain a directive commanding the Prophet Muhammad to deliver a message, using the word "Say" (*qul*).

From a structural perspective, the symmetry between the opening and closing sections is a strong example of ring composition. The sura begins (18:1–2) with an assertion of the revelation as written scripture or book (*kitab*) that is straight without any crookedness, just as it closes (18:109) with a dramatic description of revelation exhausting even a sea of ink, another implicit book image. At both the beginning and the end, it brings a warning to unbelievers (18:2, 18:103–6) and then promises eternal bliss in paradise to the faithful (18:2–3, 18:107–8). Most noteworthy is the debate section, which specifically rejects the Christian notion of incarnation (18:4–5), even as it insists that the Prophet Muhammad is only a mortal human who is inspired by God (18:110). The deceitful word of ancestral tradition (18:5) is contrasted with the limitless words of God's revelation (18:109). The consolation to the messenger who is disregarded by his people (18:6) is balanced by the declaration that he is indeed inspired (18:110). The signs of God also receive emphasis, in the beauty of the earth that is a test for humanity (18:8) and as the object of the disbelief of the misguided (18:105).

This consistent parallelism of sura 18 may be seen more easily by a juxtaposition of the introductory and closing sections:

I. Introduction and praise (8 verses)

1 Praise to the God Who revealed to His servant the Book
   that He made, not crooked,
2 But straight, so He warns of a terrible disaster,
   coming from Him;
   but He gives good news to the faithful—who do what is right—
   that they have a great reward.
   They will linger there forever.
4 Then He warns those who say God has taken a son.

5 Of this they and their fathers lack any knowledge,
   and it is a monstrous word coming from their mouths—
   they only speak lies!

6 Perhaps you [Muhammad] are hard on yourself
   because of what will befall them,
   since they did not have faith in this narration (*hadith*), to your
      sorrow.

7 We made everything upon the earth as its adornment,
   to test which of them acts best;

8 And We will make everything upon it into a wasteland.

III. Closing (8 verses)

103 Say, "Shall We tell you whose actions are most useless?

104 "Those whose effort goes wrong in this life,
   while they think they have done something beautiful!"

105 They are the ones who reject the signs of their Lord and the
      meeting with Him,
   so their deeds go wrong.
   And We won't give them any weight on Resurrection Day.

106 That will be their reward—Hell!
   Since they disbelieved, and they treated Our signs and Our
      messengers with contempt.

107 Those who have faith and do what is right
   have a lodging in Gardens of Paradise.

108 They are there forever, having no desire to leave.

109 Say, "If the ocean was ink for the words of my Lord,
   the ocean would be used up long before my Lord's words,
   even if we brought another like it to use."

110 Say, "I am only a man like you,
   to whom has been revealed that your God is One God.
   And he who hopes for the meeting with his Lord—
   let him do what is right, and not give anyone a share of the
      worship of his Lord."

The ritual opening with a hymn of praise shifts at the end of the introduction to a formula of announcement of a sacred narrative (*hadith*, 18:6), which will form the substance of the central section.

The first story in section II concerns the Companions of the Cave, commonly identified with the Christian heroes of the story of the Seven Sleepers of Ephesus, who according to tradition hid in a cave to escape the persecutions of the Roman emperor Decius (reigned 249–51 CE). Like Rip Van Winkle, they went to sleep in a cave for many years, accompanied by their dog, and a monument was built over them. When they awoke and cautiously emerged centuries later, in a world in which Christianity was triumphant, they cautiously sent one of their number into town, where his long-out-of-date coin was the first clue to the many years that had passed. This is an extremely popular story. There are numerous Christian and Muslim shrines dedicated to the Seven Sleepers, in Europe, the Middle East, and Central Asia, and these figures are still celebrated in the Orthodox and Catholic calendars. Miniature paintings depicting the Companions of the Cave are common (figure 3.1), and they also play an important role in Shi'ism.[21] Recently a twelve-part film on the Companions of the Cave, aimed at a Shi'i audience, was produced in Iran, which is available in several language versions.[22] Following the work of Louis Massignon on this topic, some recent thinkers have highlighted the Companions of the Cave as an important theme for examining commonalities between Christians and Muslims.[23]

Be that as it may, the pre-exegetical significance of the Companions of the Cave is to be sought in the way that the Qur'an recasts the narrative, which has a fairly strong tradition in the Christian East, particularly in Syriac texts. Following upon a debate passage that rejects the notion of incarnation, the telling of the story emphasizes repeatedly that its Christian heroes do not commit the sin of associating or sharing anyone but God in their worship—that is, they are not committing polytheism, along the lines of accepting Jesus as the Son of God. So in terms of prophetic rereading, sura 18 offers a strong corrective to the theology of the Christian narrative, adapting it to the familiar Qur'anic pattern of prophetic witnesses who withstand the lures of idolatry. The awakening of the Sleepers is also an implicit proof of the resurrection of the dead. As usual, the Qur'an does not provide a fully detailed version of the story, assuming instead that listeners are familiar with it; but when it is read alongside the fuller Syriac versions, those older versions help to explain details of the Qur'anic account that would otherwise be unclear, like the epitaph or inscribed tablet left outside the cave.[24] The Qur'an addresses several questions regarding the number of the Sleepers and how many years they slept, which seem to have been topics that were debated in the milieu of the Qur'an's listeners, but the answers to these questions remain somewhat mysterious. The story concludes with consolation to the Prophet and a double portrait of hell and paradise.

Figure 3.1. The Seven Sleepers, from the *Jamiʿ al-tawarikh* of Rashid al-Din. Edinburgh University Library, Special Collections Department, Ms Or 20 f.23r.

II. Narratives and Parables

A. The Companions of the Cave (24 verses)

    9 Now have you realized that the young men of the Cave and the epitaph

      were one of Our astonishing signs?

  10 When the young men sheltered in the Cave,

      then they said, "Lord, give us mercy from You,

      provide some guidance for us here!"

  11 So We sealed up their ears in the Cave

      for years of a certain number.

  12 Then We raised them up,

      to find out which party counted better

      how much time they stayed.

  13 We shall tell their story truly:

      They were young men believing in their Lord

and We increased their guidance.

14 And We bound to us their hearts when they rose up,
    so they said, "Our Lord is heaven and earth's Lord;
    we shall call on no other god besides Him—
    then we would have said something wrong.

15 "These our people have taken other gods besides Him,
    though no clear proof has come before them.
    Who is worse than one who gives the lie to God with deception?"

16 Since you went apart from them and the other gods they worship,
    so shelter in the Cave,
    and your Lord will unfold over you His mercy,
    making you a resting place from your fate.

17 And you would see the sun, when it rises,
    wander past their cave to the right.
    When it sets, it inclines over them from the left,
    and they are in its opening.
    That is one of the clearest of God's signs.
    The one God guides is on the true path,
    but one He sends astray—
    you won't find him with friend or teacher.

18 You would figure them awake though they are sleeping.
    We make them turn over, to the right and left.
    Their dog is stretching out his forelegs on the threshold.
    Had you encountered them, you would have turned and fled,
    and you would have been filled with fear of them.

19 So in this way We raised them up, so they could ask each other.
    One among them spoke: "How long have you stayed here?"
    They answered, "We have stayed a day, or part of one."
    They said, "Your Lord knows best how long you stayed.
    Send one of your number with these coins of yours to the city,
    and let him see which food is purest.
    Let him bring you some of that to eat.
    Let him act nicely, and he will not alert anyone about you.

20 "If they become aware of you, they will stone you,
    or force you back to their creed, and you will never be safe."

21 Thus We revealed them, so the people would know God's promise
       is true
    and there is no doubt about the Hour.

When the people disagreed over their fate,
some said, "Build over them a structure; their Lord knows them
   best."
Those who won the argument about them said,
"Let us make this a place of worship for them."

22 Some will say, "They are three, and their dog is the fourth."
Others say, "There are five, and their dog is the sixth,"
guessing about the unseen.
Yet others say, "They are seven, and their dog is the eighth."
Say, "My Lord knows best their number."
Just a few know them!
So don't argue about them, except on their appearance,
and don't ask anyone's opinion about them.

23 And don't ever say of anything, "I'm doing that tomorrow,"

24 Unless God wills.
Remember your Lord if you forget, and say,
"Perhaps my Lord may lead me with a closer guidance."

25 And they stayed in their Cave for three hundred years, plus
   nine.

26 Say, "God knows best how long they stayed."
The unseen part of the heavens and the earth belongs to Him.
See it, and hear! They have no other friend besides Him,
and no one shares in His wisdom.

27 Read out what He revealed to you in your Lord's book.
There is none who makes changes in His words
and you will find besides Him no other refuge.

28 Make yourself be patient,
with those who call their Lord morning and evening,
seeking His face, and don't turn your eyes from Him,
seeking the beauty of the life of this world;
and don't obey one whose heart We made forgetful of Our
   memory,
who follows his desire, outstripping all bounds.

29 And say, "The Truth is with my Lord."
Let him who wishes believe, and let him who wishes reject it.
We have readied a Fire for the unjust;
its pavilions surround them,
and if they want rain,

they will be drenched with a water like molten copper scalding
   their faces.
Terrible is the drink, and evil the resting-place.
30 As for those who have faith and act right—
We shall not omit reward for one who is virtuous in action.
31 They are the ones who hold the gardens of Eden
beneath which rivers flow
where they halt, wearing gold bracelets,
dressed in garments of green, of embroidered silk,
lying on divans beside the rivers.
Fortunate is the reward, and beautiful the resting-place!

In this way, the Qur'an has adapted the Christian tale to its own revelatory perspective.

The second and longest part in the narrative section of sura 18 begins with two parables that drive home the dependence of humanity on its Creator and the catastrophe that results from ignoring that relationship. Revelation is affirmed, though here the concept of the heavenly book as the repository of deeds makes an appearance in the context of the Day of Judgment. The focus then turns to Iblis, the only individual named in this portion, recalling the cosmic tale of sura 15 that inextricably linked opposition to prophecy with the Satanic party of Iblis. This passage then winds up with a robust debate section.

B. Parables and debate (28 verses)
  1. Parable of the two gardens
32 Strike for them a parable of two men,
to one of whom We gave two vineyards,
and We surrounded them with palm trees and placed a field
   between them.
33 One of the gardens produced, lacking nothing,
and We made a channel between them for a river.
34 It had fruit; so one told the other while they were conversing,
"I've got more than you in wealth and more power in men."
35 He went into his garden while they were conversing;
injustice was in his soul.
He said, "I don't think this will ever pass away,
36 "And I don't think the Hour is rising.
And even if I were turned back to my Lord,

surely I'd find something better than this in return."

37 His friend told him while they were conversing,
"Do you reject the One who made you from dust,
then from a sperm-drop, then turned you to a man?

38 "Here's what I say: God's my Lord,
and I'll never give anyone a share of the worship of my Lord.

39 "Why didn't you say, entering the garden,
'It's what God wished! Only God has power!'
Even though you see me with less money and children,

40 "Maybe my Lord will give me something better than your garden,
but He'll send thunder over yours from heaven
so it becomes slick wasteland;

41 "Or its water may sink so that you can't find it,

42 "And its fruit is destroyed."
He wrings his hands over what he spent on it,
and its roofs are fallen down.
He says, "I wish that I had never given anyone a share of the
worship of my Lord!"

43 But he has no gang who can help him,
other than God, so he is not triumphant.

44 Here is the dominion of God, the Truth.
He is the best for reward and the best for result.

2. Parable of life in this world

45 Strike for them the parable of life in this world,
like water that We made to fall from heaven,
from mixing with the earth's plants;
then it turns dry, so the winds blow it.
It is God who is able to do anything.

46 Money and children are the beauty of this world,
but lasting deeds of virtue are the best with your Lord for reward
and the best for hope.

47 On that day, We will make the mountains move,
and you'll see the earth laid bare;
We have raised them up, and We have left no one out.

48 They will be drawn up before your Lord in ranks.
"You have come to Us as We created you the first time,
but you claimed that We wouldn't keep this date with you."

49 The Book is set down, and you see the guilty

fearing what is in it, and they say,
"It's disaster for us, what this Book holds,
leaving no deed, great or small, uncounted!"
They will find their deeds before them,
but your Lord does wrong to no one.

50 When We told the angels, "Bow down to Adam!,"
They bowed down, all except for Iblis, who was of the jinn.
So he turned away from his Lord's command.
Will you take him and his offspring as friends in place of Me?
They are your enemy; that is a bad deal for criminals.

51 I did not let them see heaven's and earth's creation,
nor their own creation,
nor was I getting support from the deceivers.

52 And on that Day, He will say,
"Call upon My partners that you claim exist!"
And they will call on them, but they will not answer.
We have cast upon them a catastrophe.

53 And the guilty see the fire, so they think they are falling into it,
nor do they find a way to return.

54 We have coined in this Recitation every kind of parable for the
   people,
but humanity is the most quarrelsome of things.

55 Nothing stops people from believing,
when the guidance comes to them,
or from seeking their Lord's forgiveness,
except if the ancients' tradition intervenes,
or if punishment comes on them directly.

56 We only send messengers as bearers of good news and warnings.
Those who reject it argue with vanity, to refute the Truth.
They take My signs, and what they are warned about, as a joke.

57 And who is more unjust than one who is reminded of the signs of
   his Lord,
but who turns away from them,
and forgets what his hands have done?
We have placed upon their hearts coverings,
so they don't understand,
and a weight on their ears;
should you call them to guidance,

they will not ever be guided.
58 Your Lord is so forgiving, having mercy;
    if He blamed them for what they have accomplished,
    He would speed their punishment.
    But they have an appointment,
    from which they will not find release without Him.
59 These are the cities that We destroyed, when they were oppressors,
    and for their destruction We made an appointment.

This conclusion is very much in tune with the theme of punishment stories.

The next section of narrative is one of the most famous stories in the Qur'an. The spectacle of a mysterious "servant of God" instructing the incredulous Moses on the basis of special divine knowledge is a dramatic twist on the standard notion of prophetic authority. Some elusive details in this recounting call to mind other ancient Near Eastern narratives, such as Gilgamesh and his quest for immortality, a theme that also has echoes in the Alexander story that comes immediately after this. Moses' interlocutor is usually identified as al-Khidr ("the Green One," also spelled Khadir or Khizr), the deathless prophet in whose footprints green plants are said to spring up. In the section below, *he* in italics refers to Khidr. His appearance is heralded by Moses' arrival at the enigmatic "Meeting of the Oceans," where his servant (the "young man" of 18:60) cooks a fish, but the water miraculously brings it back to life so that it swims away. When they unaccountably forget this incident and move on, Moses deduces from the fish's revival that this must be the miraculous place he was seeking. When Moses attempts to follow him, this mysterious figure commits three seemingly irrational acts that Moses objects to. Before parting, Khidr reveals the secret reasons for his actions, based on the special knowledge that he received from God. Sufi interpreters view this story as the basis for mystical experience, in contrast to the limitations of knowledge based on legalistic externals.

C. The story of Moses and al-Khidr (24 verses)
    60 Then Moses said to the young man, "I won't stop till I reach
        the Meeting of the Oceans, or I'll go a long time."
    61 But when they reached the Meeting between the two,
        they forgot about their fish.
        It found its way to the ocean, tunneling.
    62 And when they moved on, he said to the young man,

"Bring our food; we find this journey of ours tiring."

63 He answered, "Did you see, when we stopped at the rock,
   that I forgot the fish?
   It was only Satan who made me to forget it.
   So it found its way to the ocean, as a wonder."

64 Moses said, "That's what we were looking for."
   So they turned back on their tracks.

65 Then they found one of Our servants,
   whom We offered Our mercy,
   teaching him Our knowledge.

66 Moses said to him, "Can I follow you, so you can teach me
   the guidance that you were taught?"

67 *He* said, "You won't have patience to bear with me.

68 "How could you be patient with knowledge you don't
      comprehend?"

69 Moses said, "You'll find me to be patient, God willing,
   nor will I disobey a command of yours."

70 *He* said, "If you follow me, you can't ask anything,
   till I discuss with you something about it."

71 So the two of them went,
   but as they rode upon a ship, *he* broke a hole in it.
   Moses said, "Did you break it to destroy these people?
   You have done something stupid!"

72 But *he* said, "Didn't I tell you? You won't have patience to bear with
      me."

73 Moses said, "Don't blame my forgetfulness, or ask something
      difficult."

74 So the two of them went,
   but as they met a youth, *he* killed him.
   Moses said, "Have you killed a pure soul,
   who hadn't killed another?
   You've done something horrible!"

75 And *he* said, "Didn't I tell you? You won't have patience to bear
      with me."

76 Moses said, "If I ask you anything after this, let me go; you have
      my forgiveness."

77 So the two of them went,
   but as they met the people of a village,

they begged them for food,
but the people refused to host them.
And they found there a wall that was falling down,
but *he* fixed it.
Moses said, "You could have been paid, if you wanted, for doing
this!"

78 *He* replied, "This is the parting between us.
I'll tell you the interpretation of the things you couldn't bear.

79 "Now the ship belonged to some poor folk who work on the ocean.
I wanted to damage it,
since they have a king ruling over them
who is seizing all the ships by force.

80 "Now the youth had two pious parents
but we were afraid he'd assault them defiantly, with unbelief.

81 "So we wanted their Lord to replace him with one of greater
purity,
one of greater kindness.

82 "Now the wall belonged to a pair of orphan youths in the city.
Beneath it was a treasure that was theirs,
and their father was an upright man.
Your Lord wanted them to reach their maturity,
and excavate their treasure as a mercy from your Lord.
All that I did I was ordered.
That's the interpretation of the things you couldn't bear."

Modern scholars have pointed out that this story has undeniable similarities with a widespread folktale. In terms of the classical repertory of folklore, the Aarne-Thompson *Motif-Index of Folk-Literature*, the story of Moses and Khidr has all the characteristics of tale type 759, "God's Justice Vindicated," also known as "the angel and the hermit." Some scholars use this functional relationship as a way to play up the literary dependency of the Qur'an on outside sources, which is the standard Orientalist exercise in one-upmanship. Taking a different tack, classical scholar and psychoanalytic theorist Norman O. Brown has found the story to be a powerful example of the apocalyptic strain of the Qur'an. Rather than seeing its folklore origin as a lack of originality, he observes that "the Koran, with characteristic monumentality, reduces the folktale to its archetypal essence and makes evident its folktale form, alerting thereby the intelligence to the problem of interpretation."[25] Although Brown was more concerned with the later impact of the Moses-Khidr story on the development of Islamic esotericism, he rightly emphasized the role of this tale in creating a sense of mystery and an awareness of the need for interpretation of these narrative sections of the Qur'an.

The fourth narrative section of sura 18 has a protagonist who is called simply "the Two-Horned One" (*dhu al-qarnayn*). This figure is commonly understood to be Alexander, both the historical Alexander the Great and the mythical hero of the same name, who is sometimes identified in Christian and Muslim sources as a prophet. For convenience he is referred to as "Alexander" in the translation below. The name "Two-Horned" is usually explained by the ram's horns of the Egyptian god Ammon, an equivalent of Zeus, with whom Alexander was identified, as seen in Hellenistic coins depicting Alexander with horns (figure 3.2). Here, too, a Syriac narrative, the *Legend of Alexander*, helps to clarify obscure parts of the story that are only hinted at in the Qur'anic version.[26] Alexander is the archetypal world ruler, to whom God has given "power on earth" (18:84). He has a supernatural ability to travel from one end of the earth to the other by celestial "pathways" (18:84, 18:85, 18:89, 18:92), reminiscent of the wormholes of modern science fiction.[27] Alexander first journeys to the west, where he finds a "muddy spring" (18:86) corresponding to a poisonous sea mentioned in the Syriac version, which Alexander tests by sending in condemned prisoners. Their death reveals that the sea is a deadly and impassable barrier that will require him to resort to celestial pathways again. The Qur'anic version, in a characteristic shift, treats the punishment of criminals as a generic administration of justice rather than the use of human guinea pigs. When Alexander then travels to the east, he meets a people who, as the Syriac story explains, have to hide from the extreme heat of the sun, from which they have no protection. On his third journey, Alexander reaches a mountain pass beyond which live people with the barbarian characteristic of speaking an incomprehensible language. This is clearly a depiction of the perennial threat of nomadic Central Asian invaders as viewed from the civilized Near East. The local people beg Alexander to protect them against these hordes of Gog and Magog—these names preserve a well-established Near Eastern and biblical portrayal of Central Asian barbarians in apocalyptic terms. Alexander agrees to build a wall of iron and brass in the mountain pass in order to hold off the invaders, but he concludes by predicting the collapse of the wall as an apocalyptic sign of Judgment Day. Later minia-

Figure 3.2. Hellenistic coin representing Alexander with ram's horn (symbol of Zeus/Ammon). Harvard Art Museums/Arthur M. Sackler Museum, Loan from the Trustees of the Arthur Stone Dewing Greek Numismatic Foundation, 1.1965.1350.

ture paintings depicting Alexander's construction of the wall portray Gog and Magog as naked savages (figure 3.3) or even as demons.

D. The Story of Two-Horned Alexander (20 verses)

    83 They will ask you of Two-Horned Alexander.
        Say, "I will tell you a story about him."
    84 We gave him power on earth,
        giving him a (celestial) pathway to all things.
    85 So he followed on a pathway.
    86 But as he reached the setting of the sun,
        he found it setting in a muddy spring,
        and he found there a people.
        We told him, "Alexander! You can either punish them, or treat
           them well."
    87 He said, "I will punish anyone who has committed crime.
        Then he will be rendered up to his Lord,
        so He will punish him terribly.
    88 "But one who has faith and who does what is right gets a beautiful
           reward.
        We will command him something easy."
    89 Then he followed on another pathway.
    90 But as he reached the rising of the sun,
        he found it rising on a people
        whom We did not give any other cover.

Figure 3.3. Miniature painting of Alexander's wall, from a *Khamsa* of Nizami.
© The British Library Board, I.O. Islamic 387, f.442v.

91 So it was, and We understood all that he knew.

92 Then he followed on another pathway.

93 But as he reached the place between two mountains,
he found beyond them a people;
they barely could understand a word.

94 [Others] said, "Alexander! Gog and Magog are causing havoc on
the earth!
Shall we pay your expense?
You can make a barrier between us and them."

95 He said, "The power that my Lord has given me is better.
Help me with your strength,
and I'll raise up a wall between you and them.

96 "Bring me iron bars."
And when they filled the gaps, he said, "Blow on it!"
And when they fired the iron, he said, "Bring me melted bronze,
so I can pour it over."

97 Gog and Magog could not get over it,
nor could they make a hole in it.

98 He said, "This wall is a mercy from my Lord.
When my Lord's Promise comes,
He will pulverize it. The Promise of my Lord is true."

99 And that day We shall leave some of them surging over others,
when the Trumpet shall be blown, and We gather all of them.

100 We will draw up Hell on display that Day for unbelievers.

101 They are the ones whose eyes were veiled from My Reminder,
and who could not hear.

102 So do the unbelievers think they can take My slaves as allies, not
Me?
We have made Hell into a lodging for the unbelievers.

By its placement as the concluding story, the Alexander narrative is made
to fit into a sequence of pre-Islamic stories that buttress the moral perspective of the Qur'an and its depiction of judgment, which is asserted through
the divine voice in the closing lines of the section.

The central role of these three pre-Islamic legends in sura 18 indicates
the breadth of the Qur'anic appropriation of previous scriptural revelations. That is, it draws upon not only Christian narratives of saintly persons (the Seven Sleepers) but also religiously charged versions of folklore

(Khidr) and epic (Alexander). The theological framework of sura 18 raises an additional question about the chronological dating of the text. That is, does the prominent critique of Christian doctrine (18:4) and the engagement with a well-known Christian legend, the Seven Sleepers, fit with the dating of this sura to the middle Meccan period? While modern scholarship generally regards sura 18 as stylistically part of the middle Meccan period, it is worth noting that there have always been hints that connect it to the Medinan period. Traditional commentators have suggested a sort of preliminary Medinan connection for sura 18, by claiming that its narratives were the answers to questions posed by the Jewish scholars of Medina to the Prophet Mohammed while he was still in Mecca.[28] Although the interest of Jewish authorities in Christian narratives is somewhat hard to imagine, this explanation may have been proposed on the assumption that Mecca itself did not have a population of Christians (or Jews) that would furnish the pretext for such a theological debate. And while it is true that some major passages rejecting the Christian notion of incarnation are clearly later, from the Medinan period (2:116, 4:171), still there are plenty of early and middle Meccan passages refuting the notion that God could have taken a son (10:68, 17:11, 19:35, 21:26, 23:91, 25:2, 39:4, 43:81, 72:2). One of these passages (19:88–93) makes a highly exaggerated caricature of the idea that God could have a son:

> They say, "The Merciful One has taken a son." You have done something monstrous! The heavens are nearly torn apart, the earth split, and the mountains fallen in ruin, because you claim that the Merciful One has a son! But it is not appropriate that the Merciful One has a son. All in heaven and the earth approach the Merciful One as a worshiper.

Here is another case where extrapolation from what is known of the prophetic biography does not help to situate the context of sura 18 with any clarity. Without imposing the sharp religious boundaries that characterize modern notions of religious identity, it may be the case that notions of divine sonship were in the air, as it were, in the Arabian environment of the Qur'an.

Yet there is one external piece of evidence indicating that at least one portion of sura 18, namely the Alexander legend, came into the text at a very late date in the Prophet's career. The Qur'anic version of this story corresponds very closely with the *Legend of Alexander*, but only up to a point. The Syriac version of the story continues with a detailed after-the-fact prophecy that can be dated to the years 628–29 CE. In this passage, Alexander prophesies that the kingdom of the Romans will annihilate the Persians in an apocalyptic and messianic triumph. Scholars have made a persuasive case for seeing this prophecy as propaganda for the attempt of the Eastern Roman (Byzantine) emperor Heraclius to rally support among the Syriac-speaking Christian communities of the East, during his decisive counterinvasion of Persia in those years. The Qur'an indeed shows elsewhere (30:1–5, late Meccan) a keen interest in the fortunes of the Eastern Roman empire and its battles with the Persians. Sura 30 is in fact named "The Romans." According to this hypothesis, the Syriac *Legend of Alexander*, with its richly apocalyptic prophecy, would have been perceived in Medina as part of the complex of Near Eastern prophecy, since Christian sources in late antiquity had attempted to tame the alarming world-emperor Alexander by transforming him into a prophet of Christian triumph. Its incorporation in the largely Meccan sura 18 — minus the prophecy of Heraclius's victory, which did not really fit the Qur'anic context — would have been a natural supplement to a dossier already containing a response to another Syriac Christian legend (the Seven Sleepers). Yet it still may be said that the literary unity of sura 18 remains strong, a sign of the successful application of the prophetic voice to the ongoing revision of the Qur'anic text. More important, the narrative complexity of sura 18 demonstrates the remarkable engagement of the Qur'an with the full range of ancient civilization. A tale of Christian martyrs, a wisdom anecdote of Moses that links back to early Mesopotamian themes, and a moralizing story about the Macedonian world emperor — all indicate the extent to which the Qur'an demands to play a role in the understanding of the full range of culture in the ancient world.

The Rhetoric of Debate and the Implied Audience of Mecca

The middle and later Meccan suras evidently were delivered over a number of years, during which time the Qur'an's audience developed a complex range of responses to the revelation. What can one tell about the nature of that audience from indications within the text of the Qur'an itself? Obviously the most distinctive addressee is the Prophet himself, addressed as "you" in the singular. There is in addition a community of worshippers, addressed in the plural, who accept the authority of revelation and are reassured by the depictions of their cosmic role and destiny; the emergence of this community has been discussed above in regard to the example of sura 15. Yet there is another disparate audience for the Qurʾan that is characterized by a hostile and critical response to its message; these voices are frequently referred to more impersonally, in the third-person plural "they." A survey of some of the major issues of contention in debates between the Qurʾan and its unreceptive auditors brings out the assumptions and conceptions that the Meccans brought to the understanding of revelation. They had well-developed ideas about miracles, magic, poetry, myth, prophecy, and angels, which they typically deployed with sarcasm and mockery. They resisted the new message on the basis of clan privilege and patriarchal tradition. The Qurʾan frequently reflects on the perverse and argumentative character of its opponents, and it considers the mystery of how God moves a soul to accept revelation or reject it. The late Meccan suras demonstrate an increasing emphasis on the notion of the Qurʾan as a scripture that fulfills previous revelations. All this suggests a climate of relatively sophisticated awareness of a range of religious topics among the Meccans, who were far from being the ignorant barbarians they are sometimes depicted as.

One of the most typical audience responses described in the middle Meccan suras consists of a combination of outright rejection of the Qurʾan's message and a demand for miracles as evidence that would ostensibly cause the Meccans to believe. Thus, in the concluding section of sura 17, "The Night Journey," a section confirming the revelation concludes by pointing out the unreceptive character of its audience: "We have expressed to the people in various ways in the Qurʾan every sort of parable, but most of the people reject anything except unbelief" (17:89). This categorical description is followed by a response, presumably depicting the obstinate Meccans, demanding a whole series of colorful miracles:

> They said, "We will not believe you until you let flow a spring from the earth, or you have a garden of date palms and grapes in which you cause rivers to flow forth, or you make heaven fall in pieces, as you claimed, or you bring God and the angels before us, or you have a house made of gold, or you ascend up to heaven; and we will not believe in your ascension until you bring down a book for us to read." Say, "Glory to my Lord! Am I anything but a human messenger?" But nothing prevented people from believing, when guidance came

to them, except that they said, "Has God sent a human messenger?"
(17:90–94)

The complex associations in this passage between prophecy and miracles embrace a range of disparate phenomena. Some of the events they demand are paradisiacal enhancements of nature, such as the flowing spring and rivers in the garden, while others, like the house of gold or shattering heaven, are extraordinary wonders. Surprisingly, the pagans of Mecca demand that the Prophet should produce God and the angels before them, clearly indicating that they had at least some sense of the theological basis of the prophetic message. It is hard to imagine, however, that the Prophet Muhammad would have made any such promises. When the Meccans describe him as claiming to make heaven fall, it seems likely that they were distorting the description of God's unleashing of Judgment Day, by attributing it to Muhammad. Yet there is evidence that Muhammad did claim to have made a heavenly ascension, and indeed the opening verse of this very sura (17:1) is typically understood as referring to such an experience. The clinching argument that seals this series of demands is the simple observation that the messenger is only a human being and not an angel. This point is reinforced both as a "Say" verse that the Prophet is commanded to recite and as a disappointed complaint of the pagan audience. In this way, the key Qur'anic doctrine of the messenger's human status becomes (for his opponents) a cause for rejecting its message altogether. In addition, the piecemeal delivery of Qur'anic revelations during the early Meccan years apparently did not yet strike these people as constituting a book, a sign of the still-unrealized process of canonization.

There is a certain slippage and ambiguity about the relationship between miracle and revelation, both in the outrageous list of wonders in the pagans' demands and in the Qur'an's own view of the revelatory process. That is, the very term used to denote a Qur'anic verse, *aya*, also means a sign of divine power, whether in the ordinary phenomena of nature or in extraordinary events decreed by God. Time and again, the opponents of the Qur'an call for a sign—or are they asking for a verse of revelation? Meanwhile, the Qur'an continually asserts the existence of signs that demonstrate the omnipotence of God. But there is something ultimately frustrating about this whole series of exchanges, since the rejecters of revelation would never be satisfied, even if all their fantasies were fulfilled. At the end of sura 20, right after a passage of consolation to the Prophet and a celebration of communal worship, the focus turns to those who resist revelation:

They said, "Let him bring a sign/verse (aya) from his Lord." But did they not receive the clarification of what is in the prior scriptures? And if We had destroyed them with punishment before then, they would have said, "Our Lord! If only You had sent us a messenger so we could follow Your signs/verses before we were humiliated and shamed!" (20:133-34)

Now this may be a generic diagnosis of opposition to prophecy as a constant theme in sacred history. But it is noteworthy that the Qur'an portrays the rejecters of revelation as being quite familiar with the category of revelation and with the notion of the fulfillment of previous prophecies, although they willfully reject the Qur'anic revelation and disingenuously fail to recognize it as an example of the category. Opponents of the Qur'an are even seen requesting revisions and alterations in the message. The Qur'an clearly distinguishes between the authority of inspiration and willful tampering with the text. "And when Our clear signs are read to them, those who do not hope for the meeting with Us say, 'Bring a different recitation (qur'an) than this, or change it!' Say, 'It is not for me to change it by myself; I only follow that by which I am inspired'" (10:15). It is worth pointing out that this verse does not exclude the possibility of revision that is undertaken by divine inspiration. At the same time, this verse points out that skeptics were willing to debate the contents of the Qur'an and even accept its revelatory format, subject to their own objections.

There are times, in fact, when the Qur'an satirizes the expectation of miracles involving the provision of wealth; houses with roofs and furnishings of silver and gold are dismissed as "enjoyment of life in this world" (43:35). Yet Pharaoh assumes that worldly wealth goes along with heavenly attributes, when he says, regarding Moses, "Am I not better than this one who is contemptible, and who can scarcely communicate? So why have gold bracelets not been placed upon him, or angels come alongside him as companions?" (43:52-53). The Meccans' desire to have it both ways — to have both miraculous wealth and heavenly inspiration — seems to have been a continuing theme that frustrated the Prophet throughout his Meccan career, to judge from a consolation verse from the later Meccan period: "It's possible that you may give up what you've been inspired with, and become depressed as a result, because they say, 'Why hasn't a treasure been sent down to him, or an angel accompanied him?' You are only a warner, and God is in charge of all things" (11:12).

Increasingly, over the course of the Meccan periods, the Qur'an focuses on both the detailed nature of the demands for miracles and the insincerity of those demands. Sura 6, "Cattle," contains several reflections on this problem, diagnosing it as a misguided attempt to produce the apocalypse on demand.

> If We had sent down to you a book on papyrus, and they touched it with their hands, the disbelievers would have said, "This is only obvious magic." And they said, "Why hasn't an angel been sent down to him?" If We had sent an angel, the command [for Judgment Day] would be executed; then they would have no respite. (6:7–8)

Ultimately, the greedy focus on miracles misses the point of the inspiration of prophecy.

> Say, "I don't tell you I have the treasures of God, I don't know the hidden, and I don't tell you that I am an angel. I only follow what I have been inspired with." Say, "Is the blind one equivalent to the one who sees? So won't you consider it?" (6:50)

The skeptical Meccans seem to have frequently invoked the assumption that revelation must be delivered by immortal angels rather than human beings. But at the same time, the Qur'an sweeps away this criticism by insisting that all messengers are human:

> Those who are unjust say, "Is this one [that is, Muhammad] anything but a human like you?" . . . But before you, We only sent men whom We inspired, so ask the people of the Reminder [that is, the recipients of earlier revelation], if you don't know. We only provided them bodies that consume food, for they were not immortals." (21:3, 7–8)

It is perhaps surprising that, although the Meccan skeptics rejected the prophetic status of Muhammad, there seems to have been at least some recognition of the concept of prophecy among the Arabs. How else can one understand the objection of those who say, "You are not a prophet" (13:43)?

Despite their apparently exaggerated expectations of the miraculous accompaniments of revelation, the Meccans also possessed a sharp sense of the category of magic as an inherently deceptive phenomenon, and they used this term as a way to discredit the Qur'anic revelation. While the term magic (*sihr*) as a negative term for the revelation occurs occasionally in early Meccan contexts (52:15, 74:24), it is a much more frequent accusation in the middle and later Meccan suras. "Magic" is a highly charged term, which in modern scholarship has been exceedingly difficult to disentangle from the category of religion. Frequently these two terms are defined as excluding each other, yet the boundaries between the two are often described in very different terms, and overlaps are common.[29] The Qur'an does not necessarily exclude magic from the domain of prophecy. The magical contests between Moses and the magicians of Pharaoh, as well as the prodigious abilities of Solomon, indicate that prophets could practice magic with equanimity. Yet the Meccans denounced the Qur'an as "obvious magic" (*sihr mubin*) so frequently that they must have felt that they knew it when they saw it. The implications of this charge are not so much that the opponents of the Qur'an detected something supernatural about the manner of its production—indeed, that was far from the case. Rather, the root meaning of *sihr* has the connotation of turning something from its proper nature into something else, in the manner of enchantment, seduction, or deception. In a positive sense, persuasive rhetorical eloquence is often known as "lawful magic" in Muslim tradition.[30] There may be a grudging recognition here that the Qur'an exerts a powerful rhetorical pull, which the skeptics acknowledged even as they rejected it.

The Meccans also dismissed the Qur'an on rhetorical grounds when they condemned it as poetry. The charge of poetry did have religious overtones, insofar as it was associated with soothsaying and possession by the demonic spirits known as jinn. So it was when the Meccans were confronted with the message of monotheism: "They became arrogant when it was said to them, 'There is no god but God,' and they said, 'Shall we abandon our gods for a possessed poet?'" (37:35–36). More often than not, poetry as a dismissive term is simply one among many, often disparate, ways in which the Meccans cast scorn upon the Qur'anic revelation as a fake invention; consistency was not the main point of these accusations. "'No,' they said, 'it's garbled dreams! No, he made it up! No, he's a poet! Let him bring us a sign, such as the ancients were sent!'" (21:5). But the accusation of poetry was serious enough that the Qur'an takes pains to reject it on more than one occasion, asserting an absolute distinction between poetry and revelation. "Nor did We teach him poetry, which is not appropriate for him. This is only a Reminder and a clear Recitation" (36:69). Surely what is offensive about the accusation of poetry is the assumption that it involves fabrication by the poet, who literally makes the text up. In contrast, the Qur'an presents itself as the report of a divine message in which no human has had a part. In one of the famous "challenge verses," which claim an unmatchable scriptural status for the Qur'an's verses, it is precisely this accusation of fabrication that causes the problem: "Or they say, 'He made it up!' So bring ten made-up suras like it!" (11:13). To be sure, part of the Meccans' objection lay in their skepticism regarding the afterlife and the resurrection: "And they said, 'This is only our life in the world; we die and live, and only time destroys us.' . . . And when it was said, 'And God's promise is true, and there is no doubt about the Hour,' you said, 'We don't know what "the Hour" is. We think it's only an opinion, and we're not convinced'" (45:24, 45:32). So the description of the Qur'an as poetry is just part of an overall rejection of it, both in style and in substance.

In tune with these techniques for dismissing the contents of the Qur'anic revelation, the Meccans also employed the strategy of labeling them as flimsy legends from the past, with the same kind of counterfactual implication that is today carried by the word "myth." The phrase that is used (repeated nine times, all but one in Meccan suras) has been translated as "fairytales of the ancients." The etymology of this phrase is disputed; the word translated as "fairytales," which is only used in the plural, is *asatir*, with a probable singular form *ustura*. This word has been variously derived from an Aramaic-Syriac term for manuscripts, or else from the Greek word *historia*, in the sense of "story, narrative."[31] In modern Arabic and cognate languages, *ustura* is indeed the normal term for "myth." What older narratives or written traditions may have been implicated by this dismissive term? Who were the "ancients" (*al-awwalun*) whose tradition is invoked? It is difficult to say in the absence of other internal evidence, but nevertheless there seems to be a category for threadbare legends of the past, here providing another pretext for rejecting the Qur'anic revelation as untrustworthy.

The Meccan opponents also found it convenient to suppose that Muhammad had a confederate who supplied him with these revelations. This critique boils down to a charge of plagiarism, or questionable authorship. Interlocutors who seem to recognize literary similarity accused the Prophet of having borrowed things that he had read elsewhere: "Thus do We express the signs in different ways, and so they say, 'You have studied'" (6:105).[32] They also maintain that his source speaks a foreign language, though the Qur'an itself is in Arabic: "And We know that they say, 'It is only a man who teaches him.' The tongue of the one they hint at is foreign, but this is a clear Arabic tongue" (16:103). There is a certain inconsistency in the way in which the critics say that Muhammad has made up the Qur'an, while at the same time they claim that he has borrowed it from others: "Those who disbelieve said, 'This is only a lie that he made up, and some other people helped him'" (25:4). Ultimately, this seems like a case of throwing together any accusations that the skeptics think will stick. "And they turned away from him, and they said, 'He's been taught, he's possessed'" (44:14).

Discussion of the Meccans' debates against the Qur'an has focused so far on the concepts implicit in their critique of the revelation, but the Qur'an also has provided commentary, diagnosing and assigning motives to these skeptical responses. One of the characteristic descriptions that the Qur'an provides for its rejecters is mockery, a charge that is applied dozens of times throughout the Qur'an. Mockery may be seen as a kind of insult that attempts to humiliate an opponent, and it casts aside the sincerity and respect that is the basis for any genuine sense of community. The Prophet Muhammad receives consolation when he is treated with such derision: "And when those who disbelieve see you, they only treat you with mockery, [saying,] 'Is this the one who mentions your gods?' While they are the ones who reject the mention of the Merciful One!" (21:36). The portrayal of rejection as mockery becomes a repeated formula, since mockery is indeed the way in which all disbelieving communities have treated their prophets: "Messengers before you were mocked, but that which they ridiculed shall befall the scoffers among them" (21:41). Needless to say, such mockery is presented as an offense that will receive due punishment in the afterlife.

The Qur'an also detects among its opponents hostile motivations based on class prejudice and the conservatism of an entrenched elite. They criticize Muhammad for putting himself forward: "And the leaders of his people, who were disbelievers, said, 'This is only a human like you, who wants to think of himself as better than you'" (23:24). They sneer that this new revelation has been given to an unimportant person: "And they said, 'Why was this Recitation not sent down upon a great man of the two cities?'" (43:31). There is even an indication of some jealousy, or perhaps just a conceited sense that the Meccan aristocrats would have been the first to discover anything of value: "And those who disbelieve say about the believers, 'If this was anything good, they would not have gotten to it before we did!'" (46:11). On one level, the rejecters of the Qur'an opposed it in the name of maintaining the tradition of their forefathers, without any question. In turn, the Qur'an pours scorn upon the social pressure that compels agreement to a doomed course: "And if it is said to them, 'Follow what God has revealed,' they replied, 'No! We follow what we discovered from our fathers.' Really? Even though the devil invites them into the punishment of blazing fire?" (31:21). But there are suggestions that the memory of the ancestral forebears of Mecca is not restricted to paganism or epicurean rejection of the afterlife. Sura 23, "The Believers," paints a portrait of the opposition to Noah that brings together many of the themes of rejection, which also seem to be applicable in the case of Mecca.

> And the leaders of these people, who disbelieve, and called the en-
> counter of the afterlife a lie, whom We exalted in the life of this
> world—they said, "This is only a human like you, who eats what you
> eat and drinks what you drink. And if you obey a human like your-
> selves, you will lose everything. Does he promise you that when you
> die, and you are dust and bones, you will be drawn forth? Beware,
> beware what you were promised! This is only our life in the world; we
> die and we live, and we are not resurrected. He is only a man who has
> made up a lie about God, and we don't have faith in him!" (23:33–38)

What is interesting about this middle Meccan passage is that, although the opponents of Noah stick to their rejection of the afterlife, the end section of the same sura echoes it in an ambiguous fashion. Now the Meccans argue the opposite case, namely, that their ancestors were promised the fiction of the afterlife and rejected it. "No, they said something just like what the ancients said. They said, 'When we die and we become dust and bones, shall we be resurrected? We were promised this before, we and our fathers. This is only fairytales of the ancients!'" (23:81–83). It seems that tradition can cut both ways. The brashness of the Meccans' skeptical rejection of the afterlife seems to conceal an uneasy memory of older debates among their forebears.

The Qur'an frequently sees its opponents as insincere, perverse, and willfully argumentative. Sometimes the pagans disingenuously claim that their worship of multiple deities is compatible with monotheism. "Those who take as friends other than Him say, 'We only worship them to become closer in station to God'" (39:3). Or are they just pagans? The following verse (39:4) rejects the notion that God could have a son, which could reflect Christian beliefs. In any case, there are frequent passages allud-ing to the difficulty of reaching this hostile audience. "It is the same for them, whether you warn them or you don't warn them; they do not believe.

You only warn the one who follows the Reminder and fears the Merciful One deeply; so give him good news of forgiveness and a generous reward" (36:10–11). And in a slight variation, mostly addressed in the plural "you" to the community of worshippers, "And if you [all] call them to guidance, they do not follow you; it is the same for you, whether you call them or if you are silent. . . . And if you call them to guidance, they do not listen, and you [Muhammad] will see them gazing at you, but they do not see" (7:193, 7:198). Quite ironically, the Meccans will even claim that their idolatry has been ordained by God: "Those who are idolaters will say, 'If God wished, we would not have been idolaters, nor our fathers'" (6:148). Indeed, in this late Meccan sura, the Qur'an in part accepts that logic, counseling Muhammad to leave the pagans alone, since they refuse to listen anyway.

> And if God had wished, they would not have been idolaters. We have not made you a guard over them, nor are you in charge of them. So don't insult those who call upon [beings] other than God, lest they unwittingly insult God. . . . And even if We had sent angels down to them, and the dead had spoken to them, and We had resurrected everything before them, they would not have believed, except if God wished; but most of them are ignorant. And thus We made for every prophet an enemy—demons of the human and the jinn; they inspire one another with fancy words in deception. But if your Lord had wished, they would not have done that. So leave them alone, and whatever they have made up, so that the hearts of those who do not believe in the afterlife may incline toward that, so they will be pleased with it, so they may gain what they gain. (6:107–8, 6:111–13)

Sura 6 exhibits an attitude toward the Meccans that is not so much conciliatory as it is frustrated. The passage just quoted is almost fatalistic in its acceptance of the divinely sanctioned role of a demonic opposition, members of which are consigned to their own fancies. Their opposition is an argumentative disposition that is practically incurable. "Those who dispute the signs of God without any authorization granted them—this is completely hateful to God, and to those who believe. Thus does God seal every arrogant and brutal heart" (40:35).

So stubborn was the problem of opposition among the pagan Meccans that the later Meccan suras treat it as resulting from the divine plan, to the degree that God has made the unbelievers blind and deaf to the truth of revelation. Many passages combine a resignation to God's will with a fierce critique of the opposition, creating thorny problems of the conflict of free will and predestination for later theologians. As sura 6 reflects, "And among them there are those who listen to you, but We have placed veils upon their hearts, and deafness on their ears, lest they should understand. And if they saw every sign, they would not believe in it, so that when they come to you, they dispute with you; those who disbelieve say, 'This is only fairytales of the ancients!'" (6:25). This deafness is an enduring problem. "And there are some of them who listen to you, but can you make the deaf hear, if they do not comprehend?" (10:42). The recurrent passages that address this resistance to revelation do in fact serve as consolation to the messenger. "For you do not make the dead hear, nor do you make the deaf hear the call, when they turn their backs. And you are no guide to the blind, from their error; it is only those who believe in Our signs whom you can make hear, for they are the submitters (*muslimun*)" (30:52–53). So strong is this sense of a divinely induced blindness and deafness that the unbelievers are made to acknowledge this themselves. "And they said, 'Our hearts are veiled from your call to us, and in our ears is deafness; there is a curtain between us and you'" (41:5). Ultimately, the mystery of the deafness and blindness of the rejecters of revelation is insoluble by ordinary means. "And if your Lord had wished, everyone on earth would have believed, all of them together. So would you compel people to become believers? It does not belong to any soul that it should believe, except with God's permission" (10:99–100).

Along with revealing the pervasive problem of hardened opposition to the Qur'anic revelation, the later Meccan suras provide suggestions that the community of believers is also subject to weakness and distraction. On several occasions, the Qur'an describes the situation of those who, in time of danger, cry out to God for help but soon forget him once they have escaped their troubles.

He is the one who makes you go on land and sea, so that when you are in the ships, and they sail with their passengers with a fair wind, and they are happy, a storm then comes to them, and the wave comes to them from every side; they imagine that they will sink. They cry to God, making their faith pure for him: "If you save us from this, we shall be thankful!" But when He saves them, then they exploit the earth wrongfully. People! You are only exploiting yourselves. (10:22–23)

This could be taken for a generic observation on the frailty of human conviction. But there are signs that the Qur'an needed to address simplistic misunderstandings of the role of suffering in the divine economy. There is first of all the question of the faithful who assume that they will be spared any suffering because of their belief. Sura 29, "The Spider," begins by correcting that misapprehension. "Do the people calculate that they will be left in peace, because they say, 'We believe,' and that they won't be chastised? But We chastised those who came before you. . . . And among the people are those who say, 'We believe in God.' But when he suffers for God, he treats chastisement by the people as if it were punishment by God. And if the victory comes from your Lord, he says, 'We were with you!' But is not God aware of what is in the breasts of creatures?" (29:2–3, 29:10). The temptation to read every success or misfortune as a sign of God's favor or displeasure too quickly assumes that the calculus of life's fortunes is transparently comprehensible by humanity.

While modern readers may find Qur'anic punishment stories to be disturbing and even morbid, one should not underestimate the extent to which they are connected to the function of consolation. These are tales that call on the imagination to portray the restoration of justice and the downfall of arrogant pretenders. But their dramatic import plays a special role in a situation where the divine message is continually being rejected. Thus one of the many functions of the narratives of prophets, and the stories of the punishment of the unbelieving communities, is to console and reassure the messenger in a time of difficulty. "And all that We tell you of reports of the prophets We do to make your heart firm. Through this the Truth comes to you and an admonition, and a Reminder for the believers" (11:120). In this respect, opposition by stubborn skeptics is simply part of the pattern of true prophecy. "And if they call you a liar, those who came before them have done the same. Their messengers came to them with clear proofs, Psalms, and the luminous Book" (35:25). Opposition, in effect, provides confirmation to the messenger.

While the middle Meccan suras offer some allusions to the question of fulfillment of earlier prophecy, the subject takes on a more central importance in the later Meccan suras. The Qur'anic revelation is depicted as having a strong family resemblance to prior scriptures. "Those to whom We gave the Book recognize it [the Qur'anic revelation] as they recognize their own sons" (6:20). With a slight variation, the possessors of previous monotheistic traditions are optimistically said to embrace the new dispensation: "Those to whom We gave the Book previously believe in it" (28:52). And readers of the Qur'an are encouraged to seek clarification of its difficult passages in previous scriptures: "And if you are in doubt about what We have revealed to you, then ask those who recite the Books that precede you" (10:94). But the relationship between these different revelations becomes complicated and contentious, at least when it comes to conversation between the different recipients. "Say, 'Who revealed the Book that Moses brought as a light and guidance for the people, which you put on papyrus that you display, though you hide much?'" (6:91). That particular exchange suggests a controversy over the contents of a scripture that is claimed by different groups, even as it underlines their common acceptance of what a scripture is. One can also see passages indicating that not all adherents of previous revelations will enthusiastically embrace the Qur'an. "Those to whom We gave the Book rejoice in what has been revealed to you, though there are factions who reject part of it. . . . So it is that We revealed it as an Arabic decree" (13:36–37). The late Meccan suras indeed contain comments that acknowledge the growth of divisions between the followers of previous prophets, which may mean erroneous interpretations of scripture. "He has instituted for you as law what He entrusted to Noah—and with which We inspired you, then entrusted to Abraham, Moses, and Jesus. [We said,] 'Establish law, and don't divide it.' . . . And they were only divided after knowledge came to them, out of jealousy for one another. . . . And those who inherited the Book after them were in anxious doubt" (42:13–14). While the growth of religious divisions may explain some debates, the main problem in the Qur'an circles back to the deep-seated disbelief that opposes all revelation.

In any case, the relation between the Qur'an and previous revelations provided an absorbing problem for consideration. Sura 28, "The Story," presents a stark juxtaposition of the Prophet Muhammad with Moses at the peak of the latter's prophetic experience. This passage occurs in the beginning of the central scriptural section of this late Meccan sura, invoking the sites (the valley of the burning bush, Midian, and Mt. Sinai) most often associated with the revelations that Moses received. This portrait underlines the extent to which Moses plays the part of the archetypal prophet, at the same time emphasizing the parallel between the Book he was given and the revelation afforded to Muhammad. While the Qur'an acknowledges the distance that separates the two figures, this passage nevertheless insists upon their essential parallelism.

And We gave Moses the Book, after We destroyed the prior generations, as proofs for the people, a guidance, and mercy, so that perhaps
they may reflect. But you were not on the western side [of the valley
of the burning bush] when We decreed the commandment to Moses,
nor were you among the witnesses. And We produced generations,
and their lives were prolonged. But you were not dwelling with the
people of Midian, reciting Our verses to them, though We were sending messengers. Nor were you beside Mt. Sinai when We called [to
Moses], but [the revelation you receive] is a mercy from your Lord,
so that you may warn a people to whom We sent no warner before
you; perhaps they may reflect. (28:43–46)

The skeptical Meccans continue to wriggle out of the situation, however,
rejecting both revelations, prompting the Qur'an to issue another challenge, daring them to produce their own scripture.

Otherwise, if a disaster befalls them, because of what they have done
before, then they will say, "Our Lord! Why didn't You send us a messenger, so we could follow your verses, and we would be believers?"
But when the Truth came to them from Us, they said, "Why was he
not given something like what Moses was given?" But didn't they reject what Moses was given before? They said, "These [revelations]
are two kinds of magic that support each other," and they said, "We
reject them both!" Say, "Then bring a Book from God that is a better
guidance than these two, and I will follow it if you are telling the
truth!" (28:47–49)

The shifting and insincere demand of the Meccans for a proper revelation
like that of Moses indicates that, despite their ultimate rejection of it, they
are quite familiar with the concept of a revealed scripture. The Qur'an concludes this particular passage with an optimistic description of the un-
swerving belief of those who previously received the Book (28: 52–54).

The assumption of harmony between different revelations remains
strong throughout the Qur'an. These late Meccan passages allude to the
possibility of debate with members of the monotheistic communities, but
they imply that it is only the unjust or unbelieving among them who will
fail to recognize the continuity between scriptures.

Only dispute with the people of the Book in the best manner, except for those of them who are unjust. And say, "We believe in that

which was revealed to us and was revealed to you, and our God and your God are one, and we submit to Him." In this way We reveal to you the Book, and those to whom We sent the Book believe in it, and some of these [Meccans] believe in it. Only the unbelievers refuse Our signs. And you did not read from any book before, nor did you write it with your right hand; then the speakers of vanity would have doubted. (29:46–48)

Remarkably, the notion of scripture is separated from the acts of studying and writing, which belong to the vocabulary of the skeptics, who object to what they call forged and made-up revelations.

It seems also to have been during the late Meccan period that the issue of the language of the Qur'anic revelation came to the fore. Passages have already been mentioned (13:37, 16:103) in which the Qur'an rejects the notion that revelation comes from a foreign language, asserting that it is presented rather in Arabic. This discussion continues in other verses, which still locate it as part of the repertoire of arguments that the Meccans employ in their unceasing debate. Perhaps the notion of a revelation in a foreign language was considered to carry with it an exotic authority, but this argument quickly falls. "If we had made it a Recitation in foreign language, they would have said, 'Why were its verses not explained? What! Foreign speech, and [we are] Arab?'" (41:44). The Meccans show no interest in canonical sources in other languages like Syriac and Hebrew, and neither does the Qur'an. Its continuity with past scriptures is entirely internal and self-sufficient. "And before it there was the Book of Moses, an example, and a mercy. And this is a Book that verifies, in an Arabic tongue, so it may warn those who are unjust and give good news to the virtuous" (46:12). This confirmatory role of the Qur'an is even vouched for by the jinn, later on in sura 46, when they hear it recited. "And when We turned a group of the jinn toward you, they wished to hear the Recitation. And when they were present for it, they said, 'Hush!' And when it was done, they turned back to their people, warning them. They said, 'Our people! We have heard a Book, which was revealed after Moses, verifying that which was before it, guiding to the Truth, and to a straight road'" (46:29–30). Although it seems like an extraordinary effort to bring in the jinn as witnesses to the confirming power of the Qur'an, this kind of hyperbole may have been seen as an appropriate response to the insensitivity of the Meccans. After all, even the jinn recognize the Qur'an!

In light of all of these debate passages from the middle and later Meccan suras, what conclusions may be drawn about the implied audience of these texts? Despite the constant objections offered to the Qur'anic revelation, it is hard to deny that the Meccans seem to have been well aware of much of the theological apparatus of prophecy and scripture. Their mocking demands for the production of miracles, their sarcastic description of the Qur'an as magic or poetry, and their insistence that angels appear, all testify to a reasonably complete acquaintance with the implications of scripture as a genre for communicating revelation. While there may well have been political and psychological issues behind this resistance to the Qur'an, those do not alter the fact that the terms of debate included the recognition of scripture and prophecy. This recognition existed despite the fact that the Arabs were not considered to have received scripture previously. As the Qur'an puts it, "We have not given them any Books that they study, nor have We sent them any warner before you" (34:44).

Part of the problem in attempting to characterize the religious parameters of this debate is that modern readers are continuously tempted to read back contemporary religious identities and issues into the text of this seventh-century document. To do so is to make the contingent historical outcomes of recent history into the essential implications of the book, which are then considered to be permanently inscribed into the religion of Islam. This kind of teleological approach assumes that current categories naturally unfold from the inevitable latency of the text. Thus, the current notion that there are clearly defined religions known as Christianity, Judaism, and Islam is often accepted at face value, although indeed it remains problematic. Debates about the nature of Jesus have taken place in circles far removed from the authoritative circles of early orthodox Christianity. Consider the example of Mani and the Manichaean tradition, and various other Gnostic groups of late antiquity, many of which engaged in serious debate over themes that others consider to be the rightful property of Christians. There is also the matter of groups that defy easy classification, such as the Jewish Christians, who accepted Jesus of Nazareth as the Messiah but retained Jewish law. And in modern times, serious readers of the New Testament have included non-Christians such as Gandhi. So it will not be easy to apply current religious labels with any confidence, particularly since it is clear that scriptural issues and religious personalities were not copyrighted or under the control of any one particular group, much as they may have wished that were the case. The most that can be said is that there is a considerable amount of evidence for awareness of prophetic and scriptural themes among the Meccan audience that received and responded, often critically, to the Qur'anic revelations announced by Muhammad. It is obvious that the dramatic power of these twinned authorities—the book of divine revelation and the person who bears it to a community—was recognized by the community of Mecca, even as they disputed its authenticity and rejected its moral claims upon them.

4

Medinan Suras

It is widely acknowledged that the Medinan suras present much greater difficulties for the interpreter than the Meccan suras, in good part because a number of them are quite long, making the determination of their structure a more difficult task. In addition, they demonstrate a range of different styles in terms of their openings and the identity of the audience. This has led a number of scholars to argue that there is a lack of coherence in the Medinan suras in comparison with the much tighter structure observed in the Meccan suras.[1] Indeed, it would be fair to say that many readers of the Qur'an have despaired of finding a literary structure in these often long and complicated compositions.

Such a defeatist reaction may not be justified, however, to judge from a number of recent researches on the longer Medinan suras. While these texts do present a greater level of difficulty, literary approaches based on ring composition and intertextual relationships with other writings offer convincing insights and promising new approaches to interpreting these texts. Certainly much remains to be done, but some encouraging results of recent scholarly analysis can be summarized and taken further here, as a useful demonstration of reading techniques and as an example for further investigation.

Before considering these new approaches, however, it would be useful to take a quick look at the Medinan suras as a whole. These are twenty-four suras, which make up about 40 percent of the totality of the Qur'an; six of these (suras 2, 3, 4, 5, 8, and 9) are among the very longest suras of the Qur'an. The composition of the Medinan suras has been described in terms of six principal registers (roughly corresponding to literary genres), which have been identified in the Meccan suras and persisted in the Medinan period, although with significant changes. The new emphases of the Medinan suras may be summarized as follows: (1) communication with the prophetic recipient (that is, Muhammad) is marked not only by the customary address to "you" in the singular but also by passages that specifically address him as "Prophet" or "Messenger," titles that did not occur in the Meccan suras; (2) debate against the pagan Arabs becomes much less visible—and in fact the punishment stories that were so prominent in the Meccan suras have almost disappeared—but there is now extensive debate in the Medinan suras directed toward Jews and Christians, collectively known as the People of the Book; (3) narratives now focus on the Israelites and their prophets, along with Jesus; (4) end-times material is considerably reduced; and the same is true of (5) the affirmation of revelation and (6) description of the signs of God in nature.[2] In addition, one may point to the prominence of legislation and references to external events in the life of the new community and the family life of the Prophet Muhammad as distinctive elements of the Medinan suras. This is one reason why many scholars advocate linking Medinan texts with the biography of the Prophet Muhammad during this period. Despite the problem of circularity that has been previously noted for the Meccan suras, in the Medinan materials more historical contexts can be either teased out of the Qur'anic text itself or taken with greater confidence from biographical sources.

So while there is considerable continuity in some ways between the Meccan and Medinan suras, there are major changes of emphasis as well as new developments, which reflect the very different audience of the new situation. This new audience has been typically viewed as the nucleus of what came to be known as the community of Muslims ("submitters"), though the lines between religious groups in Medina seem not to have been as firm initially as they later became. Fred Donner has recently argued that the language of the Qur'an indicates that the formation of a distinct Islamic religious identity among Muhammad's followers was a process that had not yet taken place in Medina.[3] The Qur'an in the Medinan suras overwhelmingly refers to its primary audience mainly as "you who believe" or "the believers" (*al-mu'minun*, which has nearly 1,000 occurrences). Much less frequently it refers to "the submitters," or as we would say today, Muslims (*al-muslimun*, which occurs about seventy-five times). As religious identity began to crystallize in the late seventh century, post-Qur'anic interpretations referred to believers and submitters as equivalent, so that in effect all of these addressees of the Qur'an were presumed to be members of a separate Muslim community. But there are clear indications within the Qur'an that there was a distinction between those who believed and those who merely submitted, since submission was on the level of external conformity that did not rise to the level of ethical commitment demanded by faith.[4] In investigating this "community of Believers," Donner marshals evidence to argue that "there is no reason to think that the Believers viewed themselves as constituting a new or separate religious confession. . . . Or, to put it the other way around, some of the early Believers were Christians or Jews."[5] This explanation, which draws chiefly on late Medinan suras as well as early Islamic historical sources, would make sense of the passages of the Qur'an that refer to the need for Jews and Christians to follow their own religious law, while the former pagans who had embraced monotheism would follow Qur'anic precepts. Such a conclusion also helps to make sense of passages from the Medinan suras—many of them marked as central principles by their pivotal position in ring compositions—that recognize religious pluralism as an undeniable fact of life. Although the later tradition that is defined as Islam has embraced these origins and made exclusive claims concerning these believers, if these sections of the Qur'an are read without presuppositions, it is easy to see how the community of Muhammad's followers could have been composed of diverse religious communities.

This chapter will present analyses of three major suras of the Medinan period (2, 3, and 5), with occasional attention to a couple of smaller suras from the same time (60 and 110). Although some readers may be particularly interested in sura 4, "The Women," for its focus on gender issues, or in suras 8 and 9 because of their attention to warfare, those questions would be most relevant for a subject-oriented approach to the Qur'an as an authoritative source of law, which is not the main concern of this book, though it is to be hoped that others will address those suras.[6] The Medinan suras that have been chosen for analysis here are particularly appropriate because of the way they demonstrate coherent structures of meaning and intertextual connections with biblical texts, with major implications for understanding the audience addressed in Medina.

Structure and Ring Composition in Sura 2 ("The Cow") and Sura 60 ("The Questioned Woman")

The scale of the problem of the Medinan suras, and the range of different approaches to them, is evident from a consideration of sura 2, "The Cow." Containing a total of 286 verses, sura 2 is half again as long as any other sura in the Qur'an, and many of its verses are lengthy and complex. In my experience teaching an upper-level university course on the Qur'an, I have found that even advanced students regularly find it difficult to make their way through a translation of sura 2 over the course of a week. It is simply too unwieldy for most readers to make sense of by itself (this is, incidentally, a good reason not to start reading the Qur'an on page 1!). What are the clues to its organization? Translations of the Qur'an that simply run the numbered verses together without any break dodge the question. But some translators implicitly mark divisions in the text by offering paragraph breaks to relieve the weight of an uninterrupted block text. Such is the case, for example, with the translation of Abdel Haleem, which adopts the paragraph division, partly as a way to answer the aesthetic expectations of readers of English, though it also aims "to clarify the meaning and structure of thoughts."[7] This particular division seems to call on thematic as well as formal elements in its organization. Following the opening verse, which consists of three isolated letters, A L M, Abdel Haleem divides the text into seventy-four paragraphs, averaging between three and four verses per paragraph. Many of the breaks occur at formal transitions where there is a direct address of an audience, such as "people" or the singular "you," which presumably addresses the Prophet Muhammad. Other principal addressees are the Children of Israel and the Prophet's followers, known as "believers." The repeated formula "remember when" occurs at verses 53, 58, 60, 67, 83, 93, and 122. Yet the suggestion of structure provided even by this articulation into paragraphs does not permit the reader to envisage an overall structure of argument or sequence that would explain why the text is as it is.

Robinson has offered a more ambitious interpretation of sura 2, which, he argues, does indeed have a coherent structure.[8] He begins by suggesting that the title of the sura, "The Cow," is incidental, taken from a mention of the Israelites' sacrifice of a cow in 2:67–71, and that it has no further bearing on the sura. Instead, he points out a crucial phrase, the hopeful description of the community of believers as "a middle people," which appropriately occurs in the mathematical center of the sura, in 2:143. This particular verse refers to the shift of the prayer direction from Jerusalem, toward which the community of believers faced in prayer, to Mecca, which subsequently became the religious center that set Muslims apart from Christians and Jews. According to most biographical accounts, this would have taken place early in the Medinan period, in the second half of 623 CE or the first half of 624 CE. Theodor Nöldeke listed sura 2 as ninety-first of the 114 suras and first of the Medinan suras.

Sura 2 evidently appeared during a time of considerable tension between Muhammad's followers and the other People of the Book in Medina. The sura calls upon Jews and Christians to join with the new dispensation, which is depicted as the true faith of Abraham, and it provides a number of legal rulings affecting religious and social practice, as a way of defining this community. Robinson divides the sura into six sections, as follows:

1. Prologue (2:1–39), on revelation, belief and unbelief, and the story of Adam
2. Criticism of the Children of Israel (2:40–121) for disobeying Moses and falling prey to Satan
3. The Abrahamic Legacy (2:122–52), calling on Jews to recognize that Muhammad was simply presenting Abraham's devotion to God
4. Legislation for the New Nation (2:153–242)
5. The Struggle to Liberate the Ka'ba (2:243–83), preparing the believers to struggle with the pagans of Mecca for control of the sanctuary
6. Epilogue (2:284–86)

This summary is a useful and accurate indication of major themes in the unfolding of sura 2. Yet the reader who follows this analysis is still faced with two sections that are eighty or ninety verses each in length, an amount that is still rather difficult to digest. With all these complex topics to evaluate, it will be hard to state with confidence what should be considered the principal point of the sura. Subsequently, other scholars have attempted to take this analysis further, paying attention to keywords, forms of address, and transitions, resulting in greater refinement of the outline of the sura.[9] The most comprehensive approach to sura 2 has been taken by Raymond Farrin, whose systematic application of the concept of ring structure to this text will be examined below.[10]

While the concept of ring composition has come up repeatedly in discussion of some of the Meccan suras, it may be useful to pause briefly to review some of the scholarship on this approach. It turns out that ring composition is widely found in many literatures of the ancient world, as anthropologist and biblical scholar Mary Douglas has recently shown.[11] As far as biblical texts are concerned, symmetrical composition has been well known since the eighteenth century under the name of chiasmus (literally, "making an X," from the shape of the Greek letter chi or X, indicating a reversal of sequence in the form AB/B′A′). A simple example would be a short biblical passage from Numbers 14:2, the complaint of the wandering Israelites:

> A If only we had died
> B in the land of Egypt.
> B′ Or in this wilderness
> A′ if only we had died.[12]

Important pioneering work on this kind of symmetrical composition in the New Testament was done by Nils Lund in 1942.[13]

Various explanations have been proposed for the popularity of such symmetrical literary forms. One view is that this kind of parallel rhetorical structure was common in preliterate societies as an aid to memory. Another theory looks to ancient "finger rhymes," games in which one would use "the five fingers of one hand to make the statement in five steps, and the fingers of the other hand for elaborating or balancing it, and bringing the two hands together at the end."[14] Some argue that ring structure is related to reading practices associated with the physical form of the scroll, the predominant portable medium for the dissemination of writing before the introduction of the bound book or codex. "When fully unrolled, a scroll creates a symmetrical perception of the overall content and leads to a focus on the content in its center."[15] It has also been pointed out that writers in ancient languages, lacking modern conventions like punctuation and capitalization, had to organize their works internally by framing and concentric parallelism to focus the reader's attention on the core message.[16] Whatever its origin, ring structure is a widespread literary form that is not easily apprehended by modern readers accustomed to linear forms of composition.

Some have thought that ring composition was peculiar to the Middle East, but that assumption seems to be a product of biblical scholars' preoccupation with texts in Hebrew and other ancient Near Eastern languages.

Beyond such biblical examples as the Book of Numbers, ring structure has been found thoroughly displayed in Homer's *Iliad*, in Chinese literature, and in the Avesta of the Iranian prophet Zoroaster. Other examples of ring structure include the great medieval *mathnawi* epics of the Persian poets Nizami and Rumi.[17] An even more complicated geometrical ring-based symmetry has been found in a Sufi romance composed in eastern Hindi in the sixteenth century, Manjhan's *Madhumalati*.[18] What is surprising about ring composition is not only its ubiquity in earlier literatures but also the extent to which modern readers consistently fail to recognize it. As a result, it has been commonplace to dismiss many texts as confusing and disorganized, when in reality they have contained a deeper structure of coherence. As Douglas puts it, "Writings that used to baffle and dismay unprepared readers, when read correctly, turn out to be marvelously controlled and complex compositions. Learning how they were constructed is like a revelation, with something of the excitement of hidden treasure. Now is a good moment for the effort of rereading."[19] This advice is particularly applicable to the study of the Qur'an.

What are the characteristics of ring composition? There are several forms of symmetry that can be found in literary texts. These include parallel construction, when related texts appear in the same sequential order (ABC/A'B'C'), and mirror construction, which extends the pattern of chiasmus (ABC/C'B'A'). In longer compositions, an especially significant form is concentric construction, where textual units are arranged symmetrically, as in mirror composition, around a central element (ABCD/X/D'C'B'A'). In this type of sequence, which involves taking a series of steps and then retracing them, "the effect is to give special emphasis to the pivotal central point."[20] Drawing upon a number of examples of long ring compositions, Douglas has summarized the conventions or rules of this kind of structure as follows:

1. There is often an introductory section or prologue that sets the stage and anticipates the turning point.
2. The composition is split into two halves, one outgoing and the other returning, that circle around the center.
3. Parallel sections match on either side of the composition, although sometimes in surprising ways.
4. Individual sections are marked off by keywords, repeated formulas, alternations, and other devices.

5. The central point is often emphasized by keywords from the prologue, which may also be found in the ending.
6. Longer compositions often feature rings within rings.
7. Closure is achieved in the ending by repeating notable keywords from the prologue and clarifying the overall theme.[21]

Douglas adds that sometimes there will be a double closure, featuring a second ending or "latch." In this case, the first ending refers back to the beginning in basic terms, while the second ending provides a larger explanatory context.[22]

In recent scholarship, the most substantial contribution to Qur'anic studies in terms of ring composition has been the work of Belgian scholar Michel Cuypers, a member of a Catholic religious community who has resided in Iran and now Egypt for many years. He has contributed a long series of studies of ring composition in the Meccan suras, complemented by a major study of sura 5, the title of which he translates as "The Banquet."[23] His remarkable conclusions regarding this late Medinan sura will be analyzed in greater detail later in this chapter, but for the moment it is important to consider his methodology as an extension of the study of ring composition. His efforts build upon the contributions of Roland Meynet to the rhetorical analysis of biblical texts, although these scholars unfortunately refer to this phenomenon as "Semitic rhetoric," despite the recognizably global extent of ring composition.[24]

The specific contribution of Cuypers to the study of written composition of the Qur'an lies in the way that he adroitly brings out the tensions between the turning point of the text and the parallel sections that frame it. He argues that the central portion of any ring composition in the Qur'an has a crucial importance on the level of universal principles or ethical teachings. In contrast, surrounding materials may often reflect temporal contingencies and conflicting situations that have a limited application. This approach does not by any means remove the tension between apparently inconsistent expressions within the same text. In this respect, rhetorical analysis differs from the doctrine of abrogation, which Muslim scholars used to iron out apparently inconsistent statements in the Qur'an. That theological method, often employed by legal scholars searching for a definitive formulation, ostensibly uses chronology to favor later Qur'anic pronouncements over earlier ones (although one wonders how often a chronology has been proposed for abrogation in order to achieve a desired interpretive result). In practice, this method tends to privilege the specific over the general. Thus, as previously mentioned, the so-called sword verse (9:5), which commands warfare against unbelievers, is held by some commentators to abrogate dozens of Qur'anic verses that proclaim patience and forgiveness for the People of the Book. They advocate this generalization of the command of warfare, despite the fact that context makes it clear that it refers only to the pagans of Mecca. These consequences of the doctrine of abrogation, from a literary perspective, are unsatisfactory. A number of apparently significant abrogated verses remain in the text, but their meaning is considered to be irrelevant, according to this standard. From a theological point of view, extensive use of abrogation also gives the unfortunate impression that God changes his mind frequently.

Cuypers's approach has the advantage of accounting for the location of central universal and ethical messages as well as conflicting historical sections in the external frames of ring compositions. In this respect, biblical intertextuality allows him to draw upon comparable examples from earlier texts. He observes that, in Near Eastern texts, "statements are often categorical, with no appeal, while they contradict others or are followed by a rider which relativizes them." This "absence of nuance" is evident in the New Testament, where at one point Jesus calls upon true disciples to hate their family members (Luke 14:26), while a little later on he demands that they honor their fathers and mothers (Luke 18:20). Although these statements seem to contradict each other, they can be put into perspective if one sees that familial love, while positive, is to be put in a secondary position relative to discipleship.[25] What is attractive about this tactic of rhetorical analysis is that it offers a comprehensive explanation of the relationship between complex and contradictory features within the text, instead of dismissing entire verses as irrelevant.

Before returning to consider the ring structure of sura 2, it would be useful to examine a shorter sura from the Medinan period, to consider how this literary approach can offer alternative readings. A good example is sura 60, "The Questioned Woman," which exhibits a number of the typical features of Medinan suras in a relatively compact thirteen verses. This sura, which takes its title from a phrase in the tenth verse, has generally been considered to be late; Nöldeke placed it at the end of the Medinan period, numbering it as 110 out of 114. Predictably, most European scholars have viewed this as a fragmentary and contradictory text. Régis Blachère regards it as being formed of two different sets of revelations mixed together, with some verses relating to the forbidding of relationships with polytheists and others emerging from the Treaty of Hudaybiyya (dating from 628 CE, between Muhammad's followers and the pagans of Mecca), concerning the treatment of pagan and believing women refugees.[26] Richard Bell, for his part, refers to the "broken structure" of the initial verses and then trails off with vague speculative comments on the possible contexts of the remainder of the sura.[27] From these remarks, one would not expect to find anything coherent in this particular sura.

A reading of sura 60 in terms of ring composition yields a very different picture, however. In the translation below, headings have been inserted to divide the text into two symmetrical halves, each composed of three sections, revolving around a central point. The first and last verses (A, A') closely mirror each other, with the same opening address to the believers and the specific directive not to treat God's enemies as allies. This is a political reference to the inappropriateness of alliance with enemy forces during a period of military conflict. Although some translators render the term *awliya'* as "friends" rather than "allies," these framing verses address an unmistakably political context, and the central turning point of the sura specifically envisages the possibility of personal relationships with enemies.[28] On the next level, the sura begins (B) by stating that it is impossible to maintain family relationships with relatives who are unbelievers. The matching section (B') deals with specific applications of that principle, involving believing women who seek refuge with the Medinan polity, including compensation to their former husbands, and the form of the oath of allegiance they should make to the Prophet. At the third level, the sura invokes the example of Abraham and his followers, who had to break from idolatrous family members (C). The repeated use here of the phrase "a beautiful model" recalls the application of the same words to Muhammad in another Medinan sura (33:21), where it is stressed that obedience to Muhammad is the same as loyalty to all the other prophets. The matching section (C') states that conditions of war make it impossible to have friendly or just relations with enemies. Finally, and most importantly, 60:7 emerges as the clear center of this composition (D), presenting an overarching principle that God can make it possible for affection to occur between those who are enemies.

A. Call to believers not to be allies with God's enemies
(1) You who believe! Do not choose My enemy and your enemy as allies

whom you treat with affection, when they have rejected the truth that
came to them, expelling the messenger and you because you believe in
God, your Lord. If you have gone forth in struggle (*jihad*) on my path,
seeking my satisfaction, do you secretly give them affection, when I know
best what you have hidden and what you have revealed? Whichever of
you has done this has deviated beyond the path.

   B. *Renouncing idolatrous relatives*
   (2) If they gain mastery over you, they will be enemies for you, and
   they will stretch out to you their hands and tongues evilly, longing for
   you to be unbelievers.
   (3) Your blood ties and children will do you no good on the day of
   resurrection. He will decide between you, for God is seeing what
   you do.
      C. *Following the model of Abraham*
      (4) There was a beautiful model for you in Abraham and those who
      were with him, when they said, "We are not responsible for you and
      that which you worship which is other than God. We have rejected
      you! Enmity and hatred has appeared between you and us forever,
      until you believe in God alone, except for what Abraham said to
      his father: 'I ask forgiveness for you, but I have nothing from God
      for you.' Our Lord! In You is our trust, towards You we return, and
      towards You is the journey.
      (5) "Our Lord! Don't make for us a temptation from those who
      disbelieve, and forgive us, our Lord! You are the glorious, the wise."
      (6) Indeed there was a beautiful model for you in them, for one who
      hopes for God and the Last Day.
         D. *Possibility of affection for enemies*
         (7) It may be that God will place affection between you and
         those among them who are your enemies; for God is the mighty
         one, and God is forgiving, merciful.
   C'. *Religious warfare prevents good relationships*
   (8) God does not forbid that you should be kind or just to those
   who have not fought you over divine service (*din*), and who did not
   expel you from your houses; for God loves those who are just.
   (9) God only forbids that you should make allies of those who fight
   you over divine service, and expel you from their homes, and help
   to exile you. Those who make allies of them are indeed the unjust.
B'. *Reclaiming refugee women*

(10) You who believe! When the believing women come to you as refugees, question them. God knows best about their faith. If you know they are believers, don't send them back to the unbelievers. They are not lawful for the unbelievers, nor are the unbelievers lawful for them, but compensate the unbelievers. And it is no sin for you to marry the women whom you have given their dowries. But don't hold on to ties with unbelieving women, and ask for compensation, and let the unbelievers ask for compensation. That is the judgment of God, who judges between you. For God is knowing, wise.

(11) And if any of your wives have departed you for the unbelievers, and you have seized their goods, then compensate accordingly those whose wives have gone, and be conscious of God, in whom you have faith.

(12) Prophet! When the believing women come to you, swearing the oath to you that they will not ascribe partners to God, nor steal, nor commit adultery, nor kill their children, nor produce any slander that they had made up by themselves, nor disobey you in anything that is right—then take their oath, and ask God for their forgiveness; God is forgiving, merciful.

A'. *Call to believers not to be allies of God's enemies*

(13) You who believe! Do not form an alliance with a people with whom God is angry, who have despaired of the afterlife as the unbelievers despair of the inhabitants of the grave.

From this review of sura 60, two conclusions emerge. First, it is not an incoherent combination of unrelated material—rather, it hangs together neatly once the ring composition is detected. One may even see an internal ring in 60:4–6, where the repeated references to the "beautiful model" frame a central prayer not to be tempted by those family members who are unbelievers. Second, despite the prevalence of conditions of war and distrust, to the extent of severing family relations, this sura preserves at its heart a sublime hope that God may make it possible for affection to exist between enemies. The structural centrality of that general principle makes it the master theme of this sura, to which the surrounding observations are subordinate. This kind of structural reading provides a contextual insight into the relationship between general ethical principles and contingent historic situations in the Qur'an.

To return to the ring composition of sura 2, Raymond Farrin proposes a reading that distinguishes two halves composed of four sections each, organized around a central point section (ABCD/E/D'C'B'A'), so that there are nine sections in all. He observes that "All sections but the introduction, middle, and conclusion—A, E, and A'—begin with formulas of address (i.e., 'O you people,' 'O Children of Israel,' or 'O you who believe'); and that all sections end with clinching statements, either relating to faith, disbelief, their respective consequences, or to God's capacity to punish. All are structurally discrete within the comprehensive ring, and indeed all sections, save the introduction which contains two small rings, constitute whole rings themselves." Farrin has organized its structure and summarized its consequent themes as follows:[29]

A. 1–20. Faith vs. unbelief
  B. 21–39. God's creation; His encompassing knowledge (here regarding Adam and Eve's sins)
    C. 40–103. Moses delivers law to Children of Israel
      D. 104–41. Abraham was tested, the Ka'ba is built by Abraham and Ishmael; responses to People of the Book
        E. 142–52. The Ka'ba is the new qibla; this is a test of faith; compete in doing good
      D'. 153–77. Muslims will be tested; the Ka'ba and Meccan pilgrimage sites; responses to polytheists
    C'. 178–253. Prophet delivers law to Muslims
  B'. 254–84. God's creation; His encompassing knowledge (regarding charity and financial dealings)
A'. 285–86. Faith vs. unbelief

All of the details of Farrin's analysis cannot be repeated here in full, but it may be observed that he makes a good case for a concentric mirror composition on the basis of the formal literary characteristics of sura 2, including the presence of internal rings and two prominent latches (see appendix B for further details). One of the interesting results of his argument is that the reference to the cow sacrifice (2:67–71), which provides the title for this sura, turns out to be central for the ring of the third section (C), so it is not so arbitrary a name after all.

What does the establishment of the ring structure tell us about the significance of sura 2? For the moment, only a brief observation will suffice. In its historical context, it is clear that this lengthy text addresses the situation of the Muslim community a couple of years into the Medinan period, and that it reflects tensions with the existing monotheistic communities that did not fully welcome the prophetic message of Muhammad. Sura 2 undertakes a lengthy critique of the Jews, in much the same tone and manner as one sees in New Testament writings, but it also rejects the Christians for their doctrine of incarnation, which is seen as a blatant transgression of the divine unity. The change of direction from Jerusalem to Mecca underscores the increasing differentiation of the proto-Muslim community from Jews and Christians, even as it is couched in terms of returning to the primordial faith of Abraham. There is also an important section (2:243–53, the latch in section C′) preparing Muhammad's community for military attack on the sanctuary of Mecca, to take control of it from its pagan masters.

Amid all these conflictive reports, Farrin agrees with Robinson that a key point in sura 2 is the identification of Muhammad's followers in 2:143 as "a middle nation" (or perhaps "a central community" or "people") standing "between the formalism of Judaism . . . and the doctrinal extravagance of Christianity. Islam is positioned as the golden mean."[30] Here is how the Qur'an addresses the shift in prayer direction from Jerusalem to Mecca in this crucial section (2:142–44):

> Fools among the people will say, "What turned them from the prayer direction that was formerly theirs?" Say, "The East and the West belong to God, who guides whom He wishes to a right path."
>
> Thus We made you a central community, so that you may be witnesses to the people, and so that the messenger may be a witness to you. We only made the prayer direction that was formerly yours so that We should know those of you who follow the messenger from those who turn upon their heels. It was a problem except for those whom God guided. God was not about to make your (earlier) faith be in vain, for God is kind and merciful to the people.
>
> We may see your face upturned to heaven;[31] then let Us turn you to a prayer direction you will be satisfied with. So turn your face toward the sacred place of worship [i.e., Mecca]. And wherever you all are, turn your faces towards it. Those who have been given the Book will know that this is the truth from their Lord, and God is not unaware of what they do.

This shift of prayer direction is no doubt a momentous event. But structural analysis indicates that the true pivot of the central section (E) lies in the following two verses: "The Truth is from your Lord, so don't be among the doubtful. And each one has a direction towards which he turns, so strive to be first in good works. Wherever you are, God brings you together; God is powerful over everything" (2:147–48). The verses indicating the change of prayer direction (2:143–44) certainly emphasize the divine authority of truth indicated by the change in prayer direction. But the central verses (2:147–48) in effect recognize both the reality of religious diversity ("each one has a direction towards which he turns") and the emptiness of religious claims that are not put into ethical practice. Sura 2 is not alone in containing such universal messages in the rhetorically central position, as will be seen from an examination of sura 5. The surrounding themes in this sura will need to be considered in the light of this central precept.

At this point, given the striking conclusions that emerge from this approach, it may be asked why patterns such as ring structure do not seem to play a major role in current Muslim interpretation of the Qur'an. Interest in the structural composition of the Qur'an can be found in traditional scholarship on the Qur'an and Arabic literature, although it cannot be said to be a major emphasis.[32] So if commentators paid relatively infrequent attention to symmetrical composition in the Qur'an, might this not be another case of the willful application of arbitrary theories by arrogant outsiders? It is indeed legitimate to raise this question, for if ring structure was not apparent to early readers, how is it possible that it is only recognized today? As a matter of fact, the same question has been raised about the application of ring structure to Homer's *Iliad* and the Hebrew Bible, among other early texts. In response, scholars have pointed out that early critics such as Cicero and other Roman commentators were quite aware of the inverted parallelism of the *Iliad*, but this awareness seems to have been gradually lost, only to be rediscovered in relatively recent times.[33] Likewise, while chiasmus and other forms of symmetrical composition in the Bible have only been recognized since the eighteenth century, progress in this area has led one scholar to assert that "Biblical works must be read chiastically [that is, in terms of symmetrical composition] if they are to reveal the primary message the author wanted to convey."[34]

Moreover, ring composition was remarkably widespread throughout the literatures of the Semitic languages of the ancient Near East, which are the historical predecessors of Arabic.[35] Thus there is not only comparative but also historical evidence for considering symmetrical composition as a feature of the most prominent of early Arabic texts, the Qur'an. It is especially important to take this historical evidence into account, in light of the tendency of modern critics to announce that Arabic poetry (and by extension, Persian, Turkish, and Urdu poetry) was basically atomistic, with completely independent lines combined together without any overall structural coherence—"Orient pearls at random strung," in the memorable phrase of Sir William Jones, describing the Persian poetry of Hafiz. Could that be one more instance of modern readers failing to recognize literary structure and contenting themselves with denouncing the text as formless and incoherent? Indeed, in a major new examination of literary structure of classical Arabic poetry, Raymond Farrin has proposed that the major structural pattern of Arabic poetry is most likely that of ring composition, which provides important keys to interpreting its meaning.[36] Against the observation that early Arabic literary critics were concerned only with the individual line of poetry and not the whole, Farrin argues that premodern Arabic literary criticism was primarily focused on moral judgment and selection of exemplars for edification or condemnation; in contrast, modern literary criticism since Coleridge has had a quite different focus on how the component parts of the poem harmonize to make a whole. If one turns away from those early critics to consider the poetry itself, as Aristotle does in his *Poetics*, it shows "a high degree of structural and thematic unity."[37]

Ring composition was thus a widespread manner of composing texts, so from this perspective it should not be surprising to find it in the Qur'an.[38] Like early Arabic literary criticism, specialized commentaries on the Qur'an were primarily addressed to extracting particular legal and theological doctrines from the text rather than engaging with it from the perspective of literary coherence. This inevitably meant a focus on line-by-line interpretation of the text and a search for authoritative rulings rather than a concern with its overall structure. The later application of aesthetic categories to the Qur'an was mainly concerned with arguing its inimitability (*i'jaz*) as a manifestation of divine creativity, which was another form of theological interpretation. So the comparative lack of attention to overall literary structure in Qur'an commentaries is quite understandable as a function of the interpretive aims of those commentaries, which actually parallel the normative interests of Arabic literary criticism.

Thus the modern approach to Qur'anic literary structure in terms of ring structure can be justified on a number of comparative and historical grounds, and its apparent novelty is really a function of changing sensibilities around the world. Like it or not, the culture of modernity has increasingly taken on new forms of aesthetic perception that make it hard for contemporary readers to recognize the kind of cultural production typical of Homer, the Bible, and the Qur'an. The fact that a new interpretive tool like ring structure makes a great deal of sense is reason enough to consider it seriously. Current research even indicates the possibility that the apparently arbitrary organization of the suras into the current canonical order may be based upon a comprehensive symmetrical structure that makes the early Meccan suras 50–56 the central section of the entire Qur'an.[39] Surely it is worth exploring such promising literary approaches, which may clarify problems that up to now have eluded solution.

Intertextuality and Religious Identity in Sura 3 ("The Family of 'Imran")

Turning to the next major sura of the Medinan period, sura 3, "The Family of 'Imran," it is immediately evident that this sura is closely related to sura 2, which it follows chronologically. It is number 97 in Nöldeke's sequence, placing it squarely in the middle of the early Medinan period. Consisting of 200 verses, this sura includes a complex range of topics, being equally focused on previous prophets (particularly Abraham and Jesus) and on the pressure faced by the community of believers in Medina. Historically, sura 3 is located not only after the successful battle of Badr in 624 CE, in which the followers of Muhammad routed the Meccans (as mentioned in 3:13), but also after the devastating defeat of the Muslims at Uhud in 625 CE (3:121–23). Robinson argues that sura 3 "constitutes a single multi-faceted response to the threat of apostasy that menaced the Muslim community after the debacle at Uhud."[40] This sura was composed, then, at a precarious moment for Muhammad and his followers, and its composition clearly reflects serious tensions and debates with both Jewish and Christian interlocutors, who seem to have challenged Muhammad's claims to prophetic authority.

Scholars are divided in their understanding of the precise structure of this sura, but many would agree with Angelika Neuwirth that it "does not seem to be a unity, but consists instead of diverse layers belonging to different periods of origin."[41] In her view, the sura can be divided into several major sections:[42]

Prologue on scriptures and prophets (3:1–3)
Commentary on female creativity, scriptural interpretation, and

divine and prophetic authority, in the context of Medina's political
crisis (3:4-32) — this is a later insertion
Narratives of Mary and Jesus (3:33-62)
Reflections on the legacy of Abraham (3:63-99)
Encouragement of the believers after defeat (3:100-200)

While this outline suggests different layers of composition, this does not
necessarily mean that the sura lacks overall unity. Although the narrative
portion of the introductory section may have been formulated prior to the
battle of Uhud, the later commentary could have been successfully integrated into the earlier sections of the sura, providing an immediate political reflection on the critical situation of Muhammad and his followers in
the early Medinan years.

More work needs to be done to establish the rhetorical structure of
sura 3, but there is an indication of an overall compositional unity in its
opening and closing prayers. Both of these prayers are introduced by the
formula "Our Lord," repeated twice at the beginning and four times at
the end. The opening prayer seeks guidance and mercy from the God who
will gather all humanity together at Judgment Day (3:8-9), setting up a
context of apocalypse and end-times. The closing prayer seeks salvation
from the fire of hell, forgiveness of sins, and fulfillment of promises made
by the prophets (3:191-94). This frame, which would belong to the final
stage of composition, suggests, on the one hand, a severe intensification of
the struggle of Muhammad's community, explicitly treating the triumphal
battle of Badr as an apocalyptic sign: "There was a sign for you in the two
bands that met, one band fighting in the path of God, and another unbelieving. . . . In that is an admonition for those with vision" (3:13). The
apocalyptic overtone is evident from the carefully balanced "Say" passages
on hell and paradise (3:12, 3:15) arranged on either side of the mention of
the battle. On the other hand, just as in sura 2, this expression of conflict
is lightened by a proclamation of universal reward and punishment in the
final lines of sura 3, where God also rewards those People of the Book who
are believers, even as the believers are encouraged to be patient and be
saved (3:199-200). This outer layer provides another interpretive perspective on the narrative history of the prophets. Just as sura 2 at its core acknowledged the fact of religious pluralism in the midst of conflict, sura 3
will raise the question of multiple interpretations of scripture at the same
time that it fiercely condemns the deliberate misuse of revelations.

The oldest portion of sura 3 may well have been the narrative of Mary and Jesus. The integrity of this section jumps out at the reader, especially if it is compared with the structure of sura 12, "Joseph." Once the early non-narrative section of sura 3 (3:4–32) is removed, the story of Mary and Jesus has a structure virtually identical to the story of Joseph. This similarity can hardly be accidental. From this comparison of the two suras, it is possible to go further and to propose that the following tripartite structure was the original nucleus of sura 3, as follows:[43]

    I. Prologue on scriptures and prophets (1–3, 33–34)
    II. Narratives of Mary and Jesus (35–43, 45–57)
    III. Conclusion, affirmation of revelation (44, 58–62)

There are verbal echoes of the Joseph story in sura 3 as well. Both narratives are summarized by the same concluding formula of mystery, pointing out that the story is a revelation, not the product of the messenger's experience: "That belongs to the tidings of the hidden, with which We have inspired you, though you were not with them . . ." (3:44, 12:102). A similar formula had been used as a tale ending in another late Meccan sura that detailed the story of Noah (11:49). The story of Mary and Jesus ends emphatically with the assertion, "This is indeed the true story" (3:62). That mention of the word "story" (*qasas*) would surely have reminded the Qur'an's audience of the concluding verse on Joseph: "In their story, there is an admonition for those who understand" (12:111). With all these signals, listeners would have been aware that sura 3 presents an important story; its divergence from the earlier account of Mary and Jesus in Meccan texts can be considered in terms of its direct contemporary significance in the Medinan period. Accordingly, articulating the structure of sura 3 begins with this story, in relation to the commentary section that is inserted in the midst of it.

In the prologue to the narrative of Mary and Jesus, sura 3 emphatically juxtaposes the revelation entrusted to Muhammad with the Torah and the Gospel: "He revealed to you the scripture with truth, confirming that which preceded it, and He revealed the Torah and the Gospel" (3:3). This explicit reference to earlier scriptures would alert readers both to the earlier writings and to their decisive reinterpretation that would emerge in the Qur'an; confirmation or fulfillment of previous scriptures generally means rewriting them. The last verses of the prologue to the narrative then proceed to invoke four key prophetic figures presented as a single genealogy. "God elected Adam, Noah, the family of Abraham, and the family of 'Imran over all humanity, descendants of one another—and God is hearing, knowing" (3:33–34). This selection of the prophetic elite of humanity marks four separate eras: the creation, the flood, monotheistic prophecy, and Mary and Jesus. At the same time, these verses distinguish two prophetic families—that of Abraham on the one hand and that of the holy family of Mary and Jesus on the other. The latter are identified as the family of 'Imran (biblical Amram, equivalent here to Mary's father Joachim), the name given in the Qur'an to the father of Mary. All this signals a preoccupation with the Jewish model of prophet (*nabi*), which emerges in the Medinan period as the more dominant term in relation to the generic notion of messenger (*rasul*) found in Meccan suras. Unlike the genealogy provided for Jesus in the Gospel of Matthew, David has no place here, since in the Qur'an there is no question of the Messiah reviving the Israelite monarchy.[44]

If the verses that intervene in the midst of the prologue to the narrative (3:4–32) were a later addition, it would make sense to see them as a commentary on the basic narrative that enhances its significance, particularly with reference to the political situation in Medina. Indeed, that commentary section begins with an amplification of the opening lines on the revealed scriptures, cautioning that the unbelievers will face a heavy punishment, for nothing is hidden from God (3:4–5). These statements are familiar, but new topics are introduced in 3:6–7 that will dramatically shift the way that both prophecy and scripture are understood. In this crucial passage, the Qur'an introduces a remarkable stress on gender in the form of female creativity, which will link up with the characters of Mary and her mother. As Neuwirth points out, "The story's predominantly 'female discourse,' centered around female purity and the sacredness of procreation, spills over into the introductory section of the sura which is primarily concerned with patriarchal prophetic discourse, centered around revelation."[45] The discussion of clear and ambiguous verses of the Qur'an in 3:7 has certainly drawn much attention from commentators, but its relationship with the gendered language that begins in 3:6 has generally been ignored. Here are the verses in question:

> It is He who has formed you in wombs, as He wishes; there is no God but He, the glorious, the wise. (3:6)
>
> It is He who revealed to you the scripture, part of which is definite verses; these are the mother of the book. Other (verses) are ambiguous. Those with deviation in their hearts are the ones who follow the

ambiguous part of it, desiring seduction and desiring its interpretation. But none knows its interpretation except God. And those who are rooted in knowledge say, "We believe in it, all is from our Lord." But only those who understand take notice. (3:7)

The parallelism of these two verses is evident from the repeated opening phrase ("It is He who . . .") that introduces God, first as creator and then as revealer of scripture. The gendered language that begins with the mention of "wombs" continues with the feminine invocation of scripture as "mother of the book," a phrase that might recall the divine feminine wisdom portrayed in parabiblical texts like the Wisdom of Solomon. The repeated reference to "desire" (*ibtigha'*) recalls the linguistically related term "whore" (*baghi*), an insult that was aimed at the unmarried mother Mary in 19:28. This vocabulary will also reverberate in the reproach of those monotheists who are opposed to each other "out of jealousy (*baghyan*) among themselves" (3:19). Likewise, the term seduction or temptation (*fitna*) commonly has negative gender connotations in Arabic.

Why would this gendered language be employed in verses relating to the interpretation of scripture? One solution is to connect this surprising symbolism with the nonpatriarchal narrative centering around Mary, which will be crucial for establishing a lineage of prophecy that can challenge the Israelite claim to be the exclusive heir of Abraham. At the same time, this argument can legitimately draw upon gendered language regarding religious loyalty (the believers adhere to the mother text rather than seductive interpretations of ambiguous verses). Likewise, authorized reading practices are associated with the Hebrew phrase for readings that have "a mother in scripture itself," that is to say, a legitimate interpretation.[46] This language in the Qur'an may have developed in discussion with Jewish circles in Medina, in which debaters raised the topic of multiple meanings (ambiguous verses) in scriptural texts, perhaps in a combative fashion. It has also been suggested that there is a parallel to the clear/ambiguous text problem in the issue of an unborn child, whose gender is not yet clear but remains ambiguous—this becomes relevant to Mary, who before she was born was consecrated to the temple, and later lived there, like a male child (3:36–37). The birth of Jesus to an unwed virgin is also an ambiguous affair. In this way, it may be said that Christology, a highly controversial topic in the Qur'an, furnishes a context for the discussion of multiple interpretations of the sacred text.[47]

However unwelcome the subtle arguments of Jewish scripture interpreters may have been, their effect upon the Qur'an in 3:7 is dramatic. Previously, the hallmark of Qur'anic self-description has been clarity, as in 12:1, where it is said, "These are the signs of the clear revelation"; there are numerous similar examples to be found in the Meccan suras. Now, however, it appears that there are two different kinds of verses in scripture, the definite (*muhkam*) and the ambiguous (*mutashabih*). The latter were sometimes identified with the mysterious isolated letters at the beginning of certain suras, which have indeed been resistant to analysis. Although the Qur'an here identifies the definite verses with the legitimate, the "mother of the book," and it casts the interpretation (*ta'wil*) of the ambiguous verses in a suspicious light, this formulation inevitably lays out the possibility of multiple meanings, some of which are only accessible to God.

Careful readers of 3:7 could not have failed to notice the implicit hierarchies of knowledge among human interpreters, signaled by phrases like "those who are rooted in knowledge" and "those who understand," which point to the existence of people with superior knowledge and insight in scriptural matters. It was also apparent that the text of 3:7 could be read grammatically in more than one way. The key section on interpretation is usually read in this fashion: "But none knows its interpretation except God. And those who are rooted in knowledge say, 'We believe in it, all is from our Lord.'" Since there is no modern punctuation in the Qur'anic text, however, it is also possible to read it in a quite different sense: "But none knows its interpretation except God *and* those who are rooted in knowledge. They say, 'We believe in it, all is from our Lord.'" According to this reading, which was accepted by early commentators such as Mujahid ibn Jabr (d. 722), there is in fact a class of individuals who know the interpretation of the ambiguous verses.[48] Understood in this sense, 3:7 became the justification for esoteric and allegorical interpretation in philosophical, Sufi, and Shi'i circles.[49] Passages immediately following in sura 3 appear to acknowledge a deeper level of interpretation, as key points are recognized by those who have vision (3:13) or attested by those who have knowledge (3:18).

After this startling juxtaposition of gender with scriptural interpretation, the remainder of this commentary section may be understood as outlining a series of dialectical oppositions. These conflicts include primarily the contrast between selfish acquisition of wealth and spending one's wealth and life for God, as well as the opposition between surrender to God's revelation and revolt against the prophets by misusing scripture. The section begins with the prayer addressed to God ("Our Lord," 3:8–9), which functions as the opening half of the frame for the entire sura, as mentioned above. The structure of the section is also marked by prominent "Say" verses addressed to the messenger (marked below in bold). It may be outlined as two small ring compositions that in turn revolve around a central pivot, which can be summarized as follows:

Ring one:
8–17 Opening prayer, double portrait of heaven and hell, sign of Badr
   18–19.5 Testimony to God's unity and surrender to Him as service
19.5–25 Punishment of unbelieving People of the Book
    Pivot:
    26–27 **Say,** praise of God's omnipotence ("Magnificat")
Ring two:
28 Believers should not take unbelievers as allies over believers
   29–30 **Say,** God knows what is in your hearts, which will be revealed on that day
   31 **Say,** love God and follow me, God will love you and forgive you
   32 **Say,** obey God and the messenger
32.5 "If they turn away, God does not love the unbelievers."

As already seen in the discussion of ring structure in sura 2, each of the small rings in this commentary section contains a central point of universal appeal that is hedged by external remarks on conflict and apocalyptic. In addition, the two rings themselves are centered on an even more important pivot that will be discussed below, what may be called the Magnificat, or praise of God's omnipotence.

Furthermore, the first section following the opening prayer (3:8–17) falls into a symmetry that is sequential rather than concentric, which is also marked by "Say" verses in this summary:

8–9 Our Lord (twice), guide us with mercy, gatherer of humanity
   10–11 Riches and progeny will not suffice, as the people of Pharaoh found
    12 **Say,** you will go to hell
13 Apocalyptic sign of the battle of Badr, an admonition for those with vision

14 People love worldly comforts and wealth
 15–17 **Say,** paradise is better, as the believers and spenders
 recognize, seeking forgiveness

This is an intricate structure, in which a single section (3:8–17) has a sequential symmetry, opens a small ring composition, and frames the sura as a whole. Both the external frames and the central points of these compositions call for further explanation.

At this point, it is appropriate to return briefly to the topic of punishment stories, which were a dominant element in narratives associated with the middle and late Meccan suras. In these tales, the standard narrative of prophecy was recounted, in which messengers are rejected by their people, who then suffer divine punishment. It is at first sight surprising that these punishment stories nearly disappear from the Medinan suras. At most, these stories are evoked in Medinan suras only by a brief line or two (for example, 3:10–11, where Pharaoh and his people are mentioned), or else their spirit is recalled by the injunction to "travel in the land and see how was the ending of the disbelievers" (3:137), where the punishment is implicit and not described. Listeners already familiar with the Meccan suras would easily have understood the reference to destroyed cities of iniquity.

Scholars have put forward various interpretations of the significance and psychological implications of these punishment stories.[50] On the one hand, it is assumed that these tales were meant to frighten the unbelieving pagans of Mecca into accepting revelation. On the other hand, the Qur'an explicitly announces that its intention is to encourage its audience: "And all that We tell you of reports of the prophets We do to make your heart firm. Through this the Truth comes to you, and an admonition, and a Reminder for the believers" (11:120). There is a problem with the view that punishment stories were intended to terrify, however. The Meccan suras repeatedly indicate that most people rejected the warnings of the Prophet, and most of them remained unbelievers. It is hard to imagine that Meccan suras continued to place so much emphasis on the punishment of unbelieving peoples as a scare tactic, if it produced no results. But punishment stories unquestionably served as encouragement and consolation to the believers, by a dramatic portrayal of the downfall of their opponents in a promised future scenario.

In Medina, however, the punishment story has been replaced by accounts of actual battles, which bear apocalyptic significance. Thus the successful battle of Badr now takes the place of punishment stories as an admonition for those who have vision (3:13). And at the unsuccessful battle of Uhud, the Qur'an discusses the promise made of thousands of angels sent down to assist the believers (3:124–25). The struggle for survival faced by the Medinan believers was intensified by the presence of people of doubtful loyalty; these included insincere supposed followers of Muhammad, known as hypocrites, as well as People of the Book, some of whom either openly or secretly rejected the authority of Muhammad. Under these circumstances, the Qur'an urgently focused on the need for complete devotion to God and his revelation and total commitment to the prophet Muhammad, even at the cost of one's possessions and one's life. It is under these circumstances that the near-disappearance of the punishment stories makes sense, since a more immediate form of encouragement was needed. Nonetheless, the encouraging sign of a successful battle is placed in the context of the ultimate reward and punishment, in parallel "Say" verses:

> Say to those who reject, "You shall be defeated and assembled in hell, an evil resting place!" (3:12)
>
> Say, "Shall I tell you of something better than that? For those who are pious, there are gardens with their Lord, beneath which flow rivers, where they are forever; and pure spouses, and satisfaction from God. And God is seeing His servants, (3:15)
>
> "Those who say, 'Our Lord, we believe, so forgive us our sins, and protect us from the punishment of the fire,' (3:16)
>
> "The patient, the truthful, the devoted, the givers, who seek forgiveness in the early mornings!" (3:17)

Giving and spending one's life and wealth is on par with the other virtues of those destined for paradise.

The central point of this first small ring composition is an important statement of the fundamental doctrine of divine unity, linked with the key term, "submitting" (*islam*), that recognizes that divine authority: "God, the angels, and those who have knowledge testify that, 'He! There is no God but He' — He is standing in justice; there is no God but He, the glorious, the wise. Devotion (*din*), with God, is submitting (*islam*)" (3:18–19). It is crucial to recognize the way in which the Qur'an deliberately employs these terms and how great a distance separates them from their modern usages. Unlike many modern translators, I do not translate the last phrase as "Religion, with God, is Islam." In the Qur'an, the term "submitting" — *islam* — is not yet used as the name of one "religion" as opposed to others, nor can the modern concept of religion be found in the Arabic word *din*, despite its common use today as a synonym for religion. Those transformations of ideological identification would only be carried out during the last two centuries, when the European concept of "religion" was successfully applied around the world in the context of colonial conquests. In the process, new concepts of identity took shape, including a concept of Islam that was self-consciously opposed to colonial domination.[51] Leaving that modern notion aside, in the immediately following verse, an idiom using a verbal form of the same word (*aslama*) reveals a much more personal and less abstract character of "submitting one's face" or "devoting oneself completely," "surrendering": "And if they argue, say: 'I have submitted (*aslamtu*) my face to God'" (3:20).[52] This phrase is equivalent to saying, "I have given my life to God," as indicated by parallel passages from early Islamic literature.[53] Likewise, *din* in Arabic conveys a primary sense of devotion, obedience, service, debt, and duty, with a secondary meaning of accepted custom or usage; in Islamic contexts, it increasingly means a devoted life contrasted with the life of this world (*dunya*).[54] In the context of this small ring composition, the central point bears witness to committed monotheism and devotion to God. Its contrasting external frames indicate the conditions of conflict that are in tension with that central creed.

The closing frame portion of the first ring composition (3:19.5–25) mirrors the opening depiction of the crisis of Badr; it illustrates the debate with the People of the Book in Medina, who are accused of rejecting the prophet who has surrendered to God (3:20); and they both reject God's revelations and kill his messengers (3:21). In this respect, the Qur'an echoes New Testament rhetoric about the killing of prophets: "O Jerusalem, Jerusalem, you who kill the prophets and stone those sent to you!" (Matthew 23:37).[55] From this account of the situation of Medina after the battle of Uhud, it appears that some Jews debated the Qur'anic revelations and rejected them, holding themselves exempt from criticism and indeed from eternal punishment, presumably because of their physical descent from the Prophet Abraham (3:23–24). In this context, the opposite of submitting is turning away (verbal form *tawalla*) from God:

> And say to those who have been given the Book, and to the unlettered, "Have you submitted?" If they surrender, then they are guided, but if they turn away, it is only your duty to announce it. (3:20)

Have you seen those who have been given a portion of the Book, calling on the Book so it may judge between them, and then a group of them turns away in aversion? (3:23)

Submitting and turning away are decisive actions. Later in the sura, it becomes more explicit that these acts define the boundary between those who accept Muhammad's authority and those who reject it.

In the central turning point of the entire commentary section (3:26–27), the Qur'an calls upon Muhammad to recite a prayer that begins as follows: "Say, 'God, Master of the kingdom, You give kingship to whom You wish, and You take away kingship from whom You wish. You empower whom You wish, and You humble whom You wish. In your hand is the good, and you have power over everything'" (3:26). This prayer has been described as "shorthand" for, or even a direct quotation of, the famous prayer of Mary in Luke 1:46–55, the song or canticle known in the Catholic tradition (from its Latin opening) as the Magnificat.[56] Indeed, the Qur'anic prayer comes very close to the core verses of Mary's prayer of praise in the New Testament, pronounced when she met Zachariah's wife Elizabeth: "He has performed mighty deeds with his arm; he has scattered those who are proud in their inmost thoughts. He has brought down rulers from their thrones but has lifted up the humble. He has filled the hungry with good things but has sent the rich away empty" (Luke 1:51–53). Noticeably absent from the Qur'an is the particularistic conclusion of Mary's prayer, asking God to be merciful "to Abraham and his descendants forever, even as he said to our fathers" (Luke 1:55). Instead, it segues (3:27) into praise of God's creative power over nature and the resurrection before returning to his sustenance of those whom he chooses.

The commentary section closes with a second ring composition (3:28–32) that also contrasts an external frame of conflict with a central message of exhortation aimed at the wavering Medinan population. The two external frames warn the believers against taking as allies (*awliya'*) those who turn away (*tawallu*), using two opposite senses of the same verbal root W-L-Y as verbal echoes that tie this ring together.

The believers should not take the unbelievers as allies (*awliya'*) instead of believers—one who does that does not belong to God in anything—except when you protect yourselves from them in fear. God warns you to be wary of Him, for the journey is to God. (3:28)

> But if they turn away (*tawallu*) — God does not love the unbelievers. (3:32.5)

The center of this second small ring composition (3:29–32) consists of a series of four verses with three "Say" commands addressed to Muhammad, calling on all listeners to commit themselves sincerely to God.

> Say, "Whether you hide what is in your hearts or display it, God knows, and He knows what is in the heavens and the earth, for God is powerful over all things. (3:29)
> "On the day when every soul finds itself summoned before the good that it has done and the evil that it has done, it will wish there was a great distance between it and them. God warns you to be wary of Him, and God is kind to his worshipers." (3:30)
> Say, "If you love God, then follow me; God will love you and forgive you your sins, for God is forgiving, merciful." (3:31)
> Say, "Obey God and the messenger." (3:32)

This is a powerful message, which focuses attention on the love of God as intimately connected with following and obeying the Prophet, an expression that resonates with Christian themes of love and salvation even as it revises their focus.

Considered as a whole, then, the commentary section of sura 3 (4–32) contains a number of topics of major importance, which reflect the situation of political crisis, in which Muhammad's Jewish and Christian allies were wavering in their loyalty or even opposing him. The opening references to female creativity and multiple interpretations of scripture acknowledge the intensity of the debate in Medina, while setting up Mary and Jesus as prophetic models that will challenge the Israelite monopoly on Abraham. Although this commentary section is framed in terms of conflict with the People of the Book, it contains three central passages that (according to the principles of ring composition) state principles aiming at universal significance:

1. Bearing witness to divine unity, and submitting to God (3:18–19.5)
2. Praising God's omnipotence (3:26–27), a revision of the Magnificat
3. Proclaiming God's knowledge, loving God, and obeying the messenger (3:29–32)

This symmetrically framed series of statements on divine and prophetic authority sets the stage for the narrative of Mary and Jesus that will immediately follow. What is at stake is the unity of God (against Christian incarnation), the universality of divine intervention (against Israelite particularism), and the acceptance of the prophecy of Muhammad.

Now the story of Mary and Jesus had already been told several years earlier in 19:16–40, in the sura named after Mary (Maryam), from the second Meccan period. Why would it be necessary to revisit this narrative in a quite different fashion later on? As usual, the Qur'an does not replicate biblical texts when it engages with them, and the first account of Mary and Jesus from sura 19 contains elements that will be both familiar and unfamiliar to readers of the New Testament. The Qur'an says nothing here about Bethlehem, the Roman census, Mary's husband Joseph, shepherds, or the manger. Sura 19 begins with an account of Zachariah praying to God for a son, who will be known as John the Baptist. Attention then shifts to Mary, who is abruptly introduced as being in seclusion, where she receives the annunciation of the birth of Jesus from an angel in human form; her virginity is no bar to this divine intervention. She withdraws to a remote location, where a palm tree and a stream provide her sustenance. She then returns to her people with a child, and their suspicious accusations are refuted by the infant Jesus, who miraculously speaks in her defense, while describing himself as a servant of God and a prophet. The Qur'an rejects the notion that God could have a child, always pointedly referring to "Jesus son of Mary." This argument does not seem to be directed here against an official Christian doctrine of the "son of God" but rather against the generic pagan notion of divine children. The account concludes with a description of divine creativity, using the same formula for the birth of Jesus as for the creation of Adam: "When He decrees something, He only says, 'Be,' and it is" (19:35), followed by affirmations of revelation.

The second version of the story of Mary and Jesus in sura 3 revises the earlier version in both structure and emphasis, in a way that will shift the genealogical understanding of Abrahamic prophecy. Although Mary is the daughter of 'Imran (Joachim), her father makes no appearance when she is born, and it is her mother who performs the symbolically important activity of naming her (3:36). Gendered terminology—womb, giving birth, female, male—is prominent in this account. This Qur'anic version has strong echoes of the life of Mary as told in the apocryphal Infancy Gospel of James, which is not surprising. Although such apocryphal texts are largely forgotten today, the Infancy Gospel of James was by far the most popular source for the life of Mary, and it was widely illustrated in Catholic and Byzantine church art (see figure 4.1 for a Byzantine portrayal of Mary in the Temple).[57] Unlike sura 19, where the stories of Zachariah and Mary are separate, sura 3 weaves them together, much as in the Gospel of Luke. Although Zachariah is supposed to be Mary's guardian, in the temple it is God who miraculously supplies her with food (3:37), so it appears that men are unnecessary to this chiefly feminine narrative. After a brief digression on Zachariah's astonishment at the prospect of a son (3:38–41), the Qur'an returns to Mary and the annunciation, this time carried out by angels, in the plural (3:42–43). Zachariah is chosen by lot as Mary's guardian (3:44), just as Joseph was chosen as Mary's husband in the Infancy Gospel, but the Qur'an minimizes or excludes male characters from this account of prophecy.

In its portrayal of Mary, sura 3 stresses her election by God and her rank above all other women, much like the Gospel of Luke. The possibility that the Qur'an is quoting the song of Mary would be an indication of familiarity with important parts of Christian liturgy; we shall see later in this chapter a similar case of reference to another New Testament song in sura 5. But the Qur'an is noticeably critical of the extreme adoration of Mary as "mother of God" in the Eastern Church.

Jesus is introduced in sura 3 as the annunciation proceeds, offering a prediction of his career in response to Mary's question about the possibility of virgin birth. This will be a supernatural creation, as with Adam, and Jesus will be taught all the scriptures (3:48). He will perform not only the miracle of bringing clay birds to life, but also the miracles of healing, raising the dead, and providing sustenance (3:49)—which are very nurturing kinds of miracles, arguably feminine in character. He will confirm the Torah and also lift some of the restrictions of the law (3:50). The proclamation of Jesus repeats his earlier declarations (19:36 and 43:64): "God is my Lord and your Lord, so worship Him. This is a straight path" (3:51). The predictions about Jesus in the annunciation shift into narrative at this point, as he experiences the typical prophetic crisis of an unbelieving people, so that he says, "Who are my helpers with God?" (3:52). The term Jesus uses for "helpers" (*ansar*) is the very term used for Muhammad's followers from Medina, setting up a clear parallel between the two prophets; when Jesus is answered enthusiastically by his disciples, Muhammad's audience must have felt called upon to do the same. God then predicts the ascension of

Figure 4.1. Mary in the Temple, Kariye Camii, Istanbul. © Dumbarton Oaks, Image Collections and Fieldwork Archives, Washington, D.C.

Jesus and the triumph of his followers, without making any reference to the crucifixion or resurrection, both of which are irrelevant here: "Then God said, 'Jesus! I am taking you to Myself, and raising you up to Me, and I am purifying you from the rejecters, and placing those who follow you above the rejecters, till the day of resurrection'" (3:55). After describing the reward of believers and the punishment of unbelievers, God explicitly compares the creation of Jesus to the creation of Adam: "The likeness of Adam, with God, is as the likeness of Jesus. He created him from dust, then said to him, 'Be!' And he was" (3:59). The conclusion of this segment (3:62) ends with exactly the same divine attributes as the beginning ("for God is the glorious, the wise," 3:6), which would lend support to the idea that this portion of sura 3 was originally an independent unit.

The elevation of the family of 'Imran in sura 3 in effect counterbalances the family of Abraham in terms of prophetic leadership. In a nonpatriarchal gesture, the family of 'Imran is presented largely through female characters plus the submissive prophet Jesus. The authority of Abraham remains intact and will be claimed in a different way, later on in sura 3, as the source of Islamic legitimacy. Yet for the moment, this alternate mode of prophecy serves to undermine exclusive Jewish claims on the prophetic heritage, though this "feminizing" move will be eclipsed by later Qur'anic assertions of Abrahamic patriarchal authority. Ironically, this shift of meaning shown in the elevation of the family of 'Imran was accomplished by engaging with techniques of arguing multiple interpretations of scripture, a method developed by the Jewish heirs of Abraham.

With the conclusion of the story of Mary and Jesus, sura 3 shifts into a new section with a direct address to the "People of the Book," a phrase that is repeated twice at the beginning of this section (3:64–65), twice more a little farther on (3:70–71), and twice more at the end (3:98–99). The thrust of this new argument is to reject any authority besides God, along with Jewish and Christian claims to be the exclusive heirs of Abraham:

> And if they turn away, God is the one who knows who are the malefactors. (3:63)
>
> Say, "People of the Book! Come to a common word between us and you, that we shall not worship anyone but God, and we shall not give Him partners at all, nor shall we take one another as lords in place of God." And if they turn away, then (all of you) say, "Bear witness that we are submitting!" (3:64)
>
> "People of the Book! Why do you argue about Abraham, when the Torah and the Gospel were not revealed until after him? Don't you understand?" (3:65)

This turning point introduces an extended debate (3:63–99) with the scriptural monotheists, at least some of whom reject the Qur'an, twist around its revelations, and see no obligation to honor agreements with the new religious community. None of this is new territory. At least twenty passages in these thirty-five verses are distinct echoes and parallels of lines from sura 2, which must have been fresh in the minds of the Qur'an's audience at the time. These deliberate reminders focus on several key issues that would have been obvious points of debate: Abraham's religious identity, prophets and angels, dietary regulations, and the Abrahamic sanctuary in Mecca.[58]

In this section, while it is difficult to detect a clear ring structure, there is an alternation of topics between externally framed conflict and debate passages and central statements of belief and allegiance. As usual, there are frequent changes of voice in which the audience shifts from the People of the Book to the believers or the messenger. The debate passages show a keen sensitivity to the different reactions among the People of the Book. Instead of painting them all with the same brush, this section is at some pains to point out that a party of the People of the Book wishes to mislead the believers (3:69, 3:72), and a faction of them turns away from or distorts the scriptures (3:78, also 3:23), but there is no blanket condemnation of the People of the Book as such. The Qur'an is careful to note that there are both trustworthy and untrustworthy members of the People of the Book (3:75), and its condemnation is reserved for those who are explicitly guilty of certain offenses. The central statements in this section concern Abraham as being neither a Jew nor a Christian (3:67–68), divine guidance bestowed on whomever God wishes (3:73.5–74), God's covenant with the prophets and prediction of Muhammad as the messenger of submission (3:81–85), the need to spend what one loves (3:92), and the teaching of Abraham, the founder of the Meccan sanctuary (3:95–97). Like the central proclamations of the commentary section of sura 3, the central statements from the Abraham section emphasize the acceptance of divine and prophetic authority in a universal context that goes beyond the Israelite genealogy.

In commenting on the topics of debate in the Abraham section, Robinson has convincingly traced relevant biblical and para-biblical texts on these issues that may have been known to the Jews and Christians of Arabia, to which the Qur'an in turn responded. One of the typical Qur'anic critiques here revolves around the excessive adoration of human prophets or angels, some of whom have been adored as "lords," or divine beings (3:64, 3:80). Such was the case with the apocryphal Apocalypse of Abraham, an early Jewish text that describes Abraham ascending to heaven with an angel, on the backs of two sacrificed birds, and witnessing the adoration of a human Messiah.[59] It is likely that Christians read this apocalyptic text in terms of the statement of Jesus (John 8:58), "Before Abraham was, I am." The Qur'an (3:79) rejects the notion that Jesus could have claimed to be a divinity or that Abraham had received a vision of Jesus' advent as Messiah. Likewise, the Qur'an rejects the assertion of Paul (Galatians 3) that God's promise to Abraham refers to Christ. Instead, the Qur'an proclaims (3:81) that God made a covenant with all the prophets, in which he prophesied a messenger who would confirm their scriptures, and whom they swore to support. That proclamation is then the basis for condemning anyone who turns away (*tawalla*, 3:82) from Muhammad's prophetic authority. And it is the believers and the followers of Muhammad (continuing the play on words derived from the root W-L-Y) who are the true heirs of Abraham: "Those of humanity who are closest (*awla*) to Abraham are those who followed him, and this prophet, and those who believe, for God is the ally (*wali*) of the believers" (3:68). In making these claims on the Abrahamic legacy, the Qur'an adopts very much the same kind of logic employed in Christian writings. The culmination of this process is undoubtedly the association of Abraham and Ishmael with the construction of the Ka'ba as a divine sanctuary and pilgrimage site in Mecca (3:96–97), a tradition that appears to have been current in Arabia in pre-Islamic times.

The final section of sura 3 is the last half (3:100–200), a lengthy sequence that is essentially a consolation and encouragement of the community of believers after a significant defeat. It begins and is repeatedly punctuated by a direct address to "You who believe" (3:100, 3:102, 3:118, 3:130, 3:156, 3:200). There are also repeated proclamations of God's sovereignty over the heavens and the earth (3:109, 3:129, 3:189). The ethical counterpart to that concept is the uselessness of worldly riches (3:116–17) and the condemnation of charging interest (3:130) or being stingy like the unbelievers (3:180–84, 3:187–88). From a historical perspective, this section contains extensive and detailed references to the defeat of the believers by the Meccan pagans at the battle of Uhud, accompanied by promises of future victory (3:121–28, 3:152–55). Such disasters are to be understood as tribulations that test the believers (3:140–44, 3:165–66). And, as already indicated, there is an overall frame structure for the entire sura, based on the prayers at the beginning and end (3:8–9, 3:191–94), intensifying the struggle with the Meccans in apocalyptic terms, even while proclaiming a universal reward and punishment for all religious groups.

Without attempting to unravel in detail the entire structure of this last half of sura 3, it is nevertheless possible to highlight a key passage at the beginning of the section, which seems to sum up the principal themes of this sura. This passage (3:102–5, 3:110–15) addresses the crucial meaning of a community held together by the bond or rope of God (*habl*, 3:103, 3:112), a metaphor for the commitment that arises from a divinely sanctioned loyalty. It offers the promise of becoming an ideal people (*umma*, 3:104, 3:110, 3:113) as a moral exemplar to humanity. It warns against the divisiveness caused by rejecting clear revelations. It concludes on the same note as the closing lines of the sura, strongly emphasizing that God dispenses reward and punishment justly to the people of all faiths.

> You who believe! Be conscious of God as awe demands, and only die when you are submitters. (3:102)
>
> And hold fast to the rope of God together, and don't separate, but remember God's favor to you, when you were enemies, and He reconciled your hearts, so that by His grace you became brothers; you were on the brink of a pit of fire, and He rescued you from it. In this way God makes His signs clear to you. Perhaps you will be guided, (3:103)
>
> So that a people will come forth from you who call to the good, and who command the right and forbid the wrong—they are the successful ones; (3:104)
>
> And so that you will not be like those who were divided and disagreed, after the clarifications came to them—there is a great punishment. (3:105)

This message is interrupted by verses (3:106–9) describing a double afterlife portrait of those whose countenances are blackened by sin or whitened by virtue and an affirmation of revelation and divine sovereignty. Since the lines preceding this depiction of the afterlife were expressed in the form of a hope, it seems appropriate to translate the succeeding verses in a subjunctive mood, articulating the hoped-for outcome:

> You would be the best people brought forth from humanity, commanding the right and forbidding the wrong, for you believe in God. And if the People of the Book had believed, it would have been better for them. Some of them are believers, though most of them are malefactors. (3:110)
>
> They will not injure you except by insult, and if they fight you, they will turn their backs, and then they will not be helped. (3:111)

They will be humbled wherever they are encountered, except (if they hold) a rope from God and a rope from humanity. They have incurred anger from God, and they are impoverished; that is because they were rejecting the signs of God, and they killed the prophets unjustly. That is because they rebelled and were aggressive. (3:112)

They are not all the same. Among the People of the Book is a people who are upright, who recite the verses of God during the night while they are prostrate. (3:113)

They believe in God and the last day, commanding the right and forbidding the wrong, and they try to be first in good deeds—they are of the righteous. (3:114)

They will not be denied the good that they do. God knows who is conscious of Him. (3:115)

Like sura 2, sura 3 expresses a strong tension between submitting to God's authority—and the Prophet's—on the one hand, and the pragmatic struggle for political survival on the other. In the midst of this struggle, the Qur'an still retains a powerful emphasis on recognizing the moral uprightness even of those who are not fully reconciled to a single bond of community.

Rewriting the Covenant in Sura 5 ("The Banquet")

Clearly all of the Medinan suras are marked by the intensity of the political and military conflict between the Medinan community of believers and their pagan antagonists in Mecca. They are also colored by the religious debates between Muhammad's followers and the People of the Book. The previous examples of suras 2, 3, and 60 have shown how valuable it is to be able to analyze these texts in terms of their structure and composition. Formal characteristics of the suras, ranging from parallel and mirror composition to shift of audience and repetition of formulas, make it possible to grasp the organization of a sura, and ring composition helps clarify its central points of emphasis. Zahniser has taken this kind of approach further in a systematic study of sura 4, "The Women," highlighting in particular the address to the Christians as the central theme of the sura, according to its structure.[60] More work needs to be done in this area; still lacking are any systematic studies of suras 8 and 9 from this point of view. Fortunately, Michel Cuypers's full-length study of sura 5, "The Banquet," offers, for the first time, a comprehensive demonstration of its mirror structure. The implications of this argument are significant, since (as seen previously in sura 2) centrally located universal proclamations outweigh framing statements of conflict, and Qur'anic revisions of earlier biblical passages provide strong statements of the new perspective of revelation.

Sura 5 is of particular importance from a chronological perspective—according to Nöldeke's sequence, sura 5 is the very last of the 114 suras to be delivered, while sura 9 is second to last, number 113. It interesting that Nöldeke here reverses the relationship of priority that parts of Islamic tradition have assigned these two suras, since the Egyptian edition places sura 5 as number 112 and sura 9 as number 113. That arrangement has the effect of placing sura 9 in the position of abrogating previous texts. If, to the contrary, sura 5 is the final revelation of the Qur'an, that raises questions about the way in which priority may be assigned to some verses over others within the abrogation scheme. It is worth noting that there is widespread agreement among traditional Muslim scholars that one important verse from the sura, 5:3, which concerns the perfection of religious service (*din*) and submission (*islam*), was the very last verse of the Qur'an to be revealed, supposedly on the occasion of the Prophet's farewell pilgrimage. It is Cuypers's contention that sura 5 demonstrates such unity of composition that, if indeed 5:3 was pronounced at the climactic finale of the Prophet's career, the same applies to the rest of the sura, at least in literary terms.[61] In short, there is good reason to regard sura 5 as the final word of the Qur'an.

Sura 5 is lengthy, with 120 verses, many of which are themselves long and complex. It covers a bewildering range of topics, starting abruptly with dietary regulations connected to the pilgrimage and then transitioning to extensive debates with the People of the Book. The title of the sura, "The Banquet," refers to a passage at the end (5:112–15), which briefly describes the Passover dinner of Jesus and his apostles as a miraculous event. The address of the audience shifts from the people to the messenger, most frequently calling upon the community of believers. Both traditional interpreters and modern European scholars have seen it as containing layers from different historical periods.[62] Cuypers, in contrast, views it as a unitary composition, and he lays out its structure as follows:

A1, A2. Entering the Covenant (5:1–26)
   B1, B2. On justice in the Muslim city (5:27–50)
      C. Status of Muslims and the People of the Book (5:51–71)
      C'. Call to Christians to convert (5:72–86)

B'. A legislative code for the community of believers (5:87–108)
A'. Jesus' and his apostles' profession of monotheistic faith (5:109–20)[63]

It would be pointless to try to replicate here all of the extensive analysis that Cuypers carries out in a book that is over 500 pages long (although a digest of this can be seen below in appendix B). To a certain extent, I would like to take as given the ring structure that has been demonstrated through this detailed illustration of parallel vocabulary and formulas of address. Instead of summarizing all of that, it will be helpful instead to take up the main topics and arguments that emerge from the interpretation of the sura as a unified structure. These key topics include the completion of religious devotion in submission to God (*islam*), criticism of the Israelite failure to keep the covenant, and rejection of the Christian doctrine of incarnation. Reflection on intertextual references to biblical passages and the central proclamations of ring compositions will permit a balanced appreciation of how the Qur'anic acceptance of pluralism relates to its powerful call for conversion.

The most impressive point made in sura 5 occurs in the center of the first section (A1, 5:1–11), in the words commonly thought to be the final statement in the Qur'an: "Today, the unbelievers despair of your devotion (*din*). So don't fear them; fear Me! Today, I have perfected your devotion for you, and I have completed My blessing to you, and I am pleased with submission (*islam*) for you as devotion" (5:3). This declaration clearly resonates with a central point highlighted earlier in sura 3: "Devotion (*din*), with God, is submitting" (3:19). Submitting (*islam*) means obedience to God and the Prophet and rejection of the worship of anything except God. Devotion or service (*din*) is not purely psychological but also constitutes the obligations collectively accepted as given by God; at times it is equivalent to obedience, or law.[64] This is not yet religion in the modern sense of a system of beliefs defining competing groups in relation to political power.[65] Nevertheless, there is a sense in which this proclamation articulates a sense of community that is evident in the address to a plural "you," consisting of those who accept obedience to God and the Prophet. Whether or not one connects this announcement to the historical event of the Prophet's farewell pilgrimage, it has a powerful sense of finality.

Strangely enough, at least to some observers, this important passage sits in the middle of a quite different set of verses (the subsection 5:1–4) that primarily concern rituals of the pilgrimage, ablutions (washing oneself) for prayer, and other matters of permitted and prohibited activities. The lack of apparent connection between this pronouncement (which is only the last half of 5:3) and the surrounding material has led some scholars to suggest that it is out of place. But according to the logic of ring composition, one begins with a framing theme, then the center introduces a new idea, after which the previous theme of the frame is resumed. The contrast caused by the introduction of the new idea creates surprise in the reader, who thereby is able to grasp that a point of major importance has been made.[66] The shift to the central point, far from being a sign of incoherence, causes that central point to linger in the mind as a contrast with the framing theme. The perfection of religious devotion therefore seems to be momentous and of lasting significance, in comparison with the historic but less weighty details of regulations for slaughtering animals (5:3.1) or training falcons (5:4).

The tendency to historicize the Qur'an has led many commentators to seize on the prominent mention of "today," repeated twice during the course of 5:3 and again in 5:5. They have identified this as referring to a particular date during the Prophet's farewell pilgrimage: 9 Dhu al-Hijja in the tenth year of the emigration (*hijra*) to Medina (July 3, 632). But comparison with similar language in the Book of Deuteronomy suggests a different interpretation that is not linked to ordinary time. There, in remarks attributed to Moses in his final testament, the frequently repeated word "today" is not so much a historical date as it is "rather the day of God's decisive intervention as he prepares to introduce his people onto the land he has given them."[67] Consider the prominent repetitions of "today" and "this day" in the following passage from Deuteronomy (29:12–15, emphasis mine):

> All of you are standing *today* in the presence of the Lord your God— your leaders and chief men, your elders and officials, and all the other men of Israel, together with your children and your wives, and the aliens living in your camps who chop your wood and carry your water. You are standing here in order to enter into a covenant with the Lord your God, a covenant the Lord is making with you *this day* and sealing with an oath, to confirm you *this day* as his people, that he may be your God as he promised you and as he swore to your fathers, Abraham, Isaac and Jacob. I am making this covenant, with its oath, not only with you who are standing here with us *today* in the presence of the Lord our God but also with those who are not here *today*.

The parallels with the Qur'anic situation are plain. In both cases, the message is presented as the final communication of the Prophet, whether Moses or Muhammad. Similarly, the conditions of this timeless day include commitment to a covenant, the completion of legislation for the community, victory over others, and establishment of a new people.[68] The fact that the word "day" occurs another half dozen times in sura 5 with the meaning of Judgment Day (5:14, 5:36, 5:64, 5:69, 5:109, 5:119) reinforces the sense that with such expressions it is evoking a time beyond the normal calculations of calendars.

The allusion to Deuteronomy in sura 5 does more than simply compare the roles of Muhammad and Moses as prophets. It sets in motion a strong revision of the biblical text that puts Muhammad's followers into the role of fulfilling prophecy, while criticizing the Jews for failing to follow the covenant. The image of the Promised Land becomes significant, as a gift that God offers to the Israelites as long as they keep the covenant. Although not specifically mentioned by name in the Qur'an, the Promised Land and the central shrine of Jerusalem stand in the background as an analogy for the holy place of worship (that is, Mecca), which has been denied to the believers by the Meccan pagans (5:2, 5:11). The difference is that Muhammad, unlike Moses, will enter the sacred land he has been promised, and so his followers are the true heirs to the Israelites; they too are entering the holy land after defeating enemies and receiving the laws that complete their devotion.[69] In rereading the symbolism of entry into the Promised Land, the Qur'an follows the precedent of the New Testament, where the Epistle to the Hebrews (3–5:10) portrays Jesus as fulfilling "the promise of entering his rest" (Hebrews 4:1), which in turn has picked up on God's anger with the wandering Israelites in Psalm 95:11, "So I declare an oath in my anger, 'They shall never enter my rest.'" The Qur'an also makes a parallel between the metaphorical entry into the holy land and Psalm 95:6, where the worshipers are invited to enter the Jerusalem Temple and prostrate themselves before God.[70] This is another example where the Qur'an takes the same approach to the Old Testament as the New Testament does, and in fact both texts claim to fulfill nearly the same biblical prophecies.

It is noteworthy that in the middle of this opening passage on the covenant (5:4–5) the Qur'an pauses to authorize as lawful good things, like hunting animals, as well as the food of the People of the Book. It is also permitted for the male believers to marry virtuous women, whether they are believers or the People of the Book. Although legal commentators will later on narrow down the acceptability of the food of Christians and Jews to make it subject to the prohibitions of Islamic law, this Qur'anic verse places no restriction on the sharing of food with monotheistic communities. While Deuteronomy forbade any intermarriage of Israelites with either male or female foreigners, the Qur'an is less restrictive, though later Islamic law will forbid Muslim women from marrying Jewish and Christian men. As with Deuteronomy, the concern here is to prevent people from turning away from the faith; the presumption is that children will be raised according to the father's community.

Just as it criticizes the Jews, sura 5 offers a strong correction to the deviations of the Christians as well. In the second part of the opening sequence (5:12–26), both Jews and Christians are charged with breaking their covenant and forgetting the revelations they received. The biographical tradition concerning Muhammad picks up the reference to the twelve tribal leaders of Israel (5:12), linking that to the twelve disciples of Jesus and again to the twelve principal helpers of Muhammad, making it clear that Muhammad both follows and fulfills the roles of previous messengers.[71] Muhammad will explain to the Jews and Christians the parts of their scripture that they had concealed (5:16) —a succinct summation of the function of prophecy as rewriting earlier revelation by bringing out its (hidden) implications. The Christian doctrine of incarnation, which has indeed been the cause of much debate among Christians (5:14), is decisively rejected (5:17), since Jesus like any other human is a created being whose life God can take. The Qur'an equally dismisses (5:18) the special privileges that Jews and Christians claim as God's favored ones.

The closing frame of this sequence (5:20–26) returns to the reproach against the Israelites who fail to enter the Promised Land, this time for fear of giants. But it singles out two men who were blessed by God, who continued to urge the Israelites, "Enter upon them by the gate; when you have entered it, you will be the victors" (5:23). These two men who fear God are clearly Joshua and Caleb, mentioned in biblical accounts (Numbers 14:5–9) as the only two Israelites who advocated obeying God and proceeding with the invasion of the Promised Land. These two would be the only ones to enter the land (Numbers 14:30, 38). These exceptional individuals among the Israelites, by entering the Promised Land, prefigure the entry into devotion and submission that is the defining feature of the community of believers; entry into the Promised Land, which has its physical counterpart in the return to Mecca (5:2), amounts to entry into Islam. The same language of "entering" occurs in the very late Medinan sura 110, which Nöldeke accepts as number 111 chronologically, despite its brevity (only three verses):

> When God's aid arrives, and the victory,
> And you have seen the people **entering** in God's service (*din*) in droves,
> Then glorify the praise of your Lord, and seek forgiveness, for He is most relenting. (110:1–3, emphasis mine)

The Qur'an is explicit here in affirming that the new community of faith supersedes its predecessors, and the metaphor of entering the faith provides a sharp contrast with the failure of most Israelites to enter the Promised Land.[72]

As far as correcting the Christians is concerned, the Qur'an focuses on Jesus and offers forceful interpretations of his role. While there is clearly a parallel between the roles of Muhammad and Jesus and their respective disciples, key differences appear in the brief reference to the banquet table that gives the sura its name (5:112–15).

> When the apostles said, "Jesus son of Mary! Is God able to send down to us a banquet table from heaven?" He said, "Be conscious of God, if you are believers!"
>
> They said, "We want to eat from it, so our hearts will be pacified, and we shall know that you have been truthful to us; then we shall be among its witnesses."
>
> Jesus and Mary said, "God, our Lord! Send down to us a banquet table from heaven, which will be a feast for us, for the first of us and the last of us, and a sign from You. Provide for us, for You are the best of providers."
>
> God said, "I am sending it down to you. Any of you who disbelieve after this I will punish with a punishment I have not inflicted on any creature."

This account, typical of the Qur'an's oblique hints at biblical references, is remarkably bare of detail, and its apparent incompleteness has led later commentators to fill in the narrative with plausible imaginative additions. Did the meal actually take place? What did it consist of? None of these details is provided in the text itself.

But the text of the banquet account offers suggestive indications that are rich with meaning relating to biblical texts. The verb "to send down" (*anzala*), normally used to describe the "sending down" of the Qur'anic revelation, is repeated here three times in different forms with reference to the heavenly banquet table. The banquet or banquet table (*ma'ida*) therefore symbolically stands for the Book that the Medinans demanded that Muhammad should produce: "The People of the Book ask that you send down to them a Book from heaven" (4:153). Simultaneously, this banquet recalls a passage from the Gospel of John (John 6:26–34), where Jesus speaks of the "food that endures to eternal life, which the Son of Man will give you" (John 6:27); it is the "bread from heaven" that sustained the Israelites in the desert (Exodus 16:4), which Jesus directly refers to (John 6:31–32), even as he claims to be the "bread of life" (John 6:35).

While the Qur'anic account eliminates any suggestion of Jesus' divinity, it accomplishes in this brief passage a many-layered intertextual reference to multiple biblical themes. The banquet table simultaneously evokes the Last Supper of Jesus and his apostles, the Jewish Passover feast, and the manna that fed the Israelites in the desert. The Qur'an describes this feast as a celebration for all times, "for the first of us and the last of us" (5:114), reflecting the biblical proclamation that the Passover feast is "for the generations to come" (Exodus 12:14). Even the doubting question of the apostles to Jesus, "Is God able to send down to us a banquet table from heaven?" (5:113), contains a clear echo of the Psalms, where the skeptical Israelites ask, "Can God spread a table in the desert?" (Psalm 78:19). Surprisingly, the Qur'an refers to the same Old Testament books but cites different verses from those that are quoted by the Gospel of John (John 6:31 quotes Psalm 78:24–25, while Qur'an 5:113 quotes both John 6:26–34 and Psalm 78:19). In other words, the Qur'an demonstrates detailed knowledge of the way that the Gospels reinterpret earlier biblical texts, but it takes an independent position in reevaluating the Old and New Testaments and its relation to both.[73]

Ultimately, repeating the anti-incarnation argument of 5:72–78, the conclusion of this sura (5:116–17) argues strongly that the divinization of Jesus is a mistake:

> And when God said, "Jesus son of Mary! Have you said to the people, 'Take me and my mother as gods apart from God'?" He said, "Glory be to You! It is not for me to say what is not true for me. If I

said it, You would have known it; You know what is in me, but I do not know what is in You. You are the knower of hidden things.

"I only said to them what You ordered me: 'Worship God, my Lord and your Lord!' And I was a witness for them while I was among them. And when You took me to Yourself, You were the watcher over them, for You are a witness to everything."

This interrogation of Jesus by God forms a dramatic parallel with the interrogations of Jesus by his opponents in the New Testament, where he is asked to declare whether he is "the Christ, the son of God" (Matthew 26:63) or "the king of the Jews" (John 18:33). In this case, Jesus firmly denies making any claim of divinity for himself or his mother Mary. While this charge does not precisely state Christian theological positions, since Mary is not technically considered divine, it does represent the logical consequences for monotheism of calling her "Mother of God," as was common in the Eastern Church. Moreover, Jesus also refuses to claim to have any divine knowledge, saying, "You know what is in me, but I do not know what is in You" (5:116). He presents his teaching as the pure monotheism commanded by God, to which he is a witness for humanity (5:117). This declaration comes close to echoing the response of Jesus to Pontius Pilate, that he "came into the world, to testify to the truth" (John 18:37).

So there is a very strong sense that, in terms of audience, sura 5 is aimed primarily at Christians, who are to be persuaded by the powerful argument that only the one God is to be worshiped. The criticism of the Jews is mainly to be understood within the rewriting of previous scriptures, the true meaning of which is now proclaimed. The contemporary political environment is one in which some of the Jews of Medina and the pagans of Mecca have taken on a position of unremitting hostility against the Prophet Muhammad (this is clearly a historical observation rather than an essential characteristic). In contrast, the Christians here are said to include priests and monks who are close in affection to the believers and profoundly receptive to the inspiration of the Qur'an (5:82–83). Indeed, the criticism of the sinners among the Jews in sura 5 follows models from the New Testament. Just as Jesus condemns the "brood of vipers" in Jerusalem who will slaughter and crucify the prophets (Matthew 23:33–37), in the same way the Qur'an condemns those who fight against God and the messenger (5:33).[74]

The completion of religious devotion (*din*) in submission to God (*islam*) was announced in a central opening passage (5:3), and it does indeed function as a key theme for this sura. If one circles back from the incomplete account of the banquet table at the end of the sura to contemplate its beginning, a powerful effect of ring composition becomes visible: the fulfillment of the annual feast proclaimed by Jesus takes place in the hajj pilgrimage ritual. It is no accident that sura 5 begins with an account of the foods that are lawful for the hajj pilgrims. So the food of a sacred feast ties the end of the sura back to its beginning. It is surely in this sense that the apostles of Jesus say, "We believe, and we bear witness that we are submitting (*muslimun*)" (5:111). That is, as portrayed in sura 5, Jesus and the apostles demonstrate that true religious devotion is submission to God, which entails submission to all the prophets, including Muhammad. This completion and perfection of religious devotion takes place not on any particular day of the calendar, but on the divine "today" of the resurrection (5:109, 5:119).[75] While this message no doubt amounts to an invitation to accept the prophecy of Muhammad, its location in the timeless realm of judgment makes it more than simply an effort to recruit converts among contemporary Christians. It is a profoundly transformed "Qur'anic version of the Christian Eucharistic feast."[76]

It is worthwhile to underline several additional examples of intertextuality in sura 5, where the Qur'an makes deliberate reference to earlier scriptures, both endorsing and transforming the previous revelations. One of these passages is 5:32, where the prohibition of murder follows on the story of Cain and Abel, just as it does Genesis 4: "Therefore We decreed to the Children of Israel that whoever kills a soul—not [as punishment] for [killing] another soul or committing corruption in the earth—it is as though he had killed all humanity; and whoever gives it life, it is as though he had given life to all humanity." The phrase "We decreed" (or "We wrote," *katabna*) is used in the Qur'an to signal a direct quotation of earlier scriptures. In this case the quotation is not from the Bible itself but from a post-biblical text in the Talmud, Mishnah Sanhedrin 4.5: "For this reason was man created alone, to teach thee that whosoever destroys a single soul of Israel, Scripture imputes [guilt] to him as though he had destroyed a complete world; and whosoever preserves a single soul of Israel, Scripture ascribes [merit] to him as though he had preserved a complete world."[77] The specific similarity of language between these passages is so close that the relationship is unmistakable. Even the restrictive phrase "of Israel" is only found in some versions of the Talmudic text.[78] In both cases, the prohibition of murder is given cosmic significance—the life or death of a single soul is equivalent to that of all humanity. A parallel example is the description of the law of retaliation in 5:45: "And We decreed for them in it [the Torah]: the life for the life, the eye for the eye, the nose for the nose, the ear for the ear, and retaliation for wounds. And whoever would waive his claims for this, it will be an atonement for him." While this verse clearly refers to the biblical law of retaliation in Exodus 21:23–25, like Qur'an 5:32 it balances a negative decree with a positive recommendation. In this way it both approves the previous scriptural decree and signals a higher moral and legal alternative.[79]

Another provocative scriptural echo occurs in 5:15–17, where the description of the Prophet Muhammad draws heavily on the end of the song or canticle of Zachariah from Luke 1:76–79. This song, also known as the Benedictus from its opening word in Latin, is one of ten hymns from the Bible (not counting the Psalms), which have long been incorporated into daily Christian worship services in both the Orthodox and the Catholic tradition.[80] Another of these canticles, the Magnificat or song of Mary (Luke 1:46–55), has already been discussed in relation to sura 3. The Benedictus follows directly after the Magnificat and is closely related to it. Reflections of these important texts in the Qur'an seem to indicate acquaintance with ritual performance among Eastern Christian communities. The song of Zachariah praises the God of Israel and prophesies the coming of a savior from the house of David, certainly a prediction of Jesus. In the closing lines, Zachariah turns to the predicted prophet and addresses him as follows:

> 76 And you, my child, will be called a prophet of the Most High;
>   for you will go on before the Lord to prepare the way for him,
> 77 to give his people the knowledge of salvation
>   through the forgiveness of their sins,
> 78 because of the tender mercy of our God,
>   by which the rising sun will come to us from heaven
> 79 to shine on those living in darkness
>   and in the shadow of death,
>   to guide our feet into the path of peace.

Consider the echoes of this biblical passage in the following Qur'anic verses:

> People of the Book! Our messenger has come to you; he makes clear for you much of the book that you have hidden, and he over-

looks much [of what you have done]. Now light has come to you from God, and a clear book. (5:15)

By this, God guides those who follow His approval on the paths of peace. He brings them out of darkness into light, with His permission, and He guides them to a right way. (5:16)

The parallels here are strong. Both prophetic figures provide knowledge of revelation—just as Jesus is "to give his people the knowledge of salvation," so Muhammad "makes clear for you much of the book that you have hidden." Likewise, the mercy of God, which Zachariah describes as a rising sun from heaven "to shine on those living in darkness," has its counterpart in the Qur'anic light that has come from God, by which he "brings them out of darkness into light." There is close agreement between the two texts in describing God's guidance to the path, or paths, of peace.

Yet the Qur'an's uncompromising insistence on monotheism requires a major qualification of this passage from the New Testament:

Those who say that God is the Messiah, the son of Mary, are indeed unbelievers. Say, "Who rules God in anything, if He wished to make perish the Messiah, the son of Mary, and his mother, and all who are on earth?" To God belongs the rule of the heavens and the earth, and what is between them. He creates what He wishes, and God is powerful over everything. (5:17)

This is a breathtakingly clear rejection of the doctrine of incarnation. The Qur'an takes very seriously the biblical texts that it invokes, and it preserves the honorary title "Messiah" (*masih*) for Jesus. Nevertheless, by presenting Jesus and Mary as ordinary mortals who eat food (5:75) and are subject to the divine will, it makes very clear that the power of God is not compromised by anything. At the same time, the Qur'an shifts the principal prophetic role directly onto Muhammad.

In view of the lengthy and complicated debates with Jews and Christians in sura 5, what can be concluded about the overall implications of this Qur'anic text for interreligious relations? This question is not amenable to a simple answer, which is an indication of its importance. There are, after all, strong acknowledgments of religious pluralism alongside statements about conflict with different religious groups, and these statements are not easily reconciled. The confident proclamation of the completion and perfection of devotion in submission (5:3), while not quite being an affirmation of religion in the modern sense, still manages to convey firmly that alternative religious views are far from perfect, and that outsiders are invited to join. Yet even though the majority of Israelites are condemned for their failure to keep the covenant, the unnamed Joshua and Caleb are praised for rightly inviting their community to salvation (5:23), implicitly acknowledging the legitimacy of at least some of the People of the Book. Likewise, while the Qur'an emphatically insists on rejecting the doctrine of incarnation, Jesus' proclamation of the Passover feast is said to be "for the first of us and the last of us," that is, for all generations. Does this not assume that the community of Jesus will continue to coexist with the followers of Muhammad? The fact that the food of the People of the Book is lawful for the believers (5:5) assumes that both groups are acknowledged as legitimate.[81]

It is true that the believers are prohibited from taking Jews and Christians as political allies (*awliya'*, 5:51; compare 60:1, 60:9). This exclusion is focused on the contemporary political situation rather than personal friendship or affection, which continues to be a possibility (5:82, 60:7). But such statements on historical conflict must be taken along with other declarations that unmistakably propose a vision of religious pluralism as part of God's plan. It is at this point that ring composition and central statements provide the key to understanding the implications of the text. It will be recalled that Cuypers divided the sura into six main sections (ABC/C'B'A'), in which the first two sections each contain two sequences (A1, A2, B1, B2, C/C', B', A'). In most cases, each of the resulting divisions contains subdivisions that are themselves concentrically arranged; there are even rings within these rings.[82] Frequently, broad statements of universal significance can be observed, which are prominently located at the center of a larger sequence or of a smaller sequence that serves as an opening or finale. Several of these have already been singled out for discussion, which have implications either for the relations between religious groups or for broad ethical considerations:

> 5:3 The perfection and completion of devotion as submission to God
>
> 5:23 The call to enter the gate of the holy land
>
> 5:32 The prohibition of murder
>
> 5:45 The law of retaliation and the possibility of atonement
>
> 5:114 Jesus' proclamation of the Passover feast
>
> 5:117 Jesus' confession of monotheistic faith

Only one of the major sections, the highly fraught call to the Christians to convert (C′, 5:72–86), appears to lack such a universal declaration, probably because of the sharp tone of debate in this section.[83]

There are three remaining universal statements in sura 5 that call for further explanation, due to their remarkable emphasis on the acceptance of religious pluralism. The first of these occurs toward the end of section B2, in the last half of a verse that begins by insisting on judgment by the scriptures. It continues, "For everyone We have established a law, and a way. If God had wished, He would have made you a single community, but this was so He might test you regarding what He sent you. So strive to be first in good deeds" (5:48). This is a remarkable statement of recognition that humanity does not form "a single community" (*umma wahida*), and that different religious groups should meet on the field of ethical behavior. It repeats the key phrase from the central verse of sura 2, "strive to be first in good deeds" (2:148), underlying the way in which ethics functions as the linchpin for both these suras.

Likewise, there is another passage that occurs at the center of a highly critical address to the People of the Book (5:65–71), right at the finale of section C and therefore at the pivot of the ring structure of the entire sura: "Those who believe, and those who are Jewish, and the Sabians, and the Christians—whoever believes in God and the last day, and does good— there is no fear upon them, nor do they sorrow" (5:69). The central position of this verse indicates its priority over the surrounding criticisms of the past failings of the monotheistic peoples. In principle, any of them (even including the mysterious Sabians, possibly a monotheistic baptizing sect) is still capable of gaining salvation by sincere belief and good actions. Moreover, they are designated by a phrase of blessing ("there is no fear upon them, nor do they sorrow") used repeatedly, especially in the Medinan period, for those who are guided by God or are his allies. Finally, in the opening subsection of B′, at the center of a lengthy passage (5:87–96) on legal prescriptions and prohibitions, there is an extraordinary statement that emphatically considers dietary infractions to be unimportant for those who believe and do good: "There is no fault for those who believe and do good deeds, regarding what they have eaten, as long as they are conscious of God, believe, and do good deeds, then again are conscious of God and believe, then again are conscious of God and are virtuous. For God loves those who are virtuous" (5:93). Contrary to the expectations of the later development of Islamic law, this verse repeatedly relegates dietary rules to a secondary position of much less significance than faith and ethical behavior.[84]

These three universal passages on religion and ethics are in tension with the more specific observations found in surrounding sections of this sura. They stand in sublime contrast with the criticisms of Jews and Christians, who elsewhere are accused of failing to adhere to their covenant and of concealing portions of their scriptures. The majority of the People of the Book are condemned for their shortcomings and urged to join the new dispensation. Yet there is a nuance that is allowed by admitting exceptions, even when it is grudgingly admitted that there may be a moderate group among them that would constitute a saved remnant (5:66). This observation is in harmony with the calm declaration that religious pluralism is a fact of human existence; this is a theological position that appears in the late articulation of the Qur'an and is attested in several late Meccan passages (11:118, 16:93, 42:8), as well as in this Medinan context. Some Muslim commentators have struggled with these passages, given the preponderant feeling that conversion to Islam should be a condition for salvation — frequently it is said that only those Jews and Christians who lived before the time of Muhammad had the possibility of salvation. Still, some Muslim thinkers have indeed accepted the straightforward meaning of these texts, that non-Muslims may achieve salvation.[85] If the principles of ring composition are accepted as relevant in this case, the meaning of these passages would be sought in the structure of the Qur'anic text itself rather than by seeking to eliminate their apparent inconsistency with other verses by the device of abrogation. From this perspective, the Qur'an patently affirms the general principle that ethics and faith are the most important criteria for all humanity, regardless of religious allegiance. At the same time, in other places it insists on rejecting theological and moral errors, and it urgently calls on believers to come to the defense of their community when it is under attack. The structural centrality of the universal proclamations suggests, however, that "they seem to be principles by which all the more circumstantial verses around them are to be interpreted."[86] This creative tension between the universal and the particular or historical is characteristic of the Qur'an's approach to major issues, and it should not be ignored by interpreters.

Conclusion

Toward a Literary Reading of the Qur'an

This book began by raising the question of how non-Muslims should read the Qur'an, followed by an account of the obstacles that make it difficult for non-Muslims to read the Qur'an at all. Most of these impediments arise from a nearly complete lack of acquaintance with the text itself, except via media-inflated claims of the contemporary relation between religion and violence. There are other cultural barriers, such as the notion that one can evaluate religious beliefs by a quick look at a text that is assumed to have only one simple meaning, or the idea that everything that people do is determined by a religious scripture from hundreds of years ago. It is also a difficulty if readers assume that the Qur'an is a foreign text that has no relation to anything familiar. Plus there is the problem that the official arrangement of the Qur'an puts the latest portions of it at the front, making it all but impossible for newcomers to read the text by following the standard sequence.

As a way around these obstacles, I have proposed to read the Qur'an in a literary and historical fashion, which means treating it as a text that can be understood through its style and structure, its reference to earlier literary productions, and its historical context, including its initial audience. This also means shifting the Qur'an out of the framework of theological authority, leaving aside for the moment the question of its status as a divine communication. The chronological approach to understanding the unfolding of the Qur'an offers instead an opportunity to grasp the way that it was received by its first listeners, as a fresh oral composition. In this way, modern readers can see how the Qur'an builds up a vocabulary and repertoire of themes and styles in dialogical communication with its audience. As a result, it becomes possible to grasp the development of the Qur'an over time, the literary structure and organization of the sura as a literary unit, and the intertextual approach of the Qur'an in its engagement with biblical and other early sources, with cautious use of external historical sources to provide a context for the explanation of particular sections of the Qur'an.

The reading of the Qur'an that has been carried out over the course of the book has followed the chronological sequence that Theodor Nöldeke initially proposed 150 years ago and which has been developed further in modern scholarship. The division of the delivery of the Qur'an into three Meccan periods (early, middle, and later) followed by the Medinan period presents a plausible case for the stylistic changes that took place in the formation of the text during the course of the prophetic career of the Prophet Muhammad. The sequential reading of the text reveals a fascinating story that is rich in implications for both religious studies and the literary history of a shared civilization (far surpassing Carlyle's dismal prediction that "it perhaps would not be so bad"!). It reveals the development of the Qur'an through liturgies of worship, which are revised in dialogue with its listeners, as it takes on the character of a canonical text. This chronological approach differs from the typical subject-oriented presentation of the Qur'an, which assumes a uniform content of the text in its canonical form and accepts later established interpretations of authoritative edicts as the norm. This literary perspective, particularly through rhetorical devices such as ring composition, permits the reader to understand different emphases within the text of the Qur'an as tensions that are mediated by its internal structure; it is no longer necessary to treat them as mere inconsistencies that need to be ironed out by a device such as the doctrine of abrogation. I hope that this book provides the tools that readers can use to continue reading the Qur'an on their own, as an enterprise that resonates with the humanistic study of religion and culture in other contexts.

Nevertheless, there are a number of questions raised by this book that call for further consideration. Some of these questions are methodological. One obvious question about the approach to the Qur'an proposed here is why the chronology proposed by modern European scholars should be considered more accurate than the sequence of suras that is accepted in traditional Muslim scholarship, or why ring composition should be considered in the Qur'an if it is not a major emphasis of traditional commentaries. In response, it is important to point out the very different kinds of questions that have been raised in these two enterprises. Traditional Qur'anic scholarship by its very nature is conservative, enshrining the views of authoritative figures and also drawing upon elaborate interpretive strategies that have been developed over many centuries. Modernist Muslim scholarship has introduced new approaches, such as "scientific" interpretation, which seeks to confirm the Qur'anic revelation by finding in it anticipations of modern scientific discoveries. While it is novel, this form of inquiry still aims to reinforce the authority of the text as the source of knowledge of God and his commandments. European scholarship introduced critical literary and historical approaches that raised a different set of questions, revolving around meaning, structure, and style, following the methods of classical Greek and Latin scholarship, Romantic approaches to literature, and the modern historical-critical study of the Bible. It is true that the work of European scholars has at times been marred by a condescending Orientalism, the assumption that the Qur'an is an inferior work that is foreign to the West, and by the conviction that only outsiders have the ability to understand this text correctly. The recent proliferation of bizarre conspiracy theories about the Qur'an has not helped the situation. There is, nevertheless, a noticeable convergence between modern Muslim and European approaches to the sura as a literary unit. All in all, the post-Orientalist approach to the Qur'an, which sees it as a significant part of humanity's global heritage, has much to offer. While the chronological reading takes the text apart, the rhetorical interpretation of structure puts it together again as a meaningful whole. This is not to say that Nöldeke's chronology is an unchallengeable fact. Rather, it is an example of an investigative procedure that proposes to try out hypotheses that can be tested and argued on the basis of comparison and theory. It can be best judged by the results emerging from analyses like the ones attempted in this book; if alternative proposals can provide more compelling conclusions, so much the better.

Another question concerns the relationship of the Qur'an to earlier scriptures. If this intertextuality is so important, why is it that Muslim scholars have typically ignored these biblical sources? The early Muslim tradition was actually much more receptive to exegetical material of pre-Islamic Near Eastern origin, which was collectively known as the Isra'iliyyat. Certain Qur'anic commentaries, such as that of al-Wahidi (d. 1075), incorporated considerable amounts of this material into their explanations, although much of it was taken from legendary and inconsistent sources with an emphasis on popular narrative rather than direct reference to scriptural texts. This material has fallen out of favor, and much of later Muslim tradition regards biblical texts as suspicious and liable to corruption.[1] So it is the rare Qur'anic commentator, such as Burhan al-Din al-Biqa'i in the fifteenth century, who has made much of an effort to study biblical texts as a way of understanding the Qur'an.[2] Ultimately speaking, it was a theological decision by Muslim scholars to ignore biblical texts; asserting that these scriptures had become corrupted provided a blanket excuse not to have to be familiar with them. Later on, when European Orientalists described the Qur'an's relation to the Bible pejoratively in terms of borrowing and plagiarism, their observations were hardly viewed with favor in Muslim circles.

If, however, there is good reason to see numerous engagements with biblical material in the Qur'an, without prejudice regarding issues of theological priority, why should readers ignore such opportunities for enriching their understanding of the text and how it operates? Defensiveness is not an effective way for Muslim scholars to respond to these comparisons, but external critics need to drop inane arguments about biblical "influence" on the Qur'an. The trite category of "influence" does not really contribute anything useful to our understanding, in any case.[3] A good argument can be made for the history of all scripture as the successive rewriting of earlier sacred writings. As Michel Cuypers remarks, "From Genesis to Revelation, the Bible can be read as a series of repetitions and re-readings of earlier writings."[4] Among these revisions, Deuteronomy ("the second law" ascribed to Moses) is a major example, as is the recapitulation of prophecy in Deutero-Isaiah, a separate prophet who is considered literally a second Isaiah. And of course the New Testament embodies a complete rereading of the Old Testament. So there is nothing remarkable in seeing this phenomenon of rewriting earlier scripture in the Qur'an.

Essentially, these methodological questions concern the appropriateness of modern scholarly analysis that does not replicate the conclusions of religious tradition. The reality is that there is always a gap between outside academic study and particular internal orthodoxies. The growth of knowledge through the vast comparative enterprises of modern scholarship makes it possible to produce new interpretations that are appropriate for today. It is interesting that Muslim scholars like Qutb and Islahi in the twentieth century for the first time began to discuss the sura as a literary unit and the relationships between suras. The emergence of such new interpretations in modern times should be a cause for celebration rather than anxiety. Indeed, while the chronological assumptions based upon the prophetic biography may still be debatable for purely historical reasons, it seems to me that no responsible reader of the Qur'an can afford to ignore the implications of ring structure and intertextual allusion. These approaches offer us the best chance of understanding how the Qur'an was perceived by its first audience.

Another set of questions emerges relating to the historical implications of this book's analysis. Who, indeed, are the various audiences presupposed by the text of the Qur'an? The issue of their religious definition is far from simple, and even in the case of the "pagans" of Mecca, it seems clear that they knew a great deal more about prophecy and revelation than has often been supposed. Another key question relates to the identity of the people who are addressed in the Medinan suras as the believers. As already indicated, there is good reason to think that this community of believers may well have included Jews and Christians, along with former pagan Arabs. While it is undeniable that a distinct Islamic religious identity emerged later, the prospect that the Qur'an in part addressed sympathetic listeners from different religious backgrounds is intriguing, to say the least.

Another issue of historical audience relates to the identities concealed behind the designation "People of the Book." A study of the Medinan suras yields information that is at some variance with the biographical tradition on the life of Muhammad. While the biographies inform us in considerable detail about the conflicts between Muhammad and the Jewish tribes of Medina, the names of these tribes are conspicuously absent from the Qur'an, and it is not easy to see how their story fits into the Qur'an without making fairly large assumptions. Christians, on the other hand, do not appear to be present in Medina, according to biographical accounts, though they are said to have lived in the north Arabian town of Tabuk after 630 CE. But overwhelming evidence from the Medinan suras (particularly 3, 4, and 5) indicates that Christians were often more important as interlocutors than Jews. It is particularly striking that the Qur'an demonstrates detailed acquaintance with the ritual performance of Christian worship service, in the form of the Magnificat and Benedictus biblical songs that are quoted and revised in suras 3 and 5. The gap between the Qur'an and the biographical tradition thus poses a problem that cannot be easily solved here. Perhaps the biographical tradition has for some reason failed to mention the presence of Christians in Medina, or else the composition of the Medinan suras underwent a longer process of revision than is commonly thought.[5] Alternatively, it is possible that we are dealing with Jewish Christians (Christians who adhere to Jewish law), or some other monotheistic group that does not fit neatly with current textbook definitions of religion. In any case, the complexity of these issues should be a warning against imposing current religious identities backward in time upon the text of the Qur'an, which seems to illustrate a more fluid situation than we are accustomed to today.

Finally, while I have attempted to exclude theology from the analytical perspective, it remains in the background as an unavoidable presence. That is, there are many religious people, of different allegiances, for whom reading the Qur'an can have theological consequences. What are the religious implications for them of a literary and historical reading of the text?

First of all, there is a possibility of an affirmative reading of the Qur'an by members of other religious faiths. Cuypers, who is after all a member of a Catholic religious order, employs a partly theological perspective, proposing to use the tools of rhetorical analysis while at the same time investigating the intertextual connections of the Qur'an to biblical literature. He says of his scholarly approach that "it suppresses nothing of the sacred nature of the text itself," and in his conclusion, he remarks that his work "is in no way an enemy of Qur'anic faith, but rather, purifying it, raising it to the level of universal ethics."[6] This may strike some as a bold approach, or even foolhardy, insofar as it seems to offer a "Christian" reading of the Qur'anic text that in a certain sense claims to improve upon traditional Muslim interpretations. Muslims are all too familiar with condescending Christian missionaries who propose to tell them what the Qur'an should actually mean. While it is always important to draw attention to the precommitments of scholars in the study of religion, at the same time one should be wary of dismissing Cuypers's contribution as one more Orientalist attempt to remake Islam in a Christian image. He received a Book of the Year award from the Iranian Ministry of Culture, in honor of *The Banquet*. Perhaps his most provocative suggestion is that intertextuality between the Qur'an and the Bible really goes both ways; in other words, "the more recent text can also shed light on the originality of the source-text."[7] So whether one likes it or not, it seems that one must take seriously the phenomenon of a theological reading of the Qur'an by non-Muslims.[8] And if one accepts the notion of the intertextuality of the Qur'an and the Bible, this means that Christians and Jews cannot afford to ignore the Qur'an as irrelevant.

Second, Muslims will continue to face the problem of how to respond to interpretation of the Qur'an by outsiders. For a long time, it has been fairly easy for Muslim authorities to dismiss the writings of Orientalists on the Qur'an as part of a colonial conspiracy aimed at undermining Islam. But despite all the criticisms that may be made regarding the limitations of Orientalist scholarship, there is so much serious and honest scholarship on the Qur'an being produced by non-Muslims that it would be absurd and paranoid to dismiss it altogether as a flawed enterprise. In the world of scholarship, honest arguments deserve honest responses. As 'Ali ibn Abi Talib advised, "Don't consider who it is who speaks, but consider what they say." Although the tradition of Muslim scholarship will undoubtedly continue to be a major resource for authoritative interpretation, it must be recognized that Muslim readers of the Qur'an are also very interested in contemporary approaches that do not rely on medieval sources. This is as true of the fundamentalist Qur'an interpretations of 'Allama Mawdudi and Sayyid Qutb as it is for the popular liberal readings of the Qur'an offered by the Syrian engineer Muhammad Shahrur.[9] And some modernist Muslim thinkers, such as the Iranian reformist politician (and first prime minister of the Islamic Republic of Iran) Mahdi Bazargan, have seriously tackled European chronological interpretations of the Qur'an in the attempt to understand the unfolding of the text over time.[10] It is also remarkable to see that empirical survey research has demonstrated that most readers of the Qur'an, whether in Arabic or English translation, understand Qur'anic verses on women's inheritance and gender equality quite differently from the readings found in traditional Muslim legal scholarship.[11] So there are evidently reasons for Muslim readers of the Qur'an to look for fresh perspectives that offer alternatives to entrenched authorities. If Muslim readers acknowledge the intertextuality of the Qur'an and the Bible, they too cannot afford to dismiss biblical texts without having given them a serious reading.[12]

In the end, reading the Qur'an from a literary and historical perspective is a humanistic exploration of the text that treats it like any other writing. This may be a cause of discomfort for Muslims who wish to regard the Qur'an as the eternal word of God, and therefore as an incomparable text that cannot be placed alongside any other book. But there needs to be a way for non-Muslims to read the Qur'an in a fair-minded way without being required to either accept or reject its authority as a divine message. The appearance of the Qur'an in a historical situation, using language and literary forms that were intelligible to its audience, is sufficient reason to approach it using the tools of scholarship. The payoff of this approach is that it promises to allow us to understand a particular voice in the Qur'an that may have been obscured by layers of tendentious readings. Interpreters, whether defensive or hostile, have either enshrined particular Islamic institutions with authority or extrapolated descriptions of historical conflict into eternal antagonisms. But if the readings offered in this book are valid, it means we need to recognize the significance of the broad statements on the fact of religious pluralism, which, as we have seen, literally hold central places in the final Medinan suras of the Qur'an. Remarkably, it is difficult to think of many analogies for these proclamations in the biblical texts to which the Qur'an so often refers. After all, the aim of the humanistic study of religious texts, as proposed here, is to increase communication between people of different backgrounds. If, as a result, people of different faiths could better understand the notion of meeting together on the field of ethics, that would be a good outcome.

Appendix A

Reading the Structure of the Meccan Suras

The following notes are designed to provide readers of the Qur'an with access to a chronological reading of the Meccan suras using the tools of literary analysis, from a precanonical and pre-exegetical perspective. This is a brief summary of the extensive and meticulous analysis provided by Angelika Neuwirth in *Studien zur Komposition der mekkanischen Suren* (most of which is available online at books.google.com). Readers interested in the details and justifications for these readings should consult that path-breaking work. Meccan suras are grouped below into three periods (early, middle, and late) and are listed by the canonical numerical order within each of those divisions. No attempt has been made to perform the same summation for the Medinan suras, since scholarly research has not yet advanced to that point.

The notations given below describe the structure of each sura according to Neuwirth's literary analysis. The first line of each entry provides the following information:

- The number and the Arabic name of each sura are given in bold.
- An outline of the sura is provided in parentheses, broken down into sections indicated by Roman numerals (except for very short suras lacking strong section divisions).
- The Roman numeral for each section is followed by a comma and then by the verses that are included within that section, numbered according to the Egyptian edition of the Qur'an.
- Sections are marked off by a semicolon.

Thus, sura 51 is listed as follows:

51. al-Dhariyyat (I, 1–23; II, 24–46; III, 47–60)

This means that, in the canonical text of the Qur'an as we have it, sura 51 is divided into three sections, in which section I consists of the verses numbered 1–23 (that is, 51:1–23), section II consists of verses 24–46 (51:24–46), and section III contains verses 47–60 (51:47–60). In some short suras where there is not a strong division into sections, just the number of verses is indicated, occasionally broken down less formally by verse groups connected by a plus sign; for example, the eight verses of sura 99 may be divided into informal clusters marked 3 + 2 + 3.

Each sura may contain two additional lines of information, "Notes" and "Structure." "Notes" are provided for suras where special features may be observed, including later additions, different verse divisions,[1] different verse order, textual emendations, repeated refrains, reference to other Qur'anic passages, and chiasmus or symmetrical composition. The "Structure" notation suggests, for every sura except for the very simplest ones, the probable earliest subdivisions of the sura. Sections in this way are further broken down by style and meaning into constituent units, to permit an easier reading of the complex changes of subject that may be found within a single section. The proposed structure is shown by the total number of verses in each subsection, which helps to clarify symmetrical features of the organization of each sura. For sura 51, we have the following:

> Structure: 9 + 14, 14 + 9, 7 + 7

This means that the 23 verses of section I are divided further into 9 + 14 verses, the 23 verses of section II are divided into 14 + 9 verses, and the 14 verses of section III are divided into 7 + 7 verses. From this breakdown, one can see that sections I and II mirror each other (9 + 14, 14 + 9), while section III consists of two equal parts. The prevalence of this kind of proportionality throughout the Qur'an is worth considering as part of its structural composition.

Readers may use this guide as a way to examine the internal structural unity and composition of the Meccan suras. One can begin by reading a series of early Meccan suras, preferably in more than one translation. Typically, the beginning and ending sections of tripartite suras consist of an affirmation of revelation, a debate, or a hymn of divine praise, at times combined with another motif. The suras often demonstrate a ring structure, in which the first and last sections are related not only in terms of their major themes but also by vocabulary and formulas. Central sections of the middle and later Meccan suras often feature extensive narratives.

Readers will find it helpful to outline suras by major section divisions and subsections containing shifts of topic; this can be done by comparing the proposed verse divisions in the "Structure" section of the notes with the actual verses in the accepted canonical text. It is especially interesting to consider cases where verses have been inserted later on, or where a different verse division may have previously existed. In such cases, the total number of verses proposed as the original structure of a sura will differ from the verse numbering of the standard Egyptian edition. Comparing the reconstructed earlier version with the accepted text of a sura permits the reader to develop a better understanding of the way the Qur'anic text developed over time. As an example, several verses from sura 53 have been identified as later insertions (53:23, 26–32). One can then try reading this sura without those verses, to see how it makes sense with a proposed original structure divided into three symmetrical groups of 24, 24, and 6 verses. Then one can consider what difference it makes to read the sura with the later insertions, and how that might have addressed a different audience.

If one then proceeds to read the middle and later Meccan suras in sequence, one can build up a sense of the developing conceptual apparatus, key topics, and essential terminology of these Qur'anic texts. By examining the textual notes, particularly those relating to later insertions in the text, one can also grasp the ongoing development and revision of the text in dialogue with its audiences.

Early Meccan Suras

1. **al-Fatiha** (1–7)
51. **al-Dhariyyat** (I, 1–23; II, 24–46; III, 47–60)
 Structure: 9 + 14, 14 + 9, 7 + 7
52. **al-Tur** (I, 1–8; II, 9–28; III, 29–47; IV, 48–49)
 Notes: Counting as two verses 52:43 (after *allah*, "God")
 Structure: 8, 20, 20, 2
53. **al-Najm** (I, 1–32; II, 33–56; III, 57–62)
 Notes: Not counting 53:23, 53:26–32, later insertions
 Structure: 24, 24, 6
55. **al-Rahman** (I, 1–13; II, 14–36; III, 37–78)
 Notes: 55:8–9, 55:33, possible later insertions (Nöldeke)
 Structure (not counting 31 repetitions of refrain): 12, 14, 21 + 1
56. **al-Waqi'a** (I, 1–56; II, 57–74; III, 75–96)

Notes: Not counting 56:8 and 56:9, as duplicates of 56:27 and 56:41; counting as two verses 56:10 (after *wal-sabiqun*, "and the forerunners"), 56:27 (after *al-yamin*, "of the right"), 56:41 (after *al-shimal*, "of the left"); 56:25–26 probably go after 56:40

Structure: 7 + 16 + 17 + 17, 18, 21 + 1

68. **al-Qalam** (I, 1–16; II, 17–34; III, 35–52)

Structure: 16, 18, 18

69. **al-Haqqa** (I, 1–12; II, 13–37; III, 38–52)

Notes: Counting as two verses 69:7 (after *thamaniya*, "eight"), 69:17 (after *arja'iha*, "around it"), 69:19 (after *bi-yaminihi*, "in his right (hand)"), 69:25 (after *bi-shimalihi*, "in his left (hand)")

Structure: 13, 7 + 7 + 14, 14 + 1

70. **al-Ma'arij** (I, 1–7; II, 8–35; III, 36–44)

Notes: Not counting 70:4, a later addition

Structure: 6, 7 + 7 + 7 + 7, 9

73. **al-Muzammil** (I, 1–9; II, 10–18; III, 19–20)

Structure: 9, 9, 2

74. **al-Mudaththir** (I, 1–10; II, 11–48; III, 49–56)

Notes: Not counting 74:31, a Medinan addition; 74:39 and 74:56, later additions

Structure: 10, 36, 7

75. **al-Qiyama** (I, 1–6; II, 7–25; III, 26–35; IV, 36–40)

Notes: Counting 75:11–12 as a single verse

Structure: 6, 6 + 6 + 6, 5 + 5, 5

77. **al-Mursalat** (I, 1–15; II, 16–45; III, 46–60)

Notes: Refrain repeated 9 times after 77:15

Structure: 15, 14 + 17, 5

78. **al-Naba'** (I, 1–16; II, 17–40)

Structure: 16, 24

79. **al-Nazi'at** (I, 1–14; II, 15–33; III, 34–46)

Notes: Not counting 79:33, a duplication of 80:32

Structure: 5 + 9, 6 + 6 + 6, 9 + 5

80. **'Abasa** (I, 1–16; II, 17–32; III, 33–42)

Structure: 16, 16, 10

81. **al-Takwir** (I, 1–14; II, 15–29)

Notes: Not counting 81:29, a later addition

Structure: 14, 14

82. **al-Infitar** (I, 1–8; II, 9–19)
    Notes: 82:13 = 83:22; 82:14 quotes 83:7 and 83:16
    Structure: 8, 11
83. **al-Mutaffifin** (I, 1–6; II, 7–28; III, 29–36)
    Structure: 6, 11 + 11, 8
84. **al-Inshiqaq** (I, 1–15; II, 16–25)
    Notes: Not counting 84:25, a later addition
    Structure: 6 + 9, 9
85. **al-Buruj** (1–6, 7–11, 12–16, 17–22)
    Notes: 85:7–11 are longer and interrupt a harmonious composition,
       a likely later addition
    Structure: 6, 5, 5, 6 (minus later additions, reconstructed as 3, 4, 4,
       4, 2)
86. **al-Tariq** (1–4, 4–10, 11–17)
    Structure: 4, 6, 6
87. **al-A'la** (I, 1–8; II, 9–15; III, 16–19)
    Notes: Chiasmus within section II (87:10 and 15, 87:11 and 14);
       references to sura 96
    Structure: 7, 7, 4
88. **al-Ghashiya** (I, 1–16; II, 17–20; III, 21–26)
    Structure: 6 + 9, 4, 6
89. **al-Fajr** (I, 1–5; II, 6–20; III, 21–30)
    Notes: Not counting 89:15–16, 89:23–24, and 89:27–30, later
       additions
    Structure: Minus later additions, reconstructed as 5, 9, 4, 4
90. **al-Balad** (1–4, 5–10, 11–16, 17–20)
    Structure: 4, 6, 6, 4
91. **al-Shams** (I, 1–10; II, 11–15)
    Structure: 10, 5
92. **al-Layl** (I, 1–13; II, 14–21)
    Structure: 13, 8
93. **al-Duha** (1–11)
94. **A-lam nashrah** (1–8)
    Structure: 4, 4
95. **al-Tin** (1–8)
    Notes: Not counting 95:6, a later insertion
96. **al-'Alaq** (1–5, 6–8, 9–18, 19)

97. **al-Qadr** (1–5)
    Notes: Similarity to 44:1–7 (middle Meccan) suggests later
      composition
99. **al-Zilzal/al-Zalzala** (3 + 2 + 3)
100. **al-ʿAdiyat** (5 + 3 + 3)
101. **al-Qariʿa** (3 + 2 + 4 + 2)
102. **al-Takathur** (2 + 2 + 2 + 2)
103. **al-ʿAsr** (1–3)
    Notes: 103:3 a later addition
104. **al-Humaza** (4 + 1 + 4)
    Notes: Syntax calls for 104:3 to begin with an interrogative particle
      (*a*) as an emendation, making it into a question
105. **al-Fil** (1 + 3 + 1)
106. **Quraysh** (2 + 2)
107. **al-Maʿun** (1–7)
    Notes: Counting 107:6–7 as a single verse
    Structure: 3 + 3
108. **al-Kawthar** (1–3)
109. **al-Kafirun** (1–6)
111. **al-Lahab/al-Masad** (2 + 3)
112. **al-Ikhlas** (1–4)
113. **al-Falaq** (1–5)
114. **al-Nas** (1–6)

Middle Meccan Suras

15. **al-Hijr** (I, 1–48; II, 49–84; III, 85–99)
    Notes: Emend 15:90 as *wa-ma anzalna*, "and We did not send down,"
      instead of *ka-ma anzalna*, "as We sent down."
    Structure: 3 + 12 + 10 + 23, 36, 15
17. **Bani Israʾil/al-Israʾ** (I, 1–21; II, 22–81; III, 82–111)
    Structure: 1 + 20, 18 + 21 + 21, 30
18. **al-Kahf** (I, 1–8; II, 9–102; III, 103–10)
    Notes: Counting as two verses 18:28 (after *dunya*, "world") and 18:77
      (after *ahlaha*, "its people")
    Structure: 8, 24 + 28 + 24 + 20, 8
19. **Maryam** (I, 1–65; II, 66–98)
    Notes: Not counting letter verse 19:1; counting as two verses 19:75

(after *maddan*, "lifespan"), and counting 19:88–89 and 19:91–92 as each a single verse

Structure: 14 + 25 + 25, 9 + 21

20. **Ta Ha** (I, 1–8; II, 9–99; III, 100–135)

Notes: Not counting letter verse 20:1; counting 20:78–79 and 20:92–93 as one verse and 20:86 as two verses (after *asifan*, "saddened")

Structure: 7 + 90 + 36

21. **al-Anbiya'** (I, 1–47; II, 48–96; III, 97–112)

Notes: Counting as two verses 21:28 (after *yashfa'una*, "[they] intercede"), and 21:66–67 as a single verse

Structure: 30 + 18, 24 + 16, 16

23. **al-Mu'minun** (I, 1–11; II, 12–77; III, 78–118)

Notes: Counting as two verses 23:109 (after *yaquluna*, "[they] say")

Structure: 11, 11 + 31 + 24, 42

25. **al-Furqan** (I, 1–34; II, 35–60; III, 61–77)

Notes: Not counting 25:51–52, later additions in the midst of creation hymn, or 25:70, a later doublet of 25:71; 25:60 goes after 25:55.

Structure: 2 + 8 + 24, 10 + 14, 16

26. **al-Shu'ara'** (I, 1–9; II, 10–191; III, 192–227)

Notes: Not counting letter verse 26:1; counting as two verses 26:49 (after *ya'maluna*, "you will know"); refrain repeated 7 times

Structure: 8, 60 + 36 + 18 + 18 + 19 + 16 + 16, 18 + 18

27. **al-Naml** (I, 1–6; II, 7–58; III, 59–93)

Structure: 6, 8 + 2 + 30 + 9, 21 + 14

36. **Ya Sin** (I, 1–12; II, 13–68; III, 69–83)

Notes: Not counting letter verse 36:1; 36:5 is a late insertion in a passage on sending prophets; 36:46 goes after 36:30.

Structure: 10, 21 + 14 + 7 + 14, 8 + 7

37. **al-Saffat** (I, 1–74; II, 75–148; III, 149–82)

Notes: 37:82 goes after 37:77; 37:112–13 are late additions; 37:178–79 are doublets of 37:174–75

Structure: 10 + 64, 8 + 16 + 13 + 9 + 10 + 6 + 10, 32

38. **al-Ahzab/al-Sad** (I, 1–11; II, 12–64; III, 65–88)

Notes: 38:27–29 go after 38:64

Structure: 2 + 9, 5 + 10 + 20 + 15, 5 + 21

43. **al-Zukhruf** (I, 1–25; II, 26–65; III, 66–89)

Notes: Not counting letter verse 43:1

Structure: 3 + 21, 20 + 20, 18 + 6

44. **al-Dukhan** (I, 1–8; II, 9–33; III, 34–59)
    Notes: Not counting letter verse 44:1
    Structure: 7, 8 + 17, 5 + 20

50. **Qaf** (I, 1–5; II, 6–35; III, 36–45)
    Structure: 5, 9 + 21, 10

54. **al-Qamar** (I, 1–8; II, 9–42; III, 43–55)
    Notes: Counting as two verses 54:9 (after *Nuh*, "Noah")
    Structure: 8, 10 + 5 + 10 + 8 + 2, 13

67. **al-Mulk** (I, 1–4; II, 5–22; III, 23–29)
    Notes: 67:29 and 67:30 should be transposed
    Structure: 4, 8 + 10, 8

71. **Nuh** (I, 1–4; II, 5–20; III, 21–28)
    Structure: 4, 16, 8

72. **al-Jinn** (I, 1–3; II, 4–19; III, 20–28)
    Structure: 3, 16, 9

76. **al-Dahr/al-Insan** (I, 1–3; II, 4–22; III, 23–31)
    Notes: Counting 76:12–13 as a single verse
    Structure: 3, 18, 9

Later Meccan Suras

6. **al-An'am** (I, 1–73; II, 74–153; III, 154–65)
   Notes: Counting 6:66–67 as a single verse
   Structure: 3 + 42 + 27, 17 + 27 + 18 + 18, 12

7. **al-A'raf** (I, 1–58; II, 59–174; III, 175–206)
   Notes: Not counting letter verse 7:1; counting 7:14–15 as a single
       verse
   Structure: 8 + 24 + 24, 44 + 54 + 18, 12 + 20

10. **Yunus** (I, 1–60; II, 61–93; III, 94–109)
    Notes: Counting 10:63–64 as a single verse
    Structure: 6 + 18 + 12 + 24, 9 + 23, 16

11. **Hud** (I, 1–24; II, 25–108; III, 109–23)
    Structure: 4 + 20, 84, 15

12. **Yusuf** (I, 1–3; II, 4–102; III, 103–11)
    Structure: 3, 54 + 45, 9

13. **al-Ra'd** (I, 1–4; II, 5–29; III, 30–43)
    Notes: Counting as two verses 13:5 (after *khalqin jadidin*, "a new
        creation"), 13:16 (after *nur*, "light"), 13:18 (after *hisab*, "reckoning")

Structure: 4, 12 + 16, 14

14. **Ibrahim** (I, 1–4; II, 5–41; III, 42–52)
    Notes: Counting 14:19–20 as a single verse; counting as two verses 14:44 (after ʿadhab, "punishment")
    Structure: 4, 13 + 5 + 18, 12

16. **al-Nahl** (I, 1–42; II, 43–89; III, 90–128)
    Notes: Counting as two verses 16:75 (after yastawuna, "are they equal"); 16:106–28 are Medinan additions
    Structure: 16 + 24, 20 + 28, 8 + 8

28. **al-Qasas** (I, 1–42; II, 43–84; III, 85–88)
    Notes: Not counting letter verse 28:1; counting as two verses 28:23 (after yasquna, "watering")
    Structure: 28 + 14, 14 + 14 + 14, 4

29. **al-ʿAnkabut** (I, 1–13; II, 14–43; III, 44–69)
    Notes: Not counting letter verse 29:1; counting as two verses 29:65 (after al-din, "religion/service")
    Structure: 12, 30, 16 + 11

30. **al-Rum** (I, 1–29; II, 30–51; III, 52–60)
    Notes: Not counting letter verse 30:1; counting as a single verse 30:48–49
    Structure: 5 + 12 + 11, 13 + 8, 9

31. **Luqman** (I, 1–11; II, 12–19; III, 20–34)
    Notes: Not counting letter verse 31:1; counting as two verses 31:32 (after al-din, "religion/service")
    Structure: 4 + 6, 8, 8 + 8

32. **al-Sajda** (I, 1–9; II, 10–22; III, 23–30)
    Notes: Not counting letter verse 32:1
    Structure: 2 + 6, 13, 8

34. **al-Sabaʾ** (I, 1–9; II, 10–27; III, 28–54)
    Structure: 9, 18, 18 + 9

35. **Fatir/al-Malaʾika** (I, 1–2; II, 3–30; III, 31–45)
    Notes: Counting as one verse 35:16–17, 35:19–21, 35:22–23
    Structure: 2, 6 + 6 + 8 + 4, 8 + 8

39. **al-Zumar** (I, 1–22; II, 23–40; III, 41–75)
    Notes: Counting as one verse 39:14–15
    Structure: 7 + 14, 18, 21 + 14

40. **al-Muʾmin/Ghafir** (I, 1–22; II, 23–76; III, 77–85)
    Structure: 3 + 18, 30 + 3 + 21, 9

41. **Ha Mim/Fussilat** (I, 1–8; II, 9–40; III, 41–54)
    Notes: Not counting letter verse 41:1
    Structure: 7, 32, 14
42. **al-Shura** (I, 1–8; II, 9–47; III, 48–53)
    Notes: Not counting letter verses 42:1–2; counting as two verses
        42:15 (after *kitab*, "book")
    Structure: 6, 8 + 8 + 12 + 12, 6
45. **al-Jathiya** (I, 1–11; II, 12–35; III, 36–37)
    Notes: Not counting letter verse 45:1
    Structure: 5 + 5, 24, 2
46. **al-Ahqaf** (I, 1–14; II, 15–28; III, 29–35)
    Notes: Not counting letter verse 46:1
    Structure: 2 + 11, 6 + 8, 7

Ring Structure in Sura 2 and Sura 5

Sura 2

The chart below outlines the symmetrical or ring composition of sura 2, "The Cow," as proposed by Raymond Farrin, "Surat al-Baqara: A Structural Analysis," *Muslim World* 100, no. 1 (2010): 17–32. For a discussion of ring composition, see chapter 4. Parallel passages are indented equally on the page. Principal sections and subsections of the sura (including internal rings and latches, or emphatic second endings) are indicated in bold, symmetrical correspondences between parallel sections are marked in italics, and the central lines of ring sections are underlined; verse numbering follows the standard Egyptian edition of the Qur'an. Subdivisions of some longer verses are occasionally indicated by decimal points (for example, 286.5 is halfway through verse 286, and 286.9 is toward the end).

A. 1–20. Faith vs. unbelief
  A.1. Internal ring on belief
1–2 Qur'an's *guidance*
   3–4 Those who believe
5 They follow *guidance*
  A.2. Internal ring on unbelief
6–7 God has made unbelievers *unperceptive*
   8–14 Hypocrites pretend to believe
15–20 Unbelievers are like the *deaf and blind*
  B. 21–39. God's creation and knowledge

21–24 Worship the Lord, challenge to produce sura, beware the
Fire

25–26.5 *Gardens of paradise, presence of spouses*

26.5–29 How can unbelievers reject faith in the Creator?

30–38 *Adam and wife expelled,* repent, *do not grieve*

39 *Unbelievers will be in the Fire*

C. 40–103. Moses delivers law to Children of Israel

40–46 *Belief and good deeds*

47–66 *Calf*

67–82 Cow

83–96 *Calf*

97–103 Most Israelites do not *believe* (a small internal ring):

97 Prophet *confirms Scriptures*

98 God opposed to those who *reject faith*

99 The perverse refuse to believe

100 Israelites *reject faith*

101 Solomon *confirmed previous scriptures* and was opposed

102–3 Solomon and his opponents **(latch)**

D. 104–41. Ka'ba built by Abraham and Ishmael;
People of the Book

D.1. Internal ring on Jews and Christians

104–10 *Believers* should not question Prophet as
Moses was questioned

111–13 *Jews and Christians think only they go to heaven*

114–15 *Pagans* prevent worship at Ka'ba

116–17 Christians say God has a son

118–19 *Pagans* ask for signs that will be punished

120 *Jews and Christians want to convert the believers*

121 Recipients of Scripture *believe* in it

D.2. Internal ring on Abrahamic foundation of
Mecca

122–23 *Children of Israel should remember God's favor* and
beware judgment

124 *God appoints Abraham as religious leader*

125 *God commands Abraham and Ishmael to purify*
Mecca

126 Abraham asked God to make Mecca a
city of peace

127 *Abraham and Ishmael build the Kaʿba*

128–29 *Abraham asked God to send a messenger*

130–33 *Not abandoning religion of Abraham, God's choice of this religion*

D.3. Internal ring responding to Jews and Christians

134 *The prophets and the Israelites will all receive what they deserve*

135 People of the Book want others to become Jews and Christians

136–38 Belief in God and the prophets without distinction

139–40 How can Jews and Christians argue when our Lord is the same?

141 *The prophets and the Israelites will all receive what they deserve*

E. 142–52. New prayer direction, faith; compete in doing good

142–43 *Prophet is a witness, change of direction is a test for believers*

144–46 Prophet, *turn towards the Sacred Mosque*

147–48 Multiple prayer directions, competition in virtue

149–50 Prophet and believers, *turn towards the Sacred Mosque*

151–52 *Believers have been sent their own messenger, should keep faith*

D'. 153–77. Muslims will be tested; Meccan pilgrimage sites; Polytheists

153–58 *Believers seek divine help in adversity*

159–60 *Jews and Christians who concealed guidance are cursed*

161–73 Unbelievers will remain in the Fire

174–76 *Jews and Christians who hide scripture will be punished*

177 *Those who pray in adversity are good*

C'. 178–253. Prophet delivers law to Muslims

178–82 *Justice, wills*

> 183–89 *Fasting, superstition*
>> 190–94 *Battle*
>>> 195–207 *Spending*, pilgrimage
>>>> 208–14 <u>Believers are wholehearted, guided,</u>
>>>> <u>tested by God</u>
>>> 215 *Spending charity*
>> 216–18 *Battle*
> 219 *Wine, gambling*
> 220–42 *Orphans, marriage and divorce, widows*
> 243–53 **(latch)**: Jihad, David and Goliath, Muhammad and
> God's plan

B'. 254–84. God's creation and knowledge

> 254 *Generosity* for believers
>> 255–60 <u>God's power and knowledge</u>
> 261–84 *Charity* and usury

A'. 285–86. Faith vs. unbelief

> 285 *Believers*
>> 285 *Forgiveness*
>>> 286 <u>God gives no soul a burden greater than it can bear</u>
>> 286.5 *Forgiveness*
> 286.9 *Unbelievers*

Sura 5

The following chart provides an outline of the structure of sura 5, "The Banquet," according to the analysis of Michel Cuypers, *The Banquet: A Reading of the Fifth Surah of the Qur'an* (Miami: Convivium Press, 2009), 61, 127, 191, 223, 267, 329, 359, 397, 451. He describes this as a mirror composition consisting of six sections, of which the first two have two separate sequences:

(A1, A2): Entering the Covenant (5:1–26)
(B1, B2): On justice in the Muslim city (5:27–50)
(C): Status of Muslims and the People of the Book (5:51–71)
(C'): Call to Christians to convert (5:72–86)
(B'): A legislative code for the community of believers (5:87–108)
(A'): Jesus' and his apostles' profession of monotheistic faith (5:109–20)

Since the alphabetical order and terminology that Cuypers uses in his book to lay out this ring structure (A1, A2, A3, A4, A5/B1, B2, B3) is different from the alphabetical order employed by other scholars like Farrin and Douglas (ABC/C′B′A′), it has been changed here to conform to that usage; the graphic layout, in any case, indicates the mirror structure in the very same fashion by parallel indentation. Likewise, the central statements of ring sections have been underlined to highlight the universal proclamations pointed out by Cuypers (*The Banquet*, 465). While Cuypers provides a far greater level of detail in his book, including a number of smaller rings and progressions, the general organization can be seen as indicated below:

A1. 1–11. The completion of the covenant in Islam
1–2 Rules of what is lawful in pilgrimage
   3 <u>The perfection of submitting to God (*islam*)</u>
4 Good things are lawful
5 Sharing food and intermarrying with the People of the Book is lawful
   6 Rituals of ablution for prayer
7–11 Reminders of covenant and its moral demands
A2. 12–26. Jews and Christians refuse to enter the covenant
12–14 Jews and Christians unfaithful to their covenant
   15–19 The Prophet is sent to the People of the Book
20–26 <u>The people of Moses refuse to enter the promised land, but two tell them to enter (5:23)</u>
     B1. 27–40. The punishment of the rebel children of Israel
     27–31 The murder of Cain
        32 <u>Murder is outlawed</u>
     32.5–40 Crimes and punishments
     B2. 41–50. The Prophet's jurisdiction over the Jews and Christians
     41–43 Muhammad's jurisdiction is refused by the Jews
        44–47 <u>The law of retaliation is in the scriptures but there is atonement (5:45)</u>
     48–50 <u>Muhammad is to judge according to the scriptures, but all should compete in good works (5.48)</u>
        C. 51–71. Status of Muslims and People of the Book
        51–58 No alliance with the People of the Book[1]
           59–64 Condemnation of the majority of the Jews
        65–71 <u>Possible salvation for Jews and Christians who believe (5:69)</u>
        C′. 72–86. Call to Christians to convert

72–77 Denunciation of Christians' errors of belief

78–86 Condemnation of the Jews, praise of Christian converts

B'. 87–108. A legislative code for the community of believers

87–96 Legal proscriptions and expectations, no sin for virtuous
believers (5:93)

97–105 Lasting divine institutions, obsolete pagan practices

106–8 Procedures for witnessing wills

A'. 109–20. Jesus' and his apostles' profession of monotheistic faith

109–11 The apostles' profession of faith

112–15 The sending down of the banquet table, the feast of Christianity
(5:114)

116–20 Jesus' monotheistic preaching, the creed of Jesus (5:117)

Suggested Interpretive Exercises

Engaged readers, whether on their own, in a class, or in a reading or discussion group, may wish to undertake some interpretive exercises to advance their understanding of the Qur'an as a text. Appendix A offers a detailed outline of the structure of the Meccan suras according to Neuwirth's
analysis, with suggestions for reading the structure of these suras in terms
of the chronological unfolding of the Qur'an. Appendix B presents sum-
maries of the ring structures present in suras 2 and 5. It is always recommended that more than one translation be used and that outlines of each
sura be made while reading, noting repeated terms and formulas as a guide
to the structure of the text. Some additional suggestions for activities are
provided below.

Adopting a Sura

In a course or in a discussion group, participants can adopt or become the
guardian of one or more suras of the Qur'an. This means the participant
takes responsibility for understanding the text of a particular sura, its literary and historical context, and perhaps something about its interpretive
tradition. To make this more interesting, in a follow-up exercise, a participant may decide to adopt one Meccan sura and one Medinan sura and then
be responsible for comparing and contrasting the two. Out of fairness, instructors or discussion leaders who adopt this activity will probably want
to assign suras randomly, excluding the shortest and longest suras to make
sure that everyone has a text of at least 10 or 12 verses but not over 100
(thanks to Bruce Lawrence for this suggestion).

Using Concordances

As with biblical study, study of the Qur'an can also benefit from examination of the multiple instances of use of any particular word in the Qur'an. This is a well-established method for enlarging one's understanding, by examining the way in which a word has been employed in different contexts. It is not necessary to know Arabic to use a concordance. An excellent English-language version is available, *A Concordance of the Qur'an*, by Hanna Kassis (University of California Press, 1983), a massive compilation of nearly 1,500 pages based on the English translation by A. J. Arberry. It is also available to subscribers of Oxford Islamic Studies Online, http://www .oxfordislamicstudies.com/Public/book_acq.html (accessed February 12, 2011), and occasionally elsewhere on the Internet. Since the main body of the concordance is organized around the roots of Arabic words, those who do not speak Arabic will need to look up the English terms of their choice in the index and then consult the appropriate Arabic words spelled in Roman transliteration; numerous examples can then be found, quoted in full context. For those who read German, Rudi Paret's *Der Koran: Kommentar und Konkordanz* (Stuttgart: W. Kohlhammer, 1977) is extremely useful.

Those who wish to examine the history of a particular term or concept over the course of the involvement of the Qur'an, after looking up a term in the concordance, can simply divide up the different quotations according to the particular period in which each verse belongs (early Meccan, middle Meccan, late Meccan, Medinan). Reflection on the different implications of particular terms in different contexts can shed light on the way in which these meanings have evolved.

Online resources are not always of high quality, but some users have had good results with YaQuB: Yet Another Qur'an Browser, http://www .quranbrowser.com/ (accessed February 12, 2011), which allows the option of tracking words in a number of different English translations.

Reading Selections Chronologically

Those who would like to read the entire Qur'an according to the chronological sequence established by modern scholarship are advised to use chart 1.2. If taking on the whole text, it is probably simplest and most efficient to read within each period (early Meccan, middle Meccan, late Meccan, and Medinan) according to the canonical order.

For those who would like to read substantial selections of the Qur'an but perhaps not the entire text, it is certainly practical to consider choosing selections that will take one through the different periods of the text's unfolding.

Over a twelve-week semester course, or for a substantial selection on one's own, the following sequence could be used (about two-thirds of the total text), which yields a roughly equivalent amount of material for each session:

1. Suras 96, 74, 111, 108, 107, 102, 105, 92, 94, 93, 97, 80, 68, 95, 103, 73, 101, 99, 53, 84 (first Meccan period)
2. Suras 100, 88, 89, 83, 51, 52, 56, 55, 112, 109, 113, 114, 1, 54 (first Meccan period)
3. Suras 36, 50, 20, 26, 15, 19 (second Meccan period)
4. Suras 23, 21, 25 (second Meccan period)
5. Suras 17, 18 (second Meccan period), 32, 30, 11 (third Meccan period)
6. Suras 14, 12, 18, 40 (third Meccan period)
7. Suras 29, 31, 42, 34, 35 (third Meccan period)
8. Suras 46, 6 (third Meccan period)
9. Sura 2 (Medinan period)
10. Suras 47, 61, 57, 4 (Medinan period)
11. Suras 63, 24, 58, 22 (Medinan period)
12. Suras 9, 5 (Medinan period)

For a short course, or for a course on comparative scripture, a briefer sequence could be used:

1. Suras 100, 88, 89, 83, 51, 52, 56, 55, 112, 109, 113, 114, 1, 54 (first Meccan period)
2. Suras 36, 50, 20, 26, 15, 19 (second Meccan period)
3. Suras 14, 12, 18, 40 (third Meccan period)
4. Suras 47, 60, 57, 5 (Medinan period)

Rendering the Qur'an into Verse

It is an interesting exercise to rewrite an existing English translation of the Qur'an in English verse. This is a way to experiment with the relation between sound and meaning in rendering a sacred text, and it is a thought-provoking way to interact with existing translations of the Qur'an and to try to see the invisible original text behind existing translations. This is most easily done with the short suras from the last portion of the Qur'an, roughly from sura 85 onward.

A variation on this exercise would be to focus on the "rider oaths" (found in 51:1–4, 77:1–6, 79:1–4, and 100:1–5) in an attempt to rewrite one or more of these highly poetic sections in verse, after paying attention to two or more different translations. It will be necessary to choose whether to interpret these verses in terms of galloping riders, winds, angels, or something else altogether, but in any case, one will need to choose a consistent literary language.

For an excellent example of thinking through the element of rhyme in different translations, see Bruce B. Lawrence, "Approximating *saj'* in English Renditions of the Qur'an: A Close Reading of Sura 93 (al-Duha) and the *basmala*," *Journal of Qur'anic Studies* 7, no. 1 (2005): 64–80.

Outlining Suras

An effective approach to grasping the structure of any particular sura is the exercise of outlining the text. Probably the best way to do that is to make detailed notes on each verse within a sura, following the standard numbering of verses. These notes can then be organized empirically into obviously related clusters, based on shifts of voice, formulas of address, changes of topic, and so on. For Meccan suras, readers can apply the general outline divisions of suras proposed by Angelika Neuwirth, summarized in appendix A. It is also possible to outline longer suras by copying and pasting translations available on the Internet and then editing them in a word processing file. One can then add appropriate subject headings and major divisions to organize the text according to its perceived structure.

Another exercise for a class is to divide up a longer Medinan sura (2 or 5) according to the outline of ring structure presented in appendix B. Individual students can then take responsibility for investigating the structure and meaning of the passage that they have been assigned.

Examining Later Insertions

This is an exercise that can be done most effectively with a class or reading group. Choose an early Meccan sura (for example, 73 or 74) that features short rhyming lines, with the single exception of a long prosaic later insertion (73:20, 74:31). Participants should read the entire sura aloud in sequence, with one verse per person, until it is concluded. The shift of voices with every verse makes it dramatically clear that the extra long verses function quite differently from the other verses, quite likely as a later explanation of a difficult or ambiguous passage. This exercise provides an excellent occasion for discussion of how the long verses relate to the rest of the sura. What does this imply about the interaction of the Qur'an with its listeners?

Likewise, one can introduce a discussion of other insertions (52:21, 55:8-9) by reading the relevant section of the sura without including the verses in question. What difference does it make to the content of the sura without the later insertions, and how do they change the earlier context? On a more extended scale, one can read sura 53 without its later insertions (53:23, 53:26-32) and ask the same questions (see also appendix A for considerations of symmetry once insertions are removed). Another exercise would be to read sura 53 but to substitute the "Satanic verses" for 53:21-22. How likely would it appear that these verses continued to be recited in this sura for several years until the early Medinan period?

Notes

Introduction

1 See my article, "From the Heart of the Qur'an Belt," *Religious Studies News*, May 2003, available online (with other sources on the controversy) at http://www.unc .edu/~cernst/quran.htm (accessed February 12, 2011).

2 For a detailed sociological study of the actual attitudes of American Muslims toward extremist violence, see David Schanzer, Charles Kurzman, and Ebrahim Moosa, "Anti-Terror Lessons of Muslim-Americans," Report for the National Institute of Justice, January 6, 2010, http://www.sanford.duke.edu/news/Schanzer_Kurzman_Moosa_ Anti-Terror_Lessons.pdf (accessed February 12, 2011). See also Charles Kurzman's collection, "Islamic Statements against Terrorism," http://www.unc.edu/~kurzman/ terror.htm (accessed February 12, 2011).

3 The extent to which we do not understand the details of this process is underlined by Andrew Rippin's foreword, in John Wansbrough, *Qur'anic Studies: Sources and Methods of Scriptural Interpretation*, ed. Andrew Rippin (Amherst, N.Y.: Prometheus, 2004 [1977]), xv–xviii.

4 Walter J. Ong, *Orality and Literacy: The Technologizing of the Word* (London: Routledge, 1988).

5 Alexander Stille, "Radical New Views of Islam and the Origins of the Koran," *New York Times*, March 2, 2002, http://www.rim.org/muslim/qurancrit.htm (accessed February 12, 2011).

6 Peter Wright, email communication, May 23, 2010.

7 Carl W. Ernst, *Following Muhammad: Rethinking Islam in the Contemporary World* (Chapel Hill: University of North Carolina Press, 2003).

8 *Journal of Qur'anic Studies*, published by Edinburgh University Press since 1999; *The Blackwell Companion to the Qur'an*, ed. Andrew Rippin (Oxford: Blackwell, 2006); *The Cambridge Companion to the Qur'an*, ed. Jane Dammen McAuliffe (Cambridge: Cambridge University Press, 2006); *The Koran*, ed. Colin Turner, Critical Concepts in Islamic Studies, 4 vols. (London: RoutledgeCurzon, 2004); *The Qur'an: An Encyclopedia*, ed. Oliver Leaman (London: Routledge, 2008); *The Encyclopaedia of the Qur'an*, ed. Jane Dammen McAuliffe, 6 vols. (Leiden: E. J. Brill, 2002–7).

9 John B. Gabel, Charles B. Miller, and Anthony York, *The Bible as Literature: An Intro-*

duction, 3rd ed. (New York: Oxford University Press, 1996), 23–42; Martin H. Manser, *Critical Companion to the Bible: A Literary Reference* (New York: Facts on File, 2009), 1–13; Kyle Keefer, *The New Testament as Literature: A Very Short Introduction* (New York: Oxford University Press, 2008).

10 One exception among general treatments of the Qur'an is Neal Robinson's judicious study, *Discovering the Qur'an: A Contemporary Approach to a Veiled Text*, 2nd ed. (Washington D.C.: Georgetown University Press, 2003), which provides a useful although somewhat technical overview of many of the historical questions surrounding the Qur'an.

11 I have laid out the presuppositions for this book earlier in "Reading Strategies for Introducing the Qur'an as Literature in an American Public University," *Islamic Studies* (Islamabad) 45, no. 3 (2006): 333–44, reprinted as *Islamic Studies Occasional Papers* 77 (Islamabad: Islamic Research Institute, 2007).

12 Benjamin D. Sommer, *A Prophet Reads Scripture: Allusion in Isaiah 40–66* (Stanford: Stanford University Press, 1998). I am indebted to Peter Wright for calling my attention to this phenomenon.

13 For an overview of the religious role of the Prophet Muhammad, see Ernst, *Following Muhammad*, 73–92; an excellent collection of articles on this topic is found in *The Cambridge Companion to Muhammad*, ed. Jonathan Brockopp (Cambridge: Cambridge University Press, 2010).

14 Carl W. Ernst, "It's Not Just Academic: Writing Public Scholarship in Middle Eastern and Islamic Studies," *Review of Middle East Studies* (forthcoming).

15 Arne A. Ambros, *A Concise Dictionary of Koranic Arabic* (Wiesbaden: Reichert Verlag, 2004); J. G. Hava, *Al-Fara'id Arabic-English Dictionary* (Beirut: Dar al-Mashriq, 1970); Edward William Lane, *Arabic-English Lexicon*, 2 vols. (Oxford: Islamic Texts Society, 1984).

16 I will not attempt to review or recommend existing English translations of the Qur'an, beyond mentioning the well-regarded translation of A. J. Arberry and the more recent useful versions by Mohammed Abdel Haleem, Alan Jones, and Thomas Cleary (see Suggested Reading). For problems in some current Qur'an translations, see Robinson, *Discovering the Qur'an*, 291; and his article, "Sectarian and Ideological Bias in Muslim Translations of the Qur'an," *Islam and Christian-Muslim Relations* 8 (1997): 261–78.

17 Angelika Neuwirth, "Orientalism in Oriental Studies? Qur'anic Studies as a Case in Point," *Journal of Qur'anic Studies* 9, no. 2 (2007): 115–27.

Chapter One

1 Thomas Carlyle, *On Heroes, Hero Worship, and the Heroic in History* (1841), available online at http://www.gutenberg.org/dirs/etext97/heros10.txt (accessed February 11, 2011).

2 Ibid.

3   For a thorough survey of early European scholarship on the Qur'an, see Hartmut Bobzin, "Pre-1800 Preoccupations of Qur'anic Studies," in *The Encyclopaedia of the Qur'an*, ed. Jane Dammen McAuliffe, 6 vols. (Leiden: E. J. Brill, 2002–7), 4:235–53.

4   For a brief overview of Orientalist scholarship, see Carl W. Ernst, *Following Muhammad: Rethinking Islam in the Contemporary World* (Chapel Hill: University of North Carolina Press, 2004), 22–24. A more upbeat evaluation of European responses to the Qur'an is provided by Ziad Elmarsafy, *The Enlightenment Qur'an: The Politics of Translation and the Construction of Islam* (Oxford: OneWorld, 2009).

5   Marco Schöller, "Post-Enlightenment Academic Study of the Qur'an," in *Encyclopaedia of the Qur'an*, 4:187–209. Nöldeke's work, though translated into Arabic and Turkish, is still unavailable in English, but the German original has been frequently reprinted, most recently in a 2005 facsimile of volumes 1 and 2 published by Elibron Classics: Theodor Nöldeke, *Geschichte des Qorans* (Leipzig: Dieterich'sche Verlagsbuchhandlung, 1909; reprint ed., N.p.: Elibron Books, 2005).

6   Schöller, "Post-Enlightenment Academic Study," 4:190.

7   Michael Sells, "The Qasida and the West: Self-Reflective Stereotype and Critical Encounter," *Al-'Arabiyya* 20 (1987): 307–57.

8   Mustansir Mir advocates a nontheological literary approach in his article "The Qur'an as Literature," *Renaissance* 10 (2000), http://www.islamic-awareness.org/Quran/Q_Studies/Mirliter.html (accessed February 11, 2011).

9   Carl W. Ernst and Richard C. Martin, "Introduction: Towards a Post-Orientalist Approach to Islamic Religious Studies," in *Rethinking Islamic Studies: From Orientalism to Cosmopolitanism*, ed. Carl W. Ernst and Richard C. Martin (Columbia: University of South Carolina Press, 2010), 1–19. I use "European" as shorthand to refer to European-language scholarship, regardless of the nationality or religion of the author concerned.

10   Abdullahi An-Na'im, cited by Bruce Lawrence, "Afterword: Competing Genealogies of Muslim Cosmopolitanism," in ibid., 305.

11   Erich Auerbach, *Mimesis: The Representation of Reality in Western Literature*, trans. Willard R. Trask (Princeton: Princeton University Press, 1953); Northrop Frye, *The Great Code: The Bible and Literature* (New York: Harvest/HBJ, 2002); Harold Bloom and David Rosenberg, *The Book of J* (New York: Grove Press, 2004). The subject of the impact of the Qur'an on later Islamicate literatures is vast and beyond the scope of this book. For an overview, see Wadad Kadi and Mustansir Mir, "Literature and the Qur'an," in *Encyclopaedia of the Qur'an*, 2:205–27.

12   Bart D. Ehrman, *The New Testament: A Historical Introduction to the Early Christian Writings*, 3rd ed. (New York: Oxford University Press, 2003).

13   John Burton, "Collection of the Qur'an," in *Encyclopaedia of the Qur'an*, 1:351–61; Harold Motzki, "Mushaf," in ibid., 3:462–66.

14   Beatrice Gruendler, "Arabic Script," in ibid., 1:135–44.

15   The Yemeni Qur'an manuscripts were referred to in a popular article by Toby Lester, "What Is the Koran?" *Atlantic Monthly* (January 1999), http://www.theatlantic.com/

doc/199901/koran (accessed February 11, 2011), which suggested the existence of major textual variations without giving any actual examples. This sensational presentation significantly overstated the available evidence on variations in the Yemeni manuscripts, which seem to be limited to the order of the suras and the spelling of individual words. A convenient summary of information about early Qur'anic manuscripts is available at http://www.islamic-awareness.org/Quran/Text/Mss/ (accessed February 11, 2011), a website that is very informative, despite its overt position of defending Islam against Christian critics.

16 Meir M. Bar-Asher, "Shi'ism and the Qur'an," in *Encyclopaedia of the Qur'an*, 4:591–95.

17 Frederik Leemhuis, "Readings of the Qur'an," in ibid., 4:353–63.

18 For scribal errors in the New Testament, see Bart D. Ehrman, *Misquoting Jesus: The Story behind Who Changed the Bible and Why* (New York: HarperOne, 2007). For a recent example of an argument that manuscript alterations were made to a particular passage in the Qur'an to conform to later doctrine, see David S. Powers, *Muhammad Is Not the Father of Any of Your Men: The Making of the Last Prophet* (Philadelphia: University of Pennsylvania Press, 2009).

19 For examples of textual emendations of scribal errors following the principles of classical scholarship, see James A. Bellamy, "Textual Criticism of the Qur'an," in *Encyclopaedia of the Qur'an*, 5:237–52, as well as the critical comment of Arne A. Ambros, in *A Concise Dictionary of Koranic Arabic* (Wiesbaden: Reichert Verlag, 2004), 19. For a balanced discussion of emendations of the Qur'an by Muslim and foreign scholars, see Devin J. Stewart, "Notes on Emendations of the Qur'an," in *The Qur'an in Its Historical Context*, ed. Gabriel Said Reynolds (London: Routledge, 2008), 225–48.

20 Andrew Higgins, "The Lost Archive: Missing for a Half Century, a Cache of Photos Spurs Sensitive Research on Islam's Holy Text," *Wall Street Journal*, January 12, 2008, available online at http://online.wsj.com/article/SB120008793352784631.html (accessed February 11, 2011). For a more thoroughly grounded discussion of the German Qur'an project and its sequels, including the mysterious death of Bergsträsser in 1932, see Gabriel Said Reynolds, "Introduction: Qur'anic Studies and Its Controversies," in Reynolds, *Qur'an in Its Historical Context*, 1–26.

21 Michael Marx, "The Lost Archive, the Myth of Philology, and the Study of the Qur'an," open letter of January 18, 2008, available online at http://www.unc.edu/courses/2008spring/reli/584/001/Reply_WSJ.pdf (accessed February 11, 2011).

22 Richard Bell, *The Qur'an Translated, with a Critical Re-arrangement of the Surahs*, 2 vols. (Edinburgh: T. and T. Clark, 1937); see also Neal Robinson, *Discovering the Qur'an: A Contemporary Approach to a Veiled Text*, 2nd ed. (Washington, D.C.: Georgetown University Press, 2003), 83–89, 94–96.

23 John Wansbrough, *Qur'anic Studies: Sources and Methods of Scriptural Interpretation*, ed. Andrew Rippin (Amherst, N.Y.: Prometheus, 2004 [1977]); the arguments raised by Wansbrough are summarized by Daniel A. Madigan, "Reflections on Some Current Directions in Qur'anic Studies," *Muslim World* 85 (1995): 345–62.

24 Patricia Crone and Michael Cook, *Hagarism: The Making of the Islamic World* (Cam-

bridge: Cambridge University Press, 1977). For an analysis, see Robinson, *Discovering the Qur'an*, 47–59.

25 Schöller, "Post-Enlightenment Academic Study," 4:202.

26 Fred M. Donner, *Muhammad and the Believers: At the Origins of Islam* (Cambridge: Harvard University Press, 2010), 56. Donner provides a useful overview of the historical sources on Islam on pp. 242–47.

27 The publications of "Ibn Warraq" (the pseudonym for a Pakistani author who writes mainly in criticism of Islam) are examples of the anti-Islamic fringe that attempts to use modern scholarship to discredit Islamic sources.

28 Franz Rosenthal, "History and the Qur'an," in *Encyclopaedia of the Qur'an*, 2:428–42.

29 Brannon Wheeler, "Arab Prophets of the Quran and Bible," *Journal of Qur'anic Studies* 8, no. 2 (2006): 24–57.

30 Brannon Wheeler, *Prophets in the Quran: An Introduction to the Quran and Muslim Exegesis* (New York: Continuum International Publications, 2002); Brannon Wheeler and Scott Noegel, *Historical Dictionary of Prophets in Islam and Judaism* (London: Scarecrow Press, 2002).

31 Robinson, *Discovering the Qur'an*, 32–35.

32 Muslim tradition commonly dates "the year of the elephant" to 570 CE, which is also said to be the year of Muhammad's birth, but this does not appear to correspond to the inscriptional evidence concerning the date of the Ethiopian governor Abraha; see Irfan Shahid, "People of the Elephant," in *Encyclopaedia of the Qur'an*, 4:44–46.

33 Robinson, *Discovering the Qur'an*, 60.

34 Uri Rubin, "Muhammad," in *Encyclopaedia of the Qur'an*, 3:440–58.

35 Robinson, *Discovering the Qur'an*, 61; Andrew Rippin, "Occasions of Revelation," in *Encyclopaedia of the Qur'an*, 3:569–73.

36 Muhammad ibn Ishaq, *The Life of Muhammad: A Translation of Ibn Ishaq's Sirat rasul Allah*, trans. A. Guillaume (Oxford: Oxford University Press, 1955); *Ibn Sa'd's Kitab al-Tabaqat al-Kabir*, trans. S. Moinul Haq and H. K. Ghazanfar (Karachi: Pakistan Historical Society, 1967–72).

37 The Ibn Ishaq material preserved by al-Tabari has been studied by Gordon D. Newby, *The Making of the Last Prophet: A Reconstruction of the Earliest Biography of Muhammad* (Columbia: University of South Carolina Press, 1989).

38 Wim Raven, "Sira and the Qur'an," in *Encyclopaedia of the Qur'an*, 5:29–51, quoting 5:49.

39 For instance, the biographies of Ibn Sa'd, which include the Prophet and his companions, need to be understood against the background of hadith transmission as an authoritative source for the development of Islamic religious sciences. Ibn Sa'd was more concerned with establishing the credentials of these transmitters of tradition than with establishing an objective history.

40 For a recent summary, see Angelika Neuwirth, "Structure and the Emergence of Community," in *The Blackwell Companion to the Qur'an*, ed. Andrew Rippin (Oxford: Blackwell, 2006), 140–58; and her *Encyclopaedia of the Qur'an* articles: "Form and Structure of the Qur'an" (2:248–66), "Sura(s)" (5:166–77), and "Verse(s)" (5:419–29); see

also Robinson, *Discovering the Qur'an*, 256–83. The fullest statement of this research is in Neuwirth's *Studien zur Komposition der mekkanischen Suren: die literarische Form des Koran—ein Zeugnis seiner Historizität?* (Berlin: de Gruyter, 1981; 2nd ed., 2007).

41 "Paul the Apostle," *International Standard Bible Encyclopedia*, ed. Geoffrey W. Bromiley (Grand Rapids, Mich.: Eerdmans, 1986), 3:706a; Gregor Schoeler, "The Codification of the Qur'an," in *The Qur'an in Context: Historical and Literary Investigations into the Qur'anic Milieu*, ed. Angelika Neuwirth, Nikolai Sinai, and Michael Marx (Leiden: Brill, 2010), 785.

42 Older European scholarship (prior to the 1960s) tended to employ the verse numbering used by Gustav Flügel in his 1834 edition of the Qur'an. This can be confusing to contemporary readers, since it differs enough from the Egyptian verse numbering to require a table to sort out the correspondences. See William Montgomery Watt and Richard Bell, *Introduction to the Qur'an* (Edinburgh: Edinburgh University Press, 1995), 202–4; see also Robinson, *Discovering the Qur'an*, 288–90.

43 Neuwirth, *Komposition*, 14–63, offers a meticulous review of alternative verse divisions in the canonical readings and in Flügel's edition, and she proposes a number of variations from the standard numbering. In many cases, the new numberings also demonstrate greater symmetry within the sura. See appendix A for examples of alternative verse divisions.

44 Although some argue that the absence of the formula of mercy from sura 9 is in accord with the military context of that sura, many traditional authorities have maintained that sura 9 was originally continuous with sura 8, and so the absence of that phrase is a result of textual division rather than a reflection of content.

45 For a compelling comparison between sura 55 and Psalm 136, on the basis of their prominent refrains, see Angelika Neuwirth, "Qur'anic Literary Structure Revisited: Surat al-Rahman between Mythic Account and Decodation of Myth," in *Storytelling in the Framework of Nonfictional Arabic Literature*, ed. S. Leder (Wiesbaden: Harrassowitz, 1998), 388–421.

46 Rudi Paret, *Der Koran: Kommentar und Konkordanz* (Stuttgart: Verlag W. Kohlhammer, 1977), 494.

47 For a survey of the problem, see Gerhard Böwering, "Chronology and the Qur'an," in *Encyclopaedia of the Qur'an*, 1:315–35.

48 Early Muslim sources in fact contain several different accounts of the precise chronology of the suras of the Qur'an, but the sequence presented in the Egyptian edition is a convenient benchmark for traditional scholarship. See, for example, three differing chronologies of the final twenty suras, listed by Régis Blachère, *Introduction au Coran*, 2nd ed. (Paris: Maisonneuve et Larose, 1991), 245. Detailed lists of five different chronologies of the Qur'an from early Muslim authorities are found in *Keys to the Arcana: Shahrastani's Esoteric Commentary on the Qur'an*, trans. Toby Mayer, Qur'anic Studies Series 6 (London: Oxford University Press, in association with the Institute of Ismaili Studies, 2009), 79–83.

49 A thoughtful analysis of the implications of Nöldeke's chronology in relation to

European and Muslim scholarship is provided by Emmanuelle Stefanidis, "The Qur'an Made Linear: A Study of the *Geschichte des Qorans'* Chronological Reordering," *Journal of Qur'anic Studies* 10, no. 2 (2008): 1–22.

50 Robinson, *Discovering the Qur'an*, 95.

51 A convenient and useful concordance is available from Hanna E. Kassis, *A Concordance of the Qur'an* (Berkeley: University of California Press, 1983).

52 Robinson, *Discovering the Qur'an*, 87–89.

53 Abu Ja'far Muhammad b. Jarir al-Tabari, *The Commentary on the Qur'an*, trans. J. Cooper, ed. W. F. Madelung and Alan Jones (London: Oxford University Press, 1987).

54 On the sura as a literary unit, see Mustansir Mir, "The Sura as a Unity: A Twentieth-Century Development in Qur'anic Exegesis," in *Approaches to the Qur'an*, ed. G. R. Hawting and A. A. Shareef (New York: Routledge, 1993), 211–24.

55 For a biblical example of chiasmus, see Mary Douglas, *In the Wilderness: The Doctrine of Defilement in the Book of Numbers* (New York: Oxford University Press, 2001). Chiasmus as a ritual process found in pre-Islamic Arabic poetry is discussed by Suzanne Pinckney Stetkevych, *The Mute Immortals Speak: Pre-Islamic Poetry and the Poetics of Ritual* (Ithaca: Cornell University Press, 1993), 56–57, 64, 70.

56 Mustansir Mir, "The Qur'anic Story of Joseph; Plot, Themes, and Characters," *Muslim World* 76 (1986): 1–15. For other examples of symmetrical structure in the Qur'an, see Robinson, *Discovering the Qur'an*, 141–42, 312n11 (sura 85), 149 (sura 12), and 151 (sura 36). It is noteworthy that Robinson later realized (p. xiii) that symmetrical or chiastic structure in the Qur'an is a topic that needed to be developed much more extensively than he had done in the first edition of his book, and his more recent publications have explored such structure in Medinan suras.

57 Robinson, *Discovering the Qur'an*, 225–34.

58 Ibid., 237–38. In the Qur'an, the council of angels actually argues with God against the creation of Adam rather than participating in the process (38:69).

59 For royal imagery in the Qur'an, see Louise Marlow, "Kings and Rulers," in *Encyclopaedia of the Qur'an*, 3:90–95.

60 Robinson, *Discovering the Qur'an*, 245–52; M. A. S. Abdel Haleem, "Grammatical Shift for Rhetorical Purposes: *Iltifat* and Related Features in the Qur'an," *Bulletin of the School of Oriental and African Studies* 55 (1992): 407–31.

61 Some biblical scholars refer to such a shift of person by the Greek term *enallage*, meaning "exchange." See David Bokovoy, "From Distance to Proximity: A Poetic Function of Enallage in the Hebrew Bible and the Book of Mormon," *Journal of Book of Mormon Studies* 9, no. 1 (2000): 60–63.

62 James W. Morris, "Dramatizing the Sura of Joseph: An Introduction to the Islamic Humanities," *Journal of Turkish Studies: Annemarie Schimmel Festschrift* 18 (1994): 201–24.

63 Neuwirth, *Komposition*, 177, describes such building blocks with the term *Gesätz*, used in German philology to describe a small independent group of verses. In this, Neuwirth follows Albert Bloch, who had applied this term to the study of Arabic poetry. See also Neuwirth, "Form and Structure of the Qur'an," in *Encyclopaedia of the Qur'an*,

2:255, where for some reason she uses the French word *enjeux* (normally meaning "stakes, challenges") as the equivalent for building blocks. Michael Marx renders the plural term *Gesätze* as "paragraphs"; see his article "The Qur'an as Process," in Neuwirth, Sinai, and Marx, *The Qur'an in Context*, 407–39, citing 419n22.

64 Angelika Neuwirth, "Structural, Linguistic, and Literary Features," in *The Cambridge Companion to the Qur'an*, ed. Jane Dammen McAuliffe (Cambridge: Cambridge University Press, 2006), 110–11.

65 Robinson, *Discovering the Qur'an*, 102, 129, 181–82; Neuwirth, "Images and Metaphors in the Introductory Sections of the Makkan Suras," in *Style and Structure*, vol. 3 of *The Koran: Critical Concepts in Islamic Studies*, ed. Colin Turner (London: RoutledgeCurzon, 2004), 244–73.

66 Neuwirth, "Rhetoric and the Qur'an," in *Encyclopaedia of the Qur'an*, 4:464–65.

67 See also Michael Sells's comments on sura 101, in *Approaching the Qur'an: The Early Revelations* (Ashland, Ore.: White Cloud Press, 1999), 24–26.

68 Stetkevych, *Mute Immortals Speak*, 18–26.

69 Similar meditations on the ephemeral nature of life are known by the Latin phrase *Ubi sunt qui ante nos in mundo fuere?* (Where are those who were before us in the world?).

70 Vernon Robbins, "Lukan and Johannine Tradition in the Qur'an: A Story of Auslegungsgeschichte and Wirkungsgeschichte," in *Moving Beyond New Testament Theology? Essays in Conversation with Heikki Räisänen*, ed. Todd Penner and Caroline Vander Stichele (Helsinki: Finnish Exegetical Society/Göttingen: Vandenhoeck and Ruprecht, 2005), 336–68, http://www.religion.emory.edu/faculty/robbins/Pdfs/RaisanenVolRRA.pdf (accessed February 11, 2011); Peter M. Wright, "Modern Qur'anic Hermeneutics" (Ph.D. diss., University of North Carolina at Chapel Hill, 2007), 137–98, particularly on the cases of Cain and Abel and second Isaiah, http://dc.lib.unc.edu/cgi-bin/showfile.exe?CISOROOT=/etd&CISOPTR=1591&filename=1582.pdf (accessed February 11, 2011). For another example of biblical intertextuality, see note 45 above.

71 For an extensive series of textual parallels, see Johann-Dietrich Thyen, *Bibel und Koran: Eine Synopse gemeinsamer Überlieferungen* (Cologne: Bölau, 2000). Some connections have even been made between Qur'anic imagery of the dark-eyed virgins of Paradise (*hur*) and the Greek goddess Hera; see Walid Saleh, "The Etymological Fallacy and Quranic Studies: Muhammad, Paradise, and Late Antiquity," in Neuwirth, Sinai, and Marx, *The Qur'an in Context*, 649–98.

72 Keith Massey, "Mysterious Letters," in *Encyclopaedia of the Qur'an*, 3:471–77.

73 Robinson, *Discovering the Qur'an*, 260–62.

74 Wael Hallaq, "Law and the Qur'an," in *Encyclopaedia of the Qur'an*, 3:149–72.

75 Fred M. Donner, "From Believers to Muslims: Confessional Self-Identity in the Early Islamic Community," *Al-Abhath* 50–51 (2002–3): 30–31.

76 Alan Jones, "Orality and Writing in Arabia," in *Encyclopaedia of the Qur'an*, 3:587–93; William A. Graham, *Beyond the Written Word: Oral Aspects of Scripture in the History of Religion* (Cambridge: Cambridge University Press, 1989); William A. Graham, *Islamic*

and Comparative Religious Studies: Selected Writings, Ashgate Contemporary Thinkers on Religion: Collected Works (Surrey: Ashgate, 2010).

77 One of many examples is the 1879 sermon "How to Read the Bible," by popular Victorian preacher Charles Spurgeon, http://www.bible-researcher.com/spurgeon2.html (accessed February 11, 2011).

78 Gerard Wiegers, "Ritual," in *Encyclopedia of Islam and the Muslim World*, ed. Richard Martin (New York: Macmillan Reference USA, 2004), 2:597–601. Wiegers, building on the work of Catherine Bell, has added to Bell's list his first category, communication, as distinctively applicable to Islamic ritual.

79 Josef Meri, "Ritual and the Qur'an," in *Encyclopaedia of the Qur'an*, 4:484–98.

80 Nasr Hamid Abu Zayd, "Everyday Life, Qur'an in," in ibid., 2:79–98.

81 John Renard, *Seven Doors to Islam: Spirituality and the Religious Life of Muslims* (Berkeley: University of California Press, 1996), 39.

82 Nasr Hamid Abu Zayd, "Everyday Life, Qur'an in," in *Encyclopaedia of the Qur'an*, 2:87, citing Ibn Hanbal, *Musnad*, nos. 19635, 19649.

83 Abu Sa'id al-Kharraz, quoted by Abu Nasr al-Sarraj, *Kitab al-Luma'*, in *Teachings of Sufism*, trans. Carl W. Ernst (Boston: Shambhala Publications, 1999), 12.

84 Kathleen Malone O'Connor, "Popular and Talismanic Uses of the Qur'an," in *Encyclopaedia of the Qur'an*, 4:163–82.

85 Anna M. Gade, "Recitation of the Qur'an," in ibid., 4:367–85; Anna M. Gade, *Perfection Makes Practice: Learning, Emotion, and the Recited Qur'an in Indonesia* (Honolulu: University of Hawaii Press, 2004).

86 Sells, *Approaching the Qur'an*, 28.

87 'Ali ibn Abi Talib, quoted by al-Tabari, *Ta'rikh al-rusul wal-muluk*, vol. 4, 48, http://www.yasoob.com/books/htm1/mo24/28/no2812.html (accessed February 12, 2011).

88 See al-Sharif al-Radi, *Nahj al-balagha*, no. 125, http://www.ahl-ul-bait.org/newlib/hadith/nahjol%20balagheh1/data/nahj4.html#ind125 (accessed February 12, 2011). I am grateful to Professor Alan Godlas of the University of Georgia for these references to 'Ali's sayings.

89 G. R. Hawting, "The Significance of the Slogan '*la hukma illa lillah*' and the References to the '*Hudud*' in the Traditions about the Fitna and the Murder of 'Uthman," *Bulletin of the School of Oriental and African Studies* 41 (1978): 453–63, citing 462.

90 Claude Gilliot, "Exegesis of the Qur'an: Classical and Medieval," in *Encyclopaedia of the Qur'an*, 2:99–124.

91 Abu Ja'far Muhammad b. Jarir al-Tabari, *The Commentary on the Qur'an*.

92 Walid A. Saleh, *The Formation of the Classical Tafsir Tradition: The Qur'an Commentary of Al-Tha'labi (d. 427/1035)*, Texts and Studies on the Qur'an, vol. 1 (Leiden: E. J. Brill, 2003); Walid A. Saleh, "Hermeneutics: al-Tha'labi," in *Blackwell Companion to the Qur'an*, 323–37.

93 Diana Steigerwald, "Twelver Shi'i *Ta'wil*," in *Blackwell Companion to the Qur'an*, 373–85.

94 *Keys to the Arcana: Shahrastani's Esoteric Commentary on the Qur'an*; Diana Steigerwald, "Isma'ili *Ta'wil*," in *Blackwell Companion to the Qur'an*, 386–400.

95 Although the commentary of al-Sulami remains untranslated, another representa-

tive early Sufi treatment of the Qur'an is discussed by Annabel Keeler, *Sufi Hermeneu-
tics: The Qur'an Commentary of Rashíd al-Dín Maybudí*, Qur'anic Studies Series 3 (Oxford:
Oxford University Press in association with the Institute of Ismaili Studies, 2006).
See also *The Minor Qur'an Commentary of Abu 'Abd ar-Rahman Muhammad b. al-Husayn as-
Sulami (d. 412/1021)*, ed. Gerhard Bowering (Beirut: Dar El-Machreq, 1997).

96 For an example of philosophical interpretation of the Qur'an, see Muhammad ibn
Ibrahim Sadr al-Din Shirazi, *On the Hermeneutics of the Light-Verse of the Qur'an*, trans.
Latimah-Parvin Peerwani (London: ICAS Press, 2004).

97 A number of commentaries are published in Arabic and English translation with the
support of a foundation established by the Jordanian royal family and are now available online at www.altafsir.com. See also the Qur'anic Studies Series published by
the Institute of Ismaili Studies.

98 Feras Hamza, Sajjad Rizvi, and Farhana Mayer, eds., *On the Nature of the Divine*, vol. 1
of *An Anthology of Qur'anic Commentaries* (Oxford: Oxford University Press in association with the Institute of Ismaili Studies, 2008); Mahmoud Ayoub, *The Qur'an and Its
Interpreters*, 2 vols. (Albany: State University of New York Press, 1984).

99 For an excellent overview of Qur'an interpretation over the centuries, see Bruce B.
Lawrence, *The Qur'an: A Biography* (New York: Atlantic Monthly Press, 2006).

100 Rotraud Weilandt, "Exegesis of the Qur'an: Modern and Contemporary," in *Encyclopaedia of the Qur'an*, 2:124–42.

101 Wright, "Modern Qur'anic Hermeneutics."

102 See Mohammed Arkoun, *Islam: To Reform or to Subvert?* (London: Saqi Essentials,
2006), esp. chapter 1, "A Critical Introduction to Qur'anic Studies," 53–92.

103 Sayyid Qutb, *In the Shade of the Qur'an*, ed. M. A. Salahi and A. A. Shamis (Leicester,
UK: Islamic Foundation, 1999); Olivier Carré, *Mysticism and Politics: A Critical Reading
of Fi Zilal Al-Qur'an by Sayyid Qutb (1906–1966)* (Leiden: Brill, 2003); Syed Abul 'Ala
Maudoodi, *The Meaning of the Quran: Arabic Text with Translation and Commentary*, ed.
M. J. Akbar and Abdul Aziz Kamal (Lahore: Islamic Publications, 1980).

104 Suha Taji-Farouki, ed., *Modern Muslim Intellectuals and the Qur'an* (Oxford: Oxford University Press in association with the Institute of Ismaili Studies, 2004).

105 John Burton, "Abrogation," in *Encyclopaedia of the Qur'an*, 1:11–19.

106 Reuven Firestone, "Jihad," in *Blackwell Companion to the Qur'an*, 308–20.

107 Although it is sometimes maintained that contemporary terrorists cite the sword
verse as abrogating the peaceful verses of the Qur'an, research indicates that Osama
bin Laden does not draw upon the theory of abrogation but instead basically takes
the most extreme position possible whenever violence is the topic. See Rosalind W.
Gwynne, "Usama bin Ladin, the Qur'an, and Jihad," *Religion* 36 (2006): 61–90.

108 Firestone, "Jihad," 317.

109 Rudolph Peters, *Jihad in Classical and Modern Islam* (Princeton: Markus Wiener, 1996).

110 Mahmud Muhammad Taha, *The Second Message of Islam* (Syracuse: Syracuse University Press, 1987); Mohamed A. Mahmoud, *Quest for Divinity: A Critical Examination of
the Thought of Mahmud Muhammad Taha* (Syracuse: Syracuse University Press, 2007).

111 Hartmut Bobzin, "Translations of the Qur'an," in *Encyclopaedia of the Qur'an*, 5:345–58.

112 Richard C. Martin, "Inimitability," in ibid., 2:526–36.

113 Navid Kermani, "The Aesthetic Perception of the Qur'an as Reflected in Early Muslim History," in *Literary Structures of Religious Meaning in the Qur'an*, ed. Issa J. Boullata (Richmond, Surrey: Curzon, 2000), 255–76.

114 Marmaduke William Pickthall [Mohammed Marmaduke Pickthall], trans., *The Meaning of the Glorious Koran, an Explanatory Translation* (London: Knopf, 1930).

115 Hussein Abdul-Raof, *Qur'an Translation: Discourse, Texture, and Exegesis* (Richmond, Surrey: Curzon, 2001).

116 Hartmut Bobzin, "'A Treasury of Heresies': Christian Polemics against the Koran," in *The Qur'an as Text*, ed. Stefan Wild (Leiden: E. J. Brill, 1996), 157–76.

117 Martin Luther, quoted in Bobzin, "Treasury," 163.

118 M. Brett Wilson, "The Qur'an after Babel: Translating and Printing the Qur'an in Late Ottoman and Modern Turkey" (Ph.D. diss., Duke University, 2009), 127–34.

119 Ernst, *Following Muhammad*, 33, 67, 100–102.

120 Wilson, "The Qur'an after Babel," 64, 172.

121 Gary R. Bunt, *iMuslims: Rewiring the House of Islam*, Islamic Civilization and Muslim Networks (Chapel Hill: University of North Carolina Press, 2009), 80–87.

122 On the tendency to interpret the Qur'an narrowly without any reference to history or culture, see Ebrahim Moosa, "Social Change," in *The Islamic World*, ed. Andrew Rippin (London: Routledge, 2008), 565–75, esp. 568–69.

123 Jalal al-Din 'Abd al-Rahman al-Suyuti, *al-Itqan fi 'ulum al-Qur'an*, 4 vols. (Cairo: al-Maktaba al-Tawfiqiyya, n.d.), 1:183, stating that the first six suras in 'Ali's copy were 96, 74, 68, 73, 111, and 81, followed by the rest of the Meccan and then the Medinan suras.

124 *The Koran*, translated from the Arabic by the Reverend J. M. Rodwell, introduction by the Reverend G. Margoliouth, Everyman's Library no. 380 (London: J. M. Dent, 1909; reprint ed., 1933), with a chart of the chronology of suras on p. xv.

125 Régis Blachère, *Le Coran: Traduction nouvelle*, Islam d'Hier et d'Aujourd'hui 4, 3 vols. (Paris: Librairie Orientale et Américaine, 1947), with chronological table of suras on 2:xv.

126 N. J. Dawood, *The Koran: A New Translation* (London: Penguin Books, 1956), 11: "The present arrangement, while not following a strictly chronological order, begins with the more poetical revelations and ends with the much longer, and often more topical, chapters. In short, it is primarily intended for the uninitiated reader, who, understandably, is often put off by such mundane chapters as 'The Cow' and 'Women,' with which the traditional arrangement of the Koran begins."

127 Jalal al-Din al-Suyuti, *Asrar Tartib al-Qur'an*, ed. 'Abd al-Qadir Ahmad 'Ata (Cairo: Dar al-I'tisam, 1976).

128 Edwin Black, "The Second Persona," *Quarterly Journal of Speech* 56 (1970): 109–19; Philip Wander, "The Third Persona: An Ideological Turn in Rhetorical Theory," *Central States Speech Journal* 35 (1984): 197–216.

Chapter Two

1 Angelika Neuwirth, *Studien zur Komposition der mekkanischen Suren: die literarische Form des Koran — ein Zeugnis seiner Historizität?* (Berlin: de Gruyter, 1981; 2nd ed., 2007), 235–37.

2 See also the examination of the "structure, sound, and meaning" of suras 103, 104, and 78, in Neal Robinson, *Discovering the Qur'an: A Contemporary Approach to a Veiled Text*, 2nd ed. (Washington, D.C.: Georgetown University Press, 2003), 162–76.

3 Neuwirth, *Komposition*, 204–5.

4 Ibid., 218–19.

5 This opening oath sequence is rendered here as a rider oath, emphasizing the semi-personification of charging horses. The imagery is elusive though highly suggestive. Later commentators try to identify the subjects as angels, stars, winds, and so on.

6 The last phrase (79:33), "as a sustenance for you and your herds," is a duplicate of a verse in the very next sura (80:32), and its lack of relation to the previous verse on hills makes its presence here seem out of place. If indeed this verse is a later insertion, then 79:27–32 originally formed a symmetrical group of six verses rather than seven.

7 Neuwirth suggests (*Komposition*, 18, 30) that 79:40–41 was originally three verses, as indicated by the rhyme (*naha, hawa, ma'wa*), with "standing before his lord" (*maqama rabbihi*) as a later explanatory addition. Then 79:34–41 would have originally been nine verses, in symmetry with 79:5–14.

8 See the chart of correspondences between suras 74 and 80 in ibid., 215.

9 Ibid., 192–200; Robinson, *Discovering the Qur'an*, 99–124.

10 R. A. Nicholson, *A Literary History of the Arabs* (London: T. Fisher Unwin, 1907), 135.

11 Jean-Yves Breuil, "The World's Largest Prehistoric Cemetery," in *Traces of Paradise: The Archaeology of Bahrain, 2500 BC–300 AD* (London: Bahrain National Museum, 2000), 35–41.

12 David L. Kennedy with Abdullah al-Saeed, "Desktop Archeology," *Saudi Aramco World* 60, no. 4 (2009): 2–9, http://www.saudiaramcoworld.com/issue/200904/desktop .archeology.htm (accessed February 12, 2011).

13 Kelly McEvers, "Will Saudi Arabia Lift the Veil for Tourism?," National Public Radio, August 8, 2009; Donna Abu-Nasr, "Digging Up the Saudi Past: Some Would Rather Not," Associated Press, August 31, 2009.

14 Brannon Wheeler, *Mecca and Eden: Ritual, Relics, and Territory in Islam* (Chicago: University of Chicago Press, 2006); Engseng Ho, *The Graves of Tarim: Genealogy and Mobility across the Indian Ocean* (Berkeley: University of California Press, 2006); 'Abd al-Qadir Muhammad Sabban, Linda Boxberger, and Awad Abdelrahim Abu Hulayqa, *Visits and Customs: The Visit to the Tomb of the Prophet Hud* (Ardmore, Pa.: American Institute for Yemeni Studies, 1998).

15 John F. Healey, *The Nabataean Tomb Inscriptions of Mada'in Salih*, Journal of Semitic Studies Supplement 1 (Oxford: Oxford University Press, 1993).

16 The story of Salih and Thamud has been brilliantly explored by Jaroslav Stetkevych, *Muhammad and the Golden Bough: Reconstructing Arabian Myth* (Bloomington: Indiana University Press, 1996).

17 Eric Voegelin, *Israel and Revelation*, vol. 1 of *Order and History* (Baton Rouge: Louisiana State University Press, 1956), 452.

18 For an overview of end-time scenarios, see Isaac Hasson, "Last Judgment," in *The Encyclopaedia of the Qur'an*, ed. Jane Dammen McAuliffe, 6 vols. (Leiden: E. J. Brill, 2002–7), 3:136–45.

19 Rudi Paret, *Mohammed und der Koran: Geschichte und Verkündigung des arabischen Propheten* (Stuttgart: Kohlhammer, 1957), 64–65, quoted in Frederik Leemhuis, "Apocalypse," in *Encyclopaedia of the Qur'an*, 1:112.

20 Patrick J. Ryan, "The Descending Scroll: A Study of the Notion of Revelation as Apocalypse in the Bible and in the Qur'an," *Ghana Bulletin of Theology* 4, no. 8 (1975): 24–39. The early Christian author Eusebius detected a similarity between the rolling up of the heavenly scroll in Isaiah and Plato's vision of the rewinding of the cosmos in *Statesman*, 269C–71A; see Eusebius of Caesarea, *Praeparatio Evangelica (Preparation for the Gospel)*, trans. E. H. Gifford (Oxford: Clarendon Press, 1903), 3:559–60, book 11, chapter 32. The word used in Revelations 6:14 for "rolling up" the sky (the Greek word *elissomenon*) is indeed related to Plato's term for "rewinding" the cosmos (Greek *aneilexis*, in *Statesman*, 270D).

21 Neuwirth, *Komposition*, 190–91; see also 92–95.

22 This section (*juz'*) is commonly known by the opening word with which it begins, in the first verse of sura 78 ('*amma*, literally "about what"), as the *juz' 'amma*.

23 Michael Sells, *Approaching the Qur'an: The Early Revelations* (Ashland, Ore.: White Cloud Press, 1999), 3.

24 Afnan H. Fatani, "Aya," in *The Qur'an: An Encyclopedia*, ed. Oliver Leaman (Oxford: Routledge, 2006), 85–103, especially 101–3.

25 Neuwirth, *Komposition*, 132–33, adds five other "teaching questions" with different formulas, to make a total of seventeen such questions in the early Meccan period; these expressions are entirely absent from the middle and later Meccan periods.

26 Theodor Nöldeke, *Geschichte des Qorans*, 2 vols. (Leipzig: Dieterich'sche Verlagsbuchhandlung, 1909; reprint ed., N.p.: Elibron Books, 2005), 1:107, observes that the last five words of 55:33 probably belong to the original composition rather than being a later addition.

27 Ibid., 1:105.

28 In some Shi'i interpretations, the front-runners were considered to be the Prophet, the Imams, and Fatima as primordially existing beings. See D. MacEoin, "al-Sabikun," in *Encyclopaedia of Islam*, ed. P. Bearman, Th. Bianquis, C. E. Bosworth, E. van Donzel, and W. P. Heinrichs (2nd ed., Leiden: Brill, 2010), available online at http://www.brillonline.nl/subscriber/entry?entry=islam_SIM-6373 (accessed January 19, 2010). Many other interpretations have been proposed for this term, indicating its mysterious character.

29 Nöldeke, *Geschichte*, 1:106, notes that some traditional commentators consider certain verses of this sura (56:74–81 or 56:94–96) to be Medinan. He also considers 56:8 and 56:9 to be duplicates of 55:27 and 55:41, added later for emphasis.

30 Behnam Sadeghi and Uwe Bergmann, "The Codex of a Companion of the Prophet and the Qur'an of the Prophet," *Arabica* 57 (2010): 343–436, quoting 346.

31 Marie Rose Séguy, *The Miraculous Journey of Mahomet: Mirâj nâmeh* (New York: G. Braziller, 1977); Frederick S. Colby and Christiane J. Gruber, eds., *The Prophet's Ascension: Cross-cultural Encounters with the Islamic Mi'raj Tales* (Bloomington: Indiana University Press, 2010).

32 Frederick S. Colby, *Narrating Muhammad's Night Journey: Tracing the Development of the Ibn 'Abbas Ascension Discourse* (Albany: State University of New York Press, 2008).

33 For details, see Shahab Ahmed, "Satanic Verses," in *Encyclopaedia of the Qur'an*, 4:531–36.

34 Neuwirth, *Komposition*, 207–9.

35 The breakdown of this sura into subgroups requires dividing 53:6 into two parts; the first vision begins in the last half of the verse.

36 53:55 closely echoes the repeated refrain of sura 55.

37 Neuwirth, *Komposition*, 208–9.

38 The language of this sura (for example, "He revealed to His slave what He revealed" in 53:10) only permits one logical interpretation, that it is God who is revealing this communication to the Prophet. Nevertheless, commentators for the most part have cautiously agreed to see here the angel Gabriel as an intermediary.

39 Ch. Pellat, "Kass," in *Encyclopaedia of Islam*, 4:733; Roberto Tottoli, *Biblical Prophets in the Qur'an and Muslim Literature* (Richmond, Surrey: Curzon Press, 2002), 86–89.

40 John Burton, "Those Are the High-Flying Cranes," *Journal of Semitic Studies* 15 (1970): 246–65.

41 Neuwirth does not follow all of Nöldeke's proposals regarding later additions to the early Meccan suras; she does not address the issue of the lateness of several passages (68:17–51, 75:16–19, 79:27–46, 96:9–19) that Nöldeke identified as additions.

Chapter Three

1 Nöldeke's criteria for distinguishing the middle Meccan period were somewhat vague, since he basically described it as transitory between the early and later periods rather than supplying clear definitions; see Emmanuelle Stefanidis, "The Qur'an Made Linear: A Study of the *Geschichte des Qorans'* Chronological Reordering," *Journal of Qur'anic Studies* 10, no. 2 (2008): 1–22.

2 The relative lengths of the middle and later Meccan suras, in terms of the number of lines they occupy on the page, are calculated on the basis of figures provided by Arne A. Ambros, *A Concise Dictionary of Koranic Arabic* (Wiesbaden: Reichert Verlag, 2004), 368–71.

3 Angelika Neuwirth, "Rhetoric," in *The Encyclopaedia of the Qur'an*, ed. Jane Dammen McAuliffe, 6 vols. (Leiden: E. J. Brill, 2002–7), 4:472–74.

4 Suzanne Pinckney Stetkevych, *The Mute Immortals Speak: Pre-Islamic Poetry and the Poetics of Ritual* (Ithaca: Cornell University Press, 1993), 3–6.

5 Angelika Neuwirth, *Studien zur Komposition der mekkanischen Suren: die literarische Form des Koran—ein Zeugnis seiner Historizität?* (Berlin: de Gruyter, 1981; 2nd ed., 2007), 242.

6 Labid, line 81, trans. Stetkevych, in Stetkevych, *Mute Immortals Speak*, 17.

7 Ibid., 51.

8 Labid, lines 8–10, in ibid., 10.

9 Ibid., 77.

10 Neuwirth, *Komposition*, 239.

11 John C. Reeves, *Trajectories in Near Eastern Apocalyptic: A Postrabbinic Jewish Apocalypse Reader* (Atlanta: Society for Biblical Literature, 2005), 7–8.

12 The classic study on this topic is Norman Cohn, *The Pursuit of the Millennium; Revolutionary Millenarians and Mystical Anarchists of the Middle Ages* (New York: Oxford University Press, 1970).

13 Neuwirth, *Komposition*, 168.

14 Although Neuwirth did not list any Medinan additions to middle Meccan suras in *Komposition*, she later proposed 20:80–82 as Medinan additions, since the direct address to the Israelites suggests a Medinan audience; see Angelika Neuwirth, "Meccan Texts—Medinan Additions? Politics and the Re-reading of Liturgical Communications," in *Words, Texts, and Concepts Cruising the Mediterranean Sea: Studies on the Sources, Contents, and Influences of Islamic Civilization and Arabic Philosophy and Science, Dedicated to Gerhard Endress on His Sixty-fifth Birthday*, ed. R. Arnzen and J. Thielmann, Orientalia Lovaniensia Analecta 139 (Leuven: Peeters, 2004), 71–93, esp. 76–79.

15 This explanation of "the sure/certain" (*al-yaqin*) as describing the Prophet's victory follows the suggestion of Jacques Berque, *Le Coran: Essai de traduction* (Paris: Albin Michel, 2002), 279.

16 The textual parallels listed below are based on the extensive list prepared by Angelika Neuwirth, "Referentiality and Textuality in *Surat al-Hijr*: Some Observations on the Qurʾanic 'Canonical Process' and the Emergence of a Community," in *Literary Structures of Religious Meaning in the Qurʾan*, ed. Issa J. Boullata (Richmond, Surrey: Curzon, 2000), 143–72, citing 170n65.

17 For the interpretation of "the Truth" (*bil-haqq*) in this verse as the Day of Judgment, see Rudi Paret, *Der Koran: Kommentar und Konkordanz* (Stuttgart: Verlag W. Kohlhammer, 1977), 278.

18 Following the persuasive emendation of Neuwirth, in *Komposition*, 265–66: "but We did not send down/reveal" (*wa-ma anzalna*); this makes more sense in context than the canonical reading "just as We sent down/revealed" (*ka-ma anzalna*).

19 Neuwirth, "Referentiality," 160, noting that the apparently earlier occurrence of ʿibad in 89:29 is a later addition to that sura.

20 Mohammed Arkoun, "Lecture de la Sourate 18," *Lectures du Coran* (Paris: G.-P. Maisonneuve et Larose, 1982), 70–86.

21 Louis Massignon, *Les Sept Dormants d'Éphèse (Ahl al-Kahf) en Islam et en Chrétienté* (Paris: Paul Geuthner, 1955).

22 These videos on the Companions of the Cave are available online at http://www.shiatv .net/search_result.php?search_id=kahf&search_cond=search_allwords&search_ typ=search_videos&submit=+ (accessed February 26, 2010).

23 See the comprehensive French website dedicated to the Companions of the Cave, at http://www.moncelon.com/ahlalkahf.htm (accessed February 26, 2010).

24 "Epitaph" is one interpretation of *al-raqim*, understood by some to be a tablet of gold or stone containing an inscription with the names of the Sleepers and their story. This interpretation is borne out in the Syriac narratives on the Seven Sleepers; see Sydney Griffith, "Christian Lore and the Arabic Qur'an: The 'Companions of the Cave' in *Surat al-Kahf* and in Syriac Christian tradition," in *The Qur'an in Its Historical Context*, ed. Gabriel Said Reynolds (London: Routledge, 2008), 109–37, esp. 125–26.

25 Norman O. Brown, "The Apocalypse of Islam," *Social Text* 8 (Winter 1983–84): 155–71, quoting 162; reprinted in Norman O. Brown, *Apocalypse and/or Metamorphosis* (Berkeley: University of California Press, 1991), 69–94. See also Norman O. Brown, *The Challenge of Islam: The Prophetic Tradition* (Santa Cruz, Calif.: New Pacific Press, 2009), 45–59. It should be noted that Brown is not sympathetic to the chronological approach to the Qur'an, preferring to see it instead as a complex work that should be grasped as a simultaneous whole, comparable to *Finnegan's Wake* by James Joyce.

26 Kevin Van Bladel, "The *Alexander Legend* in the Qur'an 18:83–102," in Reynolds, *Qur'an in Its Historical Context*, 175–203. This richly documented article is the source for the following remarks on Alexander in sura 18.

27 The concept of a "pathway" (*sabab*) in the Qur'an is like a cord or rope by which one can ascend to heaven; see Ambros, *Dictionary*, 126–27.

28 Muhammad M. Pickthall, *The Meaning of the Glorious Qur'an: Text and Explanatory Translation* (Mecca: Muslim World League, 1977), 290 (preface to sura 18), citing the *Sira* of Ibn Hisham.

29 Randall Styers, *Making Magic: Religion, Magic, and Science in the Modern World* (Oxford: Oxford University Press, 2003).

30 Edward William Lane, *Arabic-English Lexicon*, 2 vols. (Oxford: Islamic Texts Society, 1984), 1316–17.

31 Ambros, *Dictionary*, 133.

32 Commentators, perhaps expressing anxiety over the possibility of Muhammad studying other scriptures, have recorded a number of variant readings of the word "you have studied" (*darasta*), which eliminate the notion of literary dependence: "they [that is, the scriptures] have lapsed," "they have been studied," or "they have been abolished"; see Régis Blachère, *Le Coran: Traduction nouvelle*, Islam d'Hier et d'Aujourd'hui 4, 3 vols. (Paris: Librairie Orientale et Américaine, 1947), 688, note to Qur'an 6:105; and Paret, *Der Koran*, 149.

Chapter Four

1 Angelika Neuwirth, "Form and Structure of the Qur'an," in *The Encyclopaedia of the Qur'an*, ed. Jane Dammen McAuliffe, 6 vols. (Leiden: E. J. Brill, 2002–7), 2:247, 264.

2 Neal Robinson, *Discovering the Qur'an: A Contemporary Approach to a Veiled Text*, 2nd ed. (Washington, D.C.: Georgetown University Press, 2003), 196–98.

3 Fred M. Donner, "From Believers to Muslims: Confessional Self-Identity in the Early Islamic Community," *Al-Abhath* 50–51 (2002-3): 9–53.

4 See, on this point, Carl W. Ernst, *Following Muhammad: Rethinking Islam in the Contemporary World* (Chapel Hill: University of North Carolina Press, 2003), 10, 62–64.

5 Fred M. Donner, *Muhammad and the Believers: At the Origins of Islam* (Cambridge: Harvard University Press, 2010), esp. 56–57, 69–74, quoting 69.

6 Although Mohammed Arkoun never achieved his project of writing a commentary on sura 9, he has addressed some of the issues, in "Violence, the Sacred, and the Regimes of Truth," in *Proceedings of the Balzan Symposium 2008: Truth in Science, the Humanities, and Religion*, ed. M. E. H. Nicolette Mout and Werner Stauffacher, http://www .thedivineconspiracy.org/Z5245M.pdf (accessed February 22, 2011), 127–49, esp. 146–49.

7 M. A. S. Abdel Haleem, *The Qur'an: A New Translation* (New York: Oxford University Press, 2004), xxxiv.

8 Robinson, *Discovering the Qur'an*, 201–23; he bases his remarks in part on the observations of the Pakistani interpreter, Amin Ahsan Islahi.

9 A. H. Mathias Zahniser, "Major Transitions and Thematic Borders in Two Long Suras: al-Baqara and al-Nisa'," in *Literary Structures of Religious Meaning in the Qur'an*, ed. Issa J. Boullata (Richmond, Surrey: Curzon, 2000), 26–55; David E. Smith, "The Structure of al-Baqarah," *Muslim World* 91 (2001): 121–36.

10 Raymond K. Farrin, "Surat al-Baqara: A Structural Analysis," *Muslim World* 100 (2010): 17–32.

11 Mary Douglas, *Thinking in Circles: An Essay on Ring Composition*, Terry Lecture Series (New Haven: Yale University Press, 2007).

12 Ibid., 3. Most English translations of this verse do not preserve the chiastic word order, though it may be found in the Darby Bible Translation and Young's Literal Translation, available on the Biblos.com website, http://bible.cc/numbers/14-2.htm (accessed February 12, 2011).

13 Nils W. Lund, *Chiasmus in the New Testament: A Study in the Form and Function of Chiastic Structures* (Chapel Hill: University of North Carolina Press, 1942; reprint, Peabody, Mass.: Hendrickson, 1992).

14 Douglas, *Thinking in Circles*, 12.

15 Brad McCoy, "Chiasmus: An Important Structural Device Commonly Found in Biblical Literature," *Chafer Theological Seminary Journal* 9, no. 2 (2003): 18–34, citing 24.

16 John Breck, *The Shape of Biblical Language: Chiasmus in the Scriptures and Beyond* (Crestwood, N.Y.: St. Vladimir's Seminary Press, 1994), 59–60.

17 Seyed Ghahreman Safavi and Simon Weightman, *Rumi's Mystical Design: Reading the Mathnawi, Book One* (Albany: State University of New York Press, 2009), esp. 46–59.

18 Mir Sayyid Manjhan Shattari Rajgiri, *Madhumalati: An Indian Sufi Romance*, trans. Aditya Behl and Simon Weightman, Oxford World's Classics (Oxford: Oxford University Press, 2000); see especially Simon Weightman's appendix, "The Symmetry of *Madhumalati*," 229–41.

19 Douglas, *Thinking in Circles*, 1.

20 Ibid., 16.

21 Ibid., 36–38.

22 Ibid., 126.

23 Michel Cuypers, *The Banquet: A Reading of the Fifth Sura of the Qur'an*, trans. Patricia Kelly (Miami: Convivium Press, 2009). Details of Cuypers's earlier publications, all in French, are found in the bibliography to his book.

24 Cuypers's book is published in a series entitled Rhetorica Semitica. He argues that the term "Semitic" is justified for a rhetorical analysis that differs from that of Greek rhetoric, which in its impact on Islamic culture encouraged a focus on only the smallest units of text, as found in Qur'anic commentaries that proceed in a line-by-line fashion (ibid., 29–30). Others may feel that the term "Semitic" carries too much baggage of racial theory and essentialism, as well as being inadequate to account for the worldwide extent of ring composition.

25 Ibid., 475.

26 Régis Blachère, *Le Coran: Traduction nouvelle*, Islam d'Hier et d'Aujourd'hui 4, 3 vols. (Paris: Librairie Orientale et Américaine, 1947), 981n24, 1063. Remarkably, Blachère states that the abrupt beginning of sura 60 was originally preceded by a verse currently located in 59:24. Whatever the warrant for that assertion, it indicates a dissatisfaction with the canonical text of sura 60.

27 Richard Bell, *The Qur'an Translated, with a Critical Re-arrangement of the Surahs*, 2 vols. (Edinburgh: T. and T. Clark, 1937–39), 2:572.

28 Cuypers, *The Banquet*, 268.

29 Farrin, "Surat al-Baqara," 19–20, 29–30.

30 Ibid., 24.

31 For this translation of *qad nara* as "We may see," a use of *qad* with the imperfect tense in the sense of "perhaps," compare Arne A. Ambros, *A Concise Dictionary of Koranic Arabic* (Wiesbaden: Reichert Verlag, 2004), 328. It might even be rendered as a conditional clause, "Should We see."

32 Cuypers, *The Banquet*, 493–502. An equivalent term for ring structure in classical Arabic literary criticism is *al-laff wal-nashr 'ala al-'aks* (involution and evolution in reverse), cited by Mustansir Mir, "The Qur'anic Story of Joseph: Plot, Themes, and Characters," *Muslim World* 76, no. 1 (1986): 1–15. For the views of Arabic literary critics on the coherence of the Qur'an, see G. J. H. Van Gelder, *Beyond the Line: Classical Arabic Literary Critics on the Coherence and Unity of the Poem* (Leiden: E. J. Brill, 1982), 160–65.

33 Mark W. Edwards, *The Iliad: A Commentary*, vol. 5, books 17–20, general ed. G. S. Kirk (Cambridge: Cambridge University Press, 1991), 44–48, quoting 45; John W. Welch, ed., *Chiasmus in Antiquity: Structures, Analyses, Exegesis* (Hildesheim: Gerstenberg, 1981).

34 John Breck, *Scripture in Tradition: The Bible and Its Interpretation in the Orthodox Church* (Crestwood, N.Y.: St. Vladimir's Seminary Press, 2001), 98.

35 John W. Welch and Daniel B. McKinlay, *Chiasmus Bibliography* (Provo, Utah: Research Press, 1999).

36 Raymond Farrin, *Abundance from the Desert: Classical Arabic Poetry* (Syracuse: Syracuse University Press, 2011), xvii, 275. This study is based on analysis of a dozen major Arabic poems from the sixth century to the thirteenth.

37 Ibid., xvi.

38 Symmetrical composition in suras 7, 10, and 11 (all late Meccan) is addressed by Dalia Abo Haggar, "Repetition: A Key to Qur'anic Style, Structure, and Meaning" (Ph.D. diss., University of Pennsylvania, 2010).

39 Raymond Farrin, "Suras 50–56: A Structural and Thematic Analysis," paper presented at Middle East Studies Association conference, San Diego, November 2010.

40 Neal Robinson, "Surat Al 'Imran and Those with the Greatest Claim to Abraham," *Journal of Qur'anic Studies* 6, no. 2 (2004): 1–21; here he refers (in note 1) to a more detailed study, "The Dynamics of Sura Al 'Imran," which does not seem to have been published.

41 Angelika Neuwirth, "The House of Abraham and the House of Amram: Genealogy, Patriarchal Authority, and Exegetical Professionalism," in *The Qur'an in Context: Historical and Literary Investigations into the Qur'anic Milieu*, ed. Angelika Neuwirth, Nikolai Sinai, and Michael Marx (Leiden: Brill, 2010), 499–531, quoting 503. Reference will also be made to an overlapping article by Neuwirth, "Debating Christian and Jewish Traditions: Embodied Antagonisms in Surat Al 'Imran (Q 3:1–62)," in *Studien zur Semitistik und Arabistik: Festschrift für Hartmut Bobzin zum 60. Geburtstag*, ed. Otto Jastrow, Shabo Talay, and Herta Hafenrichter (Wiesbaden: Harrassowitz, 2008), 281–304.

42 Neuwirth, "Debating Christian and Jewish Traditions," 283, citing the analysis of A. H. Mathias Zahniser, "The Word of God and the Apostleship of 'Isa: A Narrative Analysis of Al 'Imran (3):33–62," *Journal of Semitic Studies* 36, no. 1 (1991): 77–112. Neuwirth and Zahniser apparently refer to the verse numbering of Flügel, who counted 198 verses in sura 4, instead of the 200 verses found in the Egyptian edition.

43 Zahniser observes, "I do not find as striking a similarity between any other two surahs in the Qur'an" ("The Word of God," 111). Zahniser's transcription of sura 3 (ibid., 110) appears to have reversed the verses numbered 45a and 43b.

44 See Neuwirth, "Debating Christian and Jewish Traditions," 293–94, where she also suggests that the similar genealogy of prophets in 19:58 is a Medinan insertion.

45 Ibid., 284. For another approach to gender in the Qur'an, see Michael Sells, *Approaching the Qur'an: The Early Revelations* (Ashland, Ore.: White Cloud Press, 1999), 197–222.

46 Neuwirth, "Debating Christian and Jewish Traditions," 287–88.

47 Neuwirth, "The House of Abraham," 519, citing Nasr Hamid Abu Zayd.

48 Jane Dammen McAuliffe, "Text and Textuality: Q. 3:7 as a Point of Intersection," in Boullata, *Literary Structures of Religious Meaning*, 56–76, citing 61.

49 Carl W. Ernst, *Words of Ecstasy in Sufism* (Albany: State University of New York Press, 1985), 19, 144.

50 David Marshall, "Punishment Stories," in *Encyclopaedia of the Qur'an*, 5:318–22.

51 Ernst, *Following Muhammad*, 38–69; Wilfred Cantwell Smith, "The Historical Development in the Islam of the Concept of Islam as an Historical Development," in Wilfred

Cantwell Smith, *On Understanding Islam: Selected Studies* (Leiden: Walter de Gruyter, 1981), 41–77.

52 Robinson, "Surat Al 'Imran," 7, points out several parallel Qur'anic idioms for "turning one's face" or "setting one's face" toward God or his service, in juxtaposition with the term *hanif*, which he sees as suggesting an inclination toward instinctive monotheism.

53 M. M. Bravmann, *The Spiritual Background of Early Islam: Studies in Ancient Arab Concepts* (Leiden: E. J. Brill, 1972), 7–26, esp. 23.

54 Ibid., 34, 36.

55 On the violent fates of the prophets, see David E. Aune, *Prophecy in Early Christianity and the Ancient Mediterranean World* (Grand Rapids, Mich.: Eerdmans, 1983), 157–59.

56 Neuwirth, "The House of Abraham," 527–28; Neuwirth, "Debating Christian and Jewish Traditions," 292–93.

57 On the Infancy Gospel of James (also known as the Protoevangelium of James), see the Early Christian Writings website, http://www.earlychristianwritings.com/infancyjames.html (accessed February 12, 2011). See also David R. Cartlidge and J. Keith Elliot, *Art and the Christian Apocrypha* (London: Routledge, 2001).

58 Robinson, "Surat Al 'Imran," 4–5.

59 Ibid., 8–9. The Apocalypse of Abraham is also evidently revised at 2:260, where Abraham's sacrifice of four birds is turned into a demonstration of God's power of resurrection.

60 A. H. Mathias Zahniser, "Sura as Guidance and Exhortation: The Composition of Surat al-Nisa," in *Humanism, Culture, and Language in the Near East: Studies in Honor of Georg Krotkoff*, ed. Asma Afsaruddin and A. H. Mathias Zahniser (Winona Lake, Ind.: Eisenbrauns, 1997), 71–86.

61 Cuypers, *The Banquet*, 482.

62 Bell, *The Qur'an Translated*, 1:92, detects three different periods in the composition of sura 5: first, years two and three of the hijra; second, the time of the Treaty of Hudaybiyya (spring 628 CE); and third, after the conquest of Mecca the following year. Blachère, *Le Coran*, 1111–46, breaks the sura down thematically into five parts.

63 Cuypers's alphabetical symbols for structural sequences have been revised here to conform to Mary Douglas's system of diagramming ring compositions.

64 Donner, "From Believers to Muslims," 14.

65 Cuypers, *The Banquet*, 77–78, follows the often suggested idea that Arabic *din* is also linked to Middle Persian *den* (Old Persian *daena*) as meaning "religion" in the sense of "a collective undertaking to follow the right path given by God." But the Old Persian term *daena* contains both subjective and objective components, denoting both the soul that perceives the truth and the truth that is seen; the evidence is discussed by Mary Boyce, *A History of Zoroastrianism: The Early Period* (Leiden: E. J. Brill, 1975; reprint, 1996), 238. It seems useful to stress both the personal and the socially accepted components of *din*.

66 Cuypers, *The Banquet*, 81–82.

67 Ibid., 85.

68 For a detailed comparison of the farewell addresses of Moses and Muhammad, see Peter Wright, "Critical Approaches to the 'Farewell Khutba' in Ibn Ishaq's Life of the Prophet," *Comparative Islamic Studies* (forthcoming).

69 Cuypers, *The Banquet*, 123. Early Muslims also conceived of the conquest of Jerusalem as a successful entry into the holy land (ibid., 182).

70 Ibid., 163, 183–85.

71 Ibid., 138–40, citing Muslim commentators who refer to Numbers 1:5–15 and the synoptic Gospels for parallels between Muhammad and the earlier prophets.

72 Ibid., 95, 97, 158.

73 Ibid., 415, 421–24.

74 Ibid., 216–17, 350.

75 Ibid., 454.

76 Ibid., 440.

77 *The Babylonian Talmud*, ed. Isadore Epstein (London: Soncino Press, 1935), vol. 27, 233, quoted by Peter M. Wright, "Modern Qur'anic Hermeneutics" (Ph.D. diss., University of North Carolina at Chapel Hill, 2007), 160.

78 Cuypers, *The Banquet*, 203.

79 Ibid., 260–61.

80 H. T. Henry, "Canticle," in *The Catholic Encyclopedia* (New York: Encyclopedia Press, 1913), 3:301–2, http://www.newadvent.org/cathen/03301a.htm (accessed February 12, 2011). It would be worth investigating whether the Qur'an contains references to any other of these canticles.

81 Cuypers, *The Banquet*, 311, 466–67.

82 See, for example, the organization of 5:41–49 into three subdivisions, each of which is concentric (ibid., 253).

83 Ibid., 464–65.

84 Cuypers even infers (*The Banquet*, 374) that the priority of belief and good deeds over diet should mitigate the prohibition of wine, which occurs in close proximity in 5:91.

85 Ibid., 301–2, lists medieval authorities Tabari, Tusi, and Ghazali, plus modern authors Muhammad 'Abduh, Rashid Rida, Mahmud Shaltut, M. Husayn Tabataba'i, and Fazlur Rahman, among those Muslim scholars who accept the salvation of non-Muslims.

86 Ibid., 464.

Conclusion

1 The decline in popularity of the Isra'iliyyat is described well by Peter Riddell, *Islam and the Malay-Indonesian World: Transmission and Responses* (Honolulu: University of Hawaii Press, 2001).

2 Michel Cuypers, *The Banquet: A Reading of the Fifth Sura of the Qur'an*, trans. Patricia Kelly (Miami: Convivium Press, 2009), 498–500; Walid A. Saleh, *In Defense of the Bible: A Critical Edition and an Introduction to al-Biqa'i's Bible Treatise* (Leiden: Brill, 2008).

3 Tony K. Stewart and Carl W. Ernst, "Syncretism," *South Asian Folklore: An Encyclopedia*,

ed. Peter J. Claus and Margaret A. Mills (New York: Garland, 2003), http://www.unc
.edu/%7Ecernst/pdf/Syncretism.pdf (accessed February 12, 2011). See also Michael
Pregill, "The Hebrew Bible and the Qur'an: The Problem of the Jewish 'Influence' on
Islam," *Religion Compass* 1, no. 6 (2007): 643–59.

4   Cuypers, *The Banquet*, 479.

5   Ibid., 487.

6   Ibid., 29, 488.

7   Ibid., 256.

8   The many publications on the Qur'an by the Right Reverend Kenneth Cragg provide
an example of a Protestant reading of the text. See most recently *The Qur'an and the
West* (Washington, D.C.: Georgetown University Press, 2006).

9   *The Qur'an, Morality, and Critical Reason: The Essential Muhammad Shahrur*, trans. Andreas
Christmann (Leiden: Brill, 2009).

10 Mahdi Bazargan, *Sayr-i tahawwul-i Qur'an*, ed. Muhammad Mahdi Ja'fari (Tehran:
Qalam, 1981), reprinted as vols. 12 and 13 of Bazargan's collected works, *Majmu'a-i
athar* (Tehran: Bunyad-i Farhangi-i Muhandis Mahdi Bazargan, 2007). An English
translation of this study, introduced by reformist politician Ibrahim Yazdi, was announced under the title *The Evolution of the Qur'an* (Houston: Institute for Research
and Islamic Studies, 1987), but it seems never to have been published. I am grateful
to Dr. Mohsen Kadivar of Duke University for drawing this work to my attention.

11 Ahmed E. Souaiaia, *Contesting Justice: Women, Islam, Law, and Society* (New York: State
University of New York Press, 2008).

12 Gabriel Said Reynolds, *The Qur'an and Its Biblical Subtext*, Routledge Studies in the
Qur'an (London: Routledge, 2010).

Appendix A

1   Neuwirth typically does not count, for numbering purposes, initial verses consisting
only of separate letters.

Appendix B

1   Cuypers argues that 5:53 and 5:54 are reversed, by analogy with 2:217; see Michel
Cuypers, *The Banquet: A Reading of the Fifth Sura of the Qur'an*, trans. Patricia Kelly
(Miami: Convivium Press, 2009), 278.

Suggested Reading

Qur'anic and Islamic Studies

Abu Zayd, Nasr Hamid. "The Dilemma of the Literary Approach to the Qur'an." *ALIF, Journal of Comparative Poetics* 23 (2003): 8–47.

Cuypers, Michel. *The Banquet: A Reading of the Fifth Sura of the Qur'an*. Translated by Patricia Kelly. Miami: Convivium Press, 2009.

Donner, Fred M. *Muhammad and the Believers: At the Origins of Islam*. Cambridge: Harvard University Press, 2010.

Ernst, Carl W. *Following Muhammad: Rethinking Islam in the Contemporary World*. Chapel Hill: University of North Carolina Press, 2003.

Lawrence, Bruce B. *The Qur'an: A Biography*. New York: Atlantic Monthly Press, 2006.

Leaman, Oliver, ed. *The Qur'an: An Encyclopedia*. London: Routledge, 2008.

McAuliffe, Jane Dammen, ed. *The Cambridge Companion to the Qur'an*. Cambridge: Cambridge University Press, 2006.

———. *The Encyclopaedia of the Qur'an*. 6 vols. Leiden: E. J. Brill, 2002–7.

Reynolds, Gabriel Said. *The Qur'an and Its Biblical Subtext*. Routledge Studies in the Qur'an. London: Routledge, 2010.

Rippin, Andrew, ed. *The Blackwell Companion to the Qur'an*. Oxford: Blackwell, 2006.

Robinson, Neal. *Discovering the Qur'an: A Contemporary Approach to a Veiled Text*. 2nd ed. Washington, D.C.: Georgetown University Press, 2003.

Sells, Michael. *Approaching the Qur'an: The Early Revelations*. Ashland, Ore.: White Cloud Press, 1999.

English Translations of the Qur'an

Abdel Haleem, M. A. S. *The Qur'an: A New Translation*. New York: Oxford University Press, 2004.

Arberry, A. J. *The Koran Interpreted: A Translation*. New York: Simon and Schuster, 1996.

Cleary, Thomas. *The Qur'an: A New Translation*. Chicago: Starlatch Press, 2004.

Jones, Alan. *The Qur'an*. Cambridge: Gibb Memorial Trust, 2007.

Index of Scriptural Citations

Qur'an

To differentiate sura and verse numbers from page numbers, sura and verse numbers are given in boldface type (for example, **2:147** for sura 2, verse 147; or simply **2** if sura 2 as a whole is under discussion). References to pages containing translated passages are given in italics.

1, 13, 118; used as prayer, 42, 59, 119
1:1–7, *111*
2, 42, 73, 155, 158–59, 167–69, 190; structure of, 159, 167, 223–26
2:7, 21
2:67–71, 158, 167
2:106, 65
2:116, 137
2:142–44, *168*, 169
2:143, 159, 168
2:147–48, *168–69*, 202
2:243–53, 168
2:260, 254 (n. 59)
3, 73, 155, 171–90; structure of, 171–72, 173
3:3, *173*
3:4–5, 175
3:4–32, 173–74
3:6–7, *174–75*, 176, 186
3:8–32, 177–78
3:10–11, 178
3:12, *179*
3:12–20, 179–80
3:13, *172*, 176, 179
3:15–17, *179*
3:18, 176, *179*
3:19, *175*, *179*, 192

3:20, *180*
3:21, 180
3:23, *181*
3:23–24, 180
3:26, *181*
3:28, *181*
3:29–32, *182*
3:33–34, *174*
3:36–37, *175*, 183, 184
3:38–44, *184*
3:44, *173*
3:48–52, 184
3:55, *185*
3:59, *186*
3:62, *173*
3:63–65, *186*
3:63–99, 187–88
3:68, *188*
3:70–71, *186*
3:79, *188*
3:81–82, 188
3:98–99, *186*
3:100–200, 188–90
3:102–5, *189*
3:110–15, *189–90*
3:124–25, 179

General Index

Abdel Haleem, Muhammad, 158

'Abduh, Muhammad, 64

Abel, 199

Abraham, 32, 54, 78, 167; opponents destroyed, 87; scripture of, 103, 150; as neither Jew nor Christian, 159, 187–88; as model, 165; Jews as descendants of, 174, 180, 181, 186; Apocalypse of Abraham, 187–88

Abrogation: of earlier Qur'anic text by later one, 16–17, 65–67, 104, 162–63, 191, 244 (n. 107); of previous scriptures by Qur'an, 65

Abu Bakr, 26

Abu Hanifah, 68

Abu Lahab, 33, 57

Abu Zayd, Abu Nasr, 65

Academic study: of Qur'an, 6–7, 14–15, 23, 24–25, 57, 207, 211; of religion, 20–21, 74, 208

'Ad, 54, 87

Adam, 32, 129, 159, 174, 184, 186

Additions to early suras. *See* Insertions in early suras

Affection between enemies, 164, 165, 166

Afterlife. *See* End-times

Alexander the Great, 13, 120, 133–38

'Ali ibn Abi Talib, 28, 63, 73, 211

Allies (*awliya'*): religious opponents rejected as, 164, 166, 181

Allusive character of Qur'anic narratives, 33, 55–56, 84

Ammon, 133, 134

Amram. *See* 'Imran

Angels, 141, 142, 179, 183, 184

Anxiety about Qur'an, 1–2, 4, 62

Apocalypse, 34, 85–92, 172, 177–78, 188

Arabic, 3, 16, 26–28, 59, 144, 150, 152, 169; Arabic script, 27–28. *See also* Pre-Islamic Arabic poetry

Archaeology, 13, 84–88

Aristotle, 170

Arkoun, Mohammed, 65, 118

Asbab al-nuzul. See Historical context of Qur'an: as presented in "occasions of revelation"

Ascension. *See* Muhammad, Prophet: ascension of

Audience of Qur'an, 6, 9, 10, 19, 73, 119, 138–39, 205, 209; hostility of, 139–54

Audio recordings of Qur'an, 29, 61, 72

Auerbach, Eric, 25

Authoritative reading of Qur'an, 17, 20, 25, 65, 72

Aya. See Signs of God in nature; Verses of Qur'an

Badr, battle of, 58, 171, 172, 177, 179, 180

Bahrain, 85

Banu Nadir, 58

Basmala, 42

Battles. *See* Badr, battle of; Uhud, battle of

Bazargan, Mahdi, 211

Believers (*mu'minun*), community of: as